MW01532024

The Lyon Families
Of
Northern Rhode Island

Compiled by
Guy Wallis

Bristol, Vermont

ii

Printed by Lulu.com

© 2013 Guy Wallis.
All rights reserved
ISBN 978-1-304-09604-3

Front cover: John Lyon [II] house, Foster. RI
Rear cover: Thomas Lyon [I] house, Sandgate, VT

Table of Contents

Forward

In the *Lyon Memorial,* a series of books written in the early 20th century there is a group of Lyon descendants referred to collectively as "John Lyon of Scituate, R. I." or "Rhode Island Lyons" or "Major Thomas Lyon of Lyon Brook, N. Y." The authors of that series of books were unable to locate information on the parentage of this group of Lyons in the various records they used. As a result of the lack of primary information the authors proposed several different progenitors.

Now, a century later the problem still exists. No primary records identifying the progenitors have been discovered and it is assumed that that those records do not exists. However, one group of them, John Lyon [I]], can be identified with good certainty from land and other town records by using dates, occupations, wife's and parents' names. The progenitors of the other group, John Lyon [II], remains improvable.

This book presents these two groups and follows their descendants as they move thru the ensuing centuries across the United States.

John Lyon [I]

The identifiable group of Lyons are descendants John Lyon [I][1] and his wife Mary Herring. John, the son of Samuel Lyon and his first wife Maria Kenrick, was born in Roxbury Massachusetts, removed to Sutton and Mendon in Massachusetts and then to Providence and East Greenwich in Rhode Island. Mary Herring, born in Dedham Massachusetts is the daughter of Thomas Herring and his wife Mehitabell.

The first record of John as an adult is found in the Worcester County land records.[2] In that record Samuel Lyon of Roxbury, mason, transferred on 20 Sep 1726 to his son John Lyon of Roxbury, yeoman, a tract of land. That transfer was "so much a part or portion of my Estate ... truly a Sixty pound value of & toward his ye s[ai]d John Portion all that my tract of ... land... containing Sixty two acres" This transfer of land effectively resolved the primogeniture problem that Samuel's second wife, Joanna Weld had with her step-son John. As Samuel's first born son, John was entitled to a double portion of his father's estate whereas Joanna's five sons were only entitled to a single portion each. When Samuel died Joanna's son Edward administered his estate.

John Lyon of Mendon, joiner, and his wife Mary, who signed with a mark, sold this tract on 3 May 1734.[3] The tract was then said to be in Sutton at the Mendon town line. Today, the town of Sutton and Mendon are not contiguous with the town of Uxbridge being in-between them.

On 20 Dec 1731, in the town of Sutton, John Lion was assigned "ye 2d seet in front gallery" of "ye meeting house".[4]

The next record of John Lyon is 4 Oct 1732 when he purchased a 10 acre tract of land along with 27 acres of woodland from John Rawson.[5] John Lyon was said to be a joiner of Sutton in this transaction. John Lyon of Mendon, joiner, and his wife sold this tract on 25 Jun 1734.[6]

In Mar 1733 John Lyon and Samuel Thayer Jr were named tithing men in Sutton.[7]

In Mar 1735 John Lyon was hired to build the new meeting house in Mendon and in August 1737 he was allowed an additional £25 to finish the meeting house.[8]

Next, in May of 1735 John Lyon of Mendon purchased 30 acres of land in Mendon from Samuel Thayer.[9] John Lyon of Mendon, joiner, sold that tract of land in two separate transactions. The first was a 5 acre portion which John Lyon of Mendon, joiner, sold on 29 Jan 1736.[10] Mary did not co-sign that sale. The second sale by John Lyon of Mendon was for 37 acres on 15 Mar 1738 which Mary co-signed with her mark.[11]

In Aug 1740 John Lyon received £8 for building the new Mendon pound.[12]

The August 1740 payment for the pound is the last information found concerning John Lyon in Massachusetts. Where he lived in the time period between Mar 1738 when he sold his last known tract of land and Nov 1749 when he appeared 20 miles to the south east in Providence Rhode Island is unknown.

In Nov 1749 John Lyon of Providence, joiner, and his wife Mary bought two tracts of land in Providence Rhode Island[13]. In Jan 1753 John Lyon, joiner, now of East Greenwich RI, sold these two tracts and Mary co-signed with her mark.[14]

---

1 Lyon Memorial, Massachusetts Families, page 42, person #115.
2 Worcester County MA Land Records Volume 4, page 398.
3 Worcester County MA Land Records Volume 5, page 371.
4 History of the Town of Sutton Massachusetts from 1704 to 1876 by Rev William A Benedict and Rev Hiram A Tracy, Sanford & Co, Worcester MA, 1878, page 46.
5 Worcester County MA Land Records Volume 4, page 397.
6 Worcester County MA Land Records Volume 5, page 361.
7 Mendon Town Records.
8 Mendon Town Records.
9 Worcester County MA Land Records Volume 7, page 85.
10 Worcester County MA Land Records Volume 11, page 153.
11 Worcester County MA Land Records Volume 10, page 117.
12 Mendon Town Records.

In Nov 1750 John Lyon] purchased two lots in East Greenwich RI[15]. He was then propounded to appear at the next court to take the oath of freeman which he did in Aug 1751.

Following becoming a freeman he was made viewer of timbers for East Greenwich a position he held until May 1755[16].

John was appointed by the town council in May 1752 to do some repair work on the court house roof. He failed to do the required repair and in May 1755 the town appointed someone else to do the repair work. This is when John lost his position as viewer of timbers. However he re-gained that position in May 1757.

The last records for John Lyon revolve around a loan he made on 14 Jun 1756 from Benjamin Gorton of West Greenwich for £54 s10 p9 to be repaid on or before 1 Nov next. If the loan wasn't repaid by that date the amount due was £116. The loan was not repaid and an arrest warrant was issued for John Lyon on 14 Dec 1756. The case was heard on the third Tuesday (17th) of January 1757 at inferior court in East Greenwich RI. The lands of John Lyon were attached. Benjamin Arnold Sheriff of Kent County sold John's land with dwelling house, lot # 94, in East Greenwich, Newtown, to Ebenezer Herr__ for £535 to satisfy the debt[17]. In that transaction he is referred to as "John Lyon late of East Greenwich" implying that he was then deceased[18].

There are no records of birth of any children. The 1749 deed for the two lots in Providence makes reference to him having a family.

In Nov 1754 Samuel Lyon of East Greenwich, also a joiner, was made a freeman in East Greenwich[19]. Samuel Lyon is assumed to be John's son as he lived in the same town and has the same trade, appears to be a generation younger and there were no other Lyon's in the East Greenwich area. When Samuel Lyon died in 1760, Thomas Lyon [I] probated his estate and was said to be Samuel Lyons' brother[20].

In 1760, Experience Lyon of East Greenwich, when she married John Spencer[21], was said to be a daughter of John Lyon.

13 Providence RI Land Records, Volume 13, page 148.

14 Providence RI Land Records, Volume 1, page 253.

[15] East Greenwich RI Land Records, Volume 7, page 67.

[16] Rhode Island Colonial Records.

[17] Rhode Island Judicial Records.

[18] East Greenwich RI Land Records, Volume 8, page 18.

[19] Rhode Island Colonial Records

[20] Cranston RI Probate Records, page 128.

[21]Arnold, *Vital Records of Rhode Island 1636-1850.*, Volume 7, Marriages of John Gorton.

John Lyon [II]

John Lyon [II] who married Martha Burlingame, a younger sister of the Huldah Burlingame that married Thomas Lyon [I] is often assumed to be a brother of Thomas Lyon [I] . That assumption is un-provable and unlikely based on the names they and their descendants used for their children which are tabulated below.

This book will treat John [I] and John [II] as two separate families linked only by marriage to the two Burlingame sisters.

The following tables compare the given names of the male children and grandchildren of John [II] and Thomas [I] Lyon.

John [II] Lyon descendants		Thomas [I] Lyon descendants	
Number of times used.	Given name	Number of times used.	Given name
4	Cyrus	3	Thomas
4	John	2	Daniel
3	Benjamin	2	Esick
3	Reuben	2	John
2	Alden	2	Samuel
2	Richmond	1	Alanson
1	Alexander	1	Alexander
1	Alford	1	Alvah
1	Christopher	1	Benjamin
1	Cyril	1	Charles
1	Daniel	1	Darus
1	Emery	1	Frank
1	Gardner	1	George
1	Hiram	1	James
1	Israel	1	Marcus
1	Richard	1	Ozro
1	Sheldon	1	Randolph
		1	Richard
		1	Rufus
		1	Sterry
		1	Theron
		1	Truxton
		1	William

Descendants of John Lyon [I]

Generation One

1. John Lyon [I][22] was born on 18 Apr 1703 at Roxbury, Suffolk County, MA. He married Mary Herring (5959), daughter of Thomas Herring and Mehitabell (--?--) on 16 Apr 1724 at Roxbury, Suffolk County, MA.[23] He died before 18 Jan 1758 when John Lyon was referred to as late of East Greenwich in the sale of his property.[24]

On 20 Sep 1726 Samuel Lyon of Roxbury, mason, gave 62 acres of land to his son John Lyon of Roxbury, yeoman, as his part of his (Samuel's) estate. This land was in Sutton, bordered both Hopkinton & Mendon and was valued at £60. The deed was witnessed by Ebenezer and Joshua Lyon. John Lyon sold this tract of land to David Bachellor on 3 May 1734 for £290.[25]

On 4 Oct 1732 John Lyon bought a 10 acre tract of land along with 27 acre woodlot from the John Rawson. That tract had previously belonged to Rawson's father Grindal Rawson and his widow still possessed her dower portion. John Lyon sold this land on 25 Jun 1734 to Samuell Thayer for the same price he had purchased it, £450.[26]

John Lyon was hired to build a new meeting house in Mendon. He received payments on this construction through Aug 1737 in Mar 1735.[27] John Lyon purchased 30 acres of land on the Mill River in Mendon from Samuel Thayer for £200 in May 1735.[28]

In Aug 1740 John Lyon received an £8 payment for building a new Mendon Town pound. This is the last date found of him being in Worcester County MA. The first record of them in Rhode Island was in Nov 1749 when John Lyon joiner, of Providence, Providence County RI bought two tracts of land in Providence. In Jan 1753 John Lyon, joiner, and his wife Mary were of East Greenwich RI when they sold the two tracts of land in Providence.[29] John and Marys' location between 1740 and 1749 has not been determined.

On 4 Nov 1750 John Lyon, joiner of Providence RI purchased lots 36 & 94 in East Greenwich RI from Jonathan Nichols.

In Aug 1751 John Lyon took the Oath of Freeman in East Greenwich RI. At the same time he was made viewer of Timbers in East Greenwich a position he held until May 1755 in Aug 1751.[30]

In May 1752 John Lyon was appointed to stop the leaks in the court house. He failed to do the repair and the town appointed someone else to do the work in 1755. On 14 Jun 1756 John Lyon of East Greenwich executed a loan from Benjamin Gorton of West Greenwich for £54 s10 p9. to be repaid on or before 1 Nov next. If the loan wasn't repaid by that date the amount due was £116. The loan was not repaid and an arrest warrant was issued for John Lyon on 14 Dec 1756. The case was heard on the third Tuesday (17th) of January 1757 at inferior court in East Greenwich RI.

The lands of John Lyon were attached. On 18 Jan 1758 Benjamin Arnold Sheriff of Kent County sold John's land in East Greenwich, Newtown with the dwelling house on lot # 94, to Ebenezer Herr__ for £535 to satisfy the debt.[31,32]

Mary Herring[33] was born on 10 Jan 1701 at Dedham, Norfolk County, MA.[34] She died after Jan 1753.

---

[22]A B & G W A Lyon, *Lyon Memorial Massachusetts Families* (Detroit. MI: William Graham Printing, 1905), page 42.

[23]Suffolk County MA, Vital Records, Vital Records of Roxbury Volume 2, page 257.

[24]East Greenwich, RI, Land Records, Volume 8, page 18.

[25]Worcester County, MA Land Records, Book 4, page 399 and Book 5 page 371.

[26]Ibid., Book 4, page 398 and book 5, page 371.

[27]Lynda K McGinnis notes and conclusions.

[28]Worcester County, MA Land Records, Book 7, page 85.

[29]Rhode Island Land Records, Providence, RI. Volume 13, pages 148 & 253.

[30]RI Colonial Records.

[31]Suit Benjamin Gorton vs John Lyon, 1756, Judicial Records Center, Pawtucket, RI.

[32]East Greenwich, RI, Land Records, Volume 8, page 18.

Known children of John Lyon [I] and Mary Herring were as follows:

2.   i.   Samuel Lyon[35] was born circa 1730 at Mendon, Worcester County, MA. He died in Dec 1760 at Cranston, Providence County, RI; Samuel's brother Thomas was appointed administrator of his estate.[36]

     Samuel was made a Freeman in East Greenwich, RI in Nov 1754.[37] He was joiner. Thomas Lyon of Cranston applied for Letters of Administration on the Estate of "late decd brother Samuel Lyon of Cranston".

     Samuels inventory filed with the Town Council was for £1058, s 1, d 12. The inventory was primarily clothing, joiners tools and notes due to him.[38]

+ 3.   ii.   Thomas [I] Lyon was born circa 1735 at Mendon, Worcester County, MA. He married Huldah Burlingame, daughter of Daniel Burlingame and Rose Briggs, on 25 Dec 1760 at Cranston, Providence County, RI. He died between 14 Apr 1806 and 16 Mar 1808.

+ 4.   iii.   Experience Lyon was born circa 1741. She married John Spencer, son of Richard Spencer and Hannah (--?--), on 25 Feb 1760 at East Greenwich, Kent County, RI.

---

[33]Robert Brand Hanson, *Vital Records of Dedham MA* (1989).

[34]Don Gleason Hill, *The Record of Births, Marriages and Deaths and Intentions of Marriage In the Town of Dedham*.

[35]Cranston Town Meeting Minutes.

[36]Ibid., page 128.

[37]RI Colonial Records.

[38]Cranston Town Meeting Minutes, page 128.

Generation Two

3. Thomas [I] Lyon (*John*) was born circa 1735 at Mendon, Worcester County, MA. He married Huldah Burlingame, daughter of Daniel Burlingame and Rose Briggs, on 25 Dec 1760 at Cranston, Providence County, RI; the married was performed by William Burton, J.P.[39] He died between 14 Apr 1806 and 16 Mar 1808; On 14 Apr 1806 Thomas Lyon gave a grant to Al Baird to permit Baird to build a dam on the river which would flood part of Thomas's land. He deed doesn't specify if this is Thomas Sr or Jr. However, when the deed was filed on 16 Mar 1808 Gurdon Hewitt testified that he was present when Thomas executed the grant and that he knew the said Thomas. The absence of Thomas to testify to the accuracy of the deed implies that it was Thomas Sr and that he was deceased by 1808.[40]/

Thomas Lyon served in Capt. Fry's Co in 1756. The unit was stationed at Fort Edward NY which is very near White Creek, Charlotte County, New York where Thomas settled by 1774. In 1757 Thomas Lyon was still serving in Capt. Fry's Co and on the alarm of 10 Aug 1757 they were called to go to the relief of Fort William Henry. However, the fort had fallen on 9 Aug and the men got no further than Connecticut and they returned home.[41] Thomas Lyon was made a Freeman of Cranston, RI in 1767. In 1767 Thomas Lyon purchased land in Cranston from Richard Sarle, Jr which he sold it back to Sarle in Feb 1774. Both Thomas and Huldah signed.[42] In 1767 Thomas Lyon was listed as a House Carpenter of Cranston and in Feb 1774 Thomas Lyon, House Carpenter, sold his land in Cranston RI.[43,44] Thomas Lyon was a resident of White Creek NY [now Salem] by 1 Dec 1774 when he signed a petition to allow the privilege of electing a representative to the assembly.[45] A record "of the Seventh Company of the first Regiment of Militia Commanded by Col John Williams in Charlotte County where of Charles Hutchison is Captain" lists 88 men including Thomas and Samuel Lyon. Both were in service and received pay between 20 June 1777 and 20 Oct 1777. Another note says that Thomas Lions had been a Lieutenant in Hutchinson's Company but enlisted in the ??? service as Sergeant but being discharged joined this Company and was in actual service till Burgoyne's defeat.

A pay record indicates Thomas belonged to Captain Hutchison's Company but transfer to Captain Edward Long's Company. For 115 days service Thomas received pay of 12.5.3 and his son Samuel Lyon who served 60 days received 5.6.8

Another "pay Roll of Captain Hutchison's Company showing the same dates and pay as above indicates that 22 men marched the 70 miles from New Perth to Ticonderoga and received one penny for each.[46] On 7 May 1779 Thomas Lyon and others petitioned The State of Vermont for a charter to the present town of Orwell in Addison County Vermont. That petition was not granted to them.[47] On 1 Feb 1791 Thomas Lyon of Sandgate, Bennington County VT sold his VT land to Robert Hopkins and on 16 Oct 1791 Thomas acknowledged the transfer of this lot. This transfer may have occurred in Chenango County NY as on 30 July 1791 Thomas Lyon had purchased his land in Chenango County NY.

On 23 April 1791 Thomas Lyon's son Samuel sold his land in Salem, Washington County, NY [formerly known as White Creek, Charlotte County, NY].

[39]James N Arnold, *Vital Records of Rhode Island 1636-1850.* (Providence RI: Narragansett Press, 1892), Cranston Marriages Records Volume 1, page 250.

[40]Chenango County, NY, Land Records, Volume K, page 466.

[41]Howard M. Chapin, *Rhode Island in the Colonial Wars, A List of Rhode Island Soldiers & Sailors in the Old French & Indian War.* (Providence, RI: Rhode Island Historical Society, 1918).

[42]Cranston, RI, Land Records, Volume 2, page 278.

[43]Cranston, Providence County, RI, Land Records, Volume 1, page 548.

[44]Ibid., Volume 2, page 278.

[45]E B O'Callaghan, *The Documentary History of the State of New York* (Albany, NY: Charles Van Benthuysen, 1851), Volume 4, page 888.

[46]William's Papers, Box 8, folder 17, New York State Archives.

[47]Vermont Secretary of State Records, Volume 21, page 70.

Huldah Burlingame[48] was born circa 1742 at Coventry, Kent County, RI. She died on 21 Aug 1804 at Oxford, Chenango County, NY; Huldah's tombstone is broken and says 21 Aug 18__. However, Huldah signed a deed on 3 Jun 1803 but she is not mentioned in the gift of land by her husband to their son on 1 May 1804 and is presumed to have died on 21 Aug 1804. She was buried at Gregory Cemetery, Oxford, Chenango County, NY.[49] Huldah received 1 silver dollar in her fathers will suggesting that she lived a distance from her father who died in Coventry, RI in 1794.

Known children of Thomas [I] Lyon and Huldah Burlingame were as follows:

+ 5.   i.   Samuel Lyon was born circa 1760. He married Maphlet Miller, daughter of John Miller and Mehitable Slawson, on 3 Jul 1777 at Church of Christ, Salem, Washington County, NY. He married Olive Rowley circa 1782. He died on 28 Nov 1828 at Oxford, Chenango County, NY.

+ 6.   ii.   Colonel Thomas [II] Lyon was born circa 1762 at RI. He married Eunice Bennett, daughter of Moses Bennett and Eunice Hurlburt, say 1780. He married Eunice Crandall (Widow) in 1798. He married Mercy Brown, daughter of Jesse Brown and Mary Boone, on 4 Apr 1802 at Presbyterian Church, Norwich, Chenango County, NY. He died on 27 Apr 1813 at York, Ontario, Canada. He was buried in May 1813 at Fort Tompkins, Sackets Harbor, Jefferson County, NY.

+ 7.   iii.   Dr. Daniel Lyon was born before 1767 at RI. He married Elizabeth Noble, daughter of Ephriam Noble, circa 1792. He died in 1811 at the Owego River, Tioga County, NY.

+ 8.   iv.   Alexander Lyon was born on 21 Apr 1776 at Sandgate, Bennington County, VT. He married Olive Van Berger, daughter of John Van Berger and Hannah Flowers, circa 1797 at Chenango County, NY. He died on 20 Feb 1851 at Hector, Tompkins County, NY, at age 74.

+ 9.   v.   Anna B. Lyon was born say 1780 at Sandgate, Bennington County, VT. She married Daniel Gregory, son of Jachin Gregory, circa 1794. She married (--?--) Tanner after 1804. She died on 27 Oct 1824.

  10.   vi.   John Lyon was born circa 1780 at Sandgate, Bennington County, VT.

                There are no primary sources to link John to his assumed parents of Thomas Lyon [I] and Huldah Burlingame. It is assumed that they were his parents based on his witnessing the sale of land by Thomas Lyon [I] and Thomas Lyon[II].[50]

  11.   vii.   Esick Lyon[51] was born in 1781 at Sandgate, Bennington County, VT. He died on 18 May 1802 at NY. He was buried at Gregory Cemetery, Oxford, Chenango County, NY.[52]

                There are no primary sources to link Esick to his assumed parents of Thomas Lyon [I] and Huldah Burlingame. It is assumed that they were his parents based on his witnessing the sale of land by Thomas Lyon [I] and Thomas Lyon[II].[53]

4. Experience Lyon (*John*)[54] was born circa 1741. She married John Spencer, son of Richard Spencer and Hannah (--?--), on 25 Feb 1760 at East Greenwich, Kent County, RI; Arnold has date as 26 Dec 1760 under the Spencer heading but as 25 Feb 1760 under the Lyon heading. The town records say 25 Feb 1760.
The marriage was performed by Elder John Gorton pastor of the Warwick and East Greenwich Baptist Church whose records give the date as 21 Feb 1760 and say Experience Lyon was daughter of John and was of East Greenwich.[55,56]

John Spencer[57] was born on 7 Oct 1730 at East Greenwich, Kent County, RI.[58]

[48]Arnold, *Vital Records of Rhode Island 1636-1850.*, Cranston Marriages Records Volume 1, page 250.

[49]Gone but Not Forgotten, Oxford Burial Grounds,, Chenango Co. Historian, 45 Rexford St., Norwich, Chenango County, NY.

[50]Chenango County, NY, Land Records, Volume O, page 460.

[51]Tombstone, Gregory Cemetery, Oxford, Chenango County, NY.

[52]DAR NY Cemetery, Church, & Town Records, 1930, Volume 26, page 184.

[53]Chenango County, NY, Land Records, Volume O, page 460.

[54]Arnold, *Vital Records of Rhode Island 1636-1850.*, Volume 7, Marriages of John Gorton.

[55]East Greenwich, RI, Vital Records, Volume 2, page 16.

[56]Arnold, *Vital Records of Rhode Island 1636-1850.*, Volume 7, Marriages of John Gorton.

Known children of Experience Lyon and John Spencer were as follows:

12. i. John Spencer Jr was born on 9 Oct 1761 at East Greenwich, Kent County, RI; Arnold has birth year as 1781 which is incorrect.[59] He married Hope Pearce in 1784.[60]

13. ii. Captain Simmons Spencer was born on 23 Jun 1766 at East Greenwich, Kent County, RI.[61] He married Amey Briggs, daughter of Joseph Briggs and Lydia Miller, on 7 Jun 1789 at Warwick, Kent County, RI.[62] He married Ruth Miller on 11 Nov 1792 at East Greenwich, Kent County, RI.[63] He died on 27 May 1849 at age 82.[64]

   Amey Briggs[65] was born on 1 Feb 1779 at Warwick, Kent County, RI.[66]
   Ruth Miller[67] was born circa 1766.[68] She died on 21 Jul 1860. She was buried at East Greenwich Cemetery, East Greenwich, Kent County, RI.[69]

14. iii. Lydia Spencer was born on 27 Feb 1770 at RI.[70] She married Ebenezer Williams on 31 Oct 1793 at East Greenwich, Kent County, RI.[71] She died on 4 Jan 1867 at East Greenwich, Kent County, RI, at age 96.[72] She was buried at East Greenwich Cemetery, East Greenwich, Kent County, RI.[73]

   Her birth 27 Feb 1770 isn't recorded in the East Greenwich vital records. Her marriage to Ebenezer Williams lists her as Lydia Spencer of John.[74]
   Ebenezer Williams was born circa 1768.[75] He died on 1 Oct 1825.[76] He was buried at East Greenwich Cemetery, East Greenwich, Kent County, RI.[77]

[57]Ibid., East Greenwich, Volume 2, page 16.
[58]Louise Brownell Clarke, *The Greene's of Rhode Island* (New York, 1903), page 81-2.
[59]East Greenwich, RI, Vital Records, Volume 2, page 229.
[60]Clarke, *The Greene's of Rhode Island*, page 81-2.
[61]East Greenwich, RI, Vital Records, Volume 2, page 128.
[62]Arnold, *Vital Records of Rhode Island 1636-1850.*, Warwick, Volume 2, page 182.
[63]East Greenwich, RI, Vital Records, Volume 2, page 82.
[64]Tombstone.
[65]Arnold, *Vital Records of Rhode Island 1636-1850.*, Warwick, Volume 2, page 252.
[66]Ibid.
[67]Clarke, *The Greene's of Rhode Island*, page 81-2.
[68]Find A Grave www.findagrave.com.
[69]Ibid.
[70]Tombstone.
[71]East Greenwich, RI, Vital Records, Volume 2, page 83.
[72]Tombstone.
[73]Find A Grave.
[74]East Greenwich, RI, Vital Records.
[75]Tombstone.
[76]Ibid.
[77]Find A Grave.

Generation Three

5. Samuel Lyon (*Thomas, John*) was born circa 1760; his tombstone gives his age as 68 years.[78] He married Maphlet Miller, daughter of John Miller and Mehitable Slawson, on 3 Jul 1777 at Church of Christ, Salem, Washington County, NY.[79] He married Olive Rowley circa 1782. He died on 28 Nov 1828 at Oxford, Chenango County, NY. He was buried at Gregory Cemetery, Oxford, Chenango County, NY.[80]

A record "of the Seventh Company of the First Regiment of Militia Commanded by Col John Williams in Charlotte County where of Charles Hutchison is Captain" lists 88 men including Thomas and Samuel Lyon. Both were in service and received pay between 20 June 1777 and 20 Oct 1777. Samuel Lyon served 60 days and received 5.6.8

He also served in Col Warner's Vermont Rangers and in Captain Munro's Company 1, New Hampshire Regiment.[81,82]

Maphlet Miller[83] was born say 1757.
There were no known children of Samuel Lyon and Maphlet Miller.

Olive Rowley was born circa 1763; her tombstone gives her age at death as being 61 years. She died on 2 May 1824 at Oxford, Chenango County, NY. She was buried at Gregory Cemetery, Oxford, Chenango County, NY.[84]

Known children of Samuel Lyon and Olive Rowley were as follows:

+ 15.   i.   Daniel Lyon was born say 1785. He married Asenath Cook.
+ 16.   ii.   Elizabeth Lyon was born on 7 Dec 1786. She married Ira Burlingame, son of Lt Israel Burlingame and Eunice Crandall, circa 1803 at Chenango County, NY. She died on 4 Jul 1864 at Franklinville, Carraraugus County, NY, at age 77. She was buried at Cadiz Cemetery, Franklinville, Cattaraugus County, NY.
+ 17.   iii.   Samuel Lyon was born circa 1789. He married (--?--) Betsey circa 1815. He died on 2 May 1867. He was buried at North Norwich Cemetery, North Norwich, Chenango County, NY.
+ 18.   iv.   Mary Lyon was born circa 1794 at NY. She married Samuel Pollard, son of James Pollard and Mercy Barlett.
+ 19.   v.   Sally Lyon was born circa 1795 at NY. She married Greene Rathbun, son of Greene Rathbun and Sarah Nichols, in 1818.
+ 20.   vi.   Huldah Lyon was born in 1796 at NY. She married Charles Smith.
+ 21.   vii.   George Rowley Lyon was born on 16 Aug 1800. He married Susanne Lyon, daughter of David Lyon and Charity Wilson, on 28 Dec 1822. He died on 19 Jul 1887 at age 86. He was buried at Sylvan Lawn Cemetery, Greene, Chenango County, NY.
+ 22.   viii.   Lucina Lyon was born on 1 Apr 1803 at NY. She married John Pollard, son of James Pollard and Mercy Barlett, circa 1825. She died on 25 Mar 1881 at Vernon County, WI, at age 77. She was buried at Liberty Pole Cemetery, Viroqua, Vernon County, WI.

[78] Tombstone, Gregory Cemetery, Oxford, Chenango County, NY.

[79] Nelson B. Tiffany, *Revolutionary War Veterans, Chenango County, New York* (Norwich, NY: Chenango County Historical Society, c 1998).

[80] Gone but Not Forgotten.

[81] William's Papers, Box 8, folder 17.

[82] Tiffany, *Revolutionary War Veterans, Chenango.*

[83] Ibid.

[84] Gone but Not Forgotten.

23. ix. Lucina Lyon married (--?--) Baker.[85]

        She was also known as Lucinda Lyon. The Lyon Memorials, based on information given by Anna Holcomb says this person, Lucina Lyon, married a person named Baker, and is a twin of Lovina who married John Pollard.

        There is a Lucinda, born 1794 who married a Silas Baker and is buried in the Pitcher Congregational Church Cemetery, Chenango County, NY. Further, the 1850 and 1860 census say she was born in Vermont whereas the 1870 census gives he birth as NY. If she was a Lyon her twin sister would be Mary (Polly) Lyon who was also born in 1794 and not the sister that married John Pollard who was named Lucina Lyon and born 1 Apr 1803.[86]

+ 24. x. Lovisa Lyon was born on 14 Aug 1806. She married William T Smith circa 1832. She died on 9 Oct 1884 at age 78. She was buried at Sylvan Lawn Cemetery, Greene, Chenango County, NY.

25. xi. Ira Lyon.[87]

6. Colonel Thomas [II] Lyon (*Thomas, John*)[88,89] was born circa 1762 at RI. He married Eunice Bennett, daughter of Moses Bennett and Eunice Hurlburt, say 1780. He married Eunice Crandall (Widow) in 1798.[90] He married Mercy Brown, daughter of Jesse Brown and Mary Boone, on 4 Apr 1802 at Presbyterian Church, Norwich, Chenango County, NY.[91] He died on 27 Apr 1813 at York, Ontario, Canada. He was buried in May 1813 at Fort Tompkins, Sackets Harbor, Jefferson County, NY; Captain Thomas Lyon, General Zebulon M Pike, Captain Benjamin Nicholson and probably Col John L Tuttle were all buried within the ramparts of Fort Tompkins. Their remands have been moved at least three times since and the exact location of their grave in the military burial ground is uncertain.

There is a family tombstone in Mt Hope Cemetery, Norwich NY that implies he is buried there. However, that tombstone was paid for and erected by the estate of his granddaughter Mary Elizabeth Knapp. Her will states the tombstone was to be erected "where my grandmother Mercy Lyon, my father and my mother are buried" which implies that Captain Thomas Lyon is not buried there.

Emily M (Coburn) Austin in her book, <u>Mormonism or life among the Mormons</u> implies he was buried in Norwich, NY and Olive Buckley, a great granddaughter of Hezekiah Brown, in a 1931 letter says that Hezekiah brought the body back to Norwich.[92,93]

Notes located in the Chenango County Historian's Office indicate that Thomas Lyon was married 4 times and had 16 children.

History of Chenango County says that Thomas took a seat on the bench of Common Pleas Court as an associate Judge in Oct 1805 and <u>The Annals of Oxford</u> say Major Lyon "led a regiment of State Troops from the County of Chenango in the War of 1812. Toward the close of 1813 General Dearborn, under whom Major Lyon served, crossed Lake Erie with seventeen hundred men with the intention of attacking York [now Toronto] and then the chief depot of the British posts in the West. A landing was made before York on the 27th of April under hot fire, but the Americans pushed on and the enemy was driven from the works. The Americans were still pressing toward the main works when a powder magazine exploded." The magazine contained about 200 barrels of powder and may have been a trap set by the British. "Two hundred Americans were killed or wounded, among the mortally wounded being Major Lyon who lost a leg and was

[85] Dr G. W. A. Lyon, *Lyon Memorial, NY Families* (Detroit MI: William Graham, 1907), page 322.
[86] Ibid.
[87] Ibid.
[88] Military Minutes of the Council of Appointments of the State of New York, Council of Appointment, Military 1783-1821, 1901, New York State Library.
[89] Kenneth A Perry, *The Fitch Gazetteer an Annotated Index to the Manuscript History of Washington County NY* (MD: Heritage Books, 1999), page 241.
[90] James H. Smith, *History of Chenango and Madison Counties 1784-1880* (1880).
[91] Court Deposition ~1860 relative to Mercy Lyon's Pension.
[92] *National Cemetery at Sackets Harbor, NY*, (Watertown, NY: Watertown Daily Times, 27 Apr 1946), Clipping file 132/4, Plattsburgh NY SUNY.
[93] Emily M. Austin, *Mormonism or life among the Mormons* (Madison, WI: 1882), page 8.

carried on board the Commodore's vessel where he died." <u>The Lyon Memorial, New York Families</u> adds "in fact, the troops who were engaged were under the command of General Zebulon M. Pike, and that officer, with two of his aides, one of them very possibly Major Lyon, were mortally injured in the explosion. General Pike lingered long enough to receive the British flag which was under his head as a pillow when he died."

In spite of General Dearborn's orders to the contrary, public buildings of York were burned. This set off a chain of burnings which ultimately led to the burning of Washington, DC in 1814.

During the battle of York Thomas Lyon was serving as captain in the 16th Regiment of Infantry, Col. Pearce commanding. He held the rank of Major and Lieutenant Colonel at other times. Captain Lyon's rifle company with 1 Captain, 1 Lieutenants, 1 Ensigns, 2 Sergeants, and 24 rank and file was listed under Col William Claus on 7 Jul 1812 at Ft George, Ontario, Canada.[94] Thomas Lyon's military positions are as follows:

1797, he was a Lieutenant in John Fitch's Company, Benjamin Hovey's Regiment.

1802, Thomas Lyon Jr was a Captain and his uncle Samuel Lyon was a Major. Later that year Daniel Lyon was a Surgeon.

1804, Thomas Lyon Jr was a First Major. The use of the term Jr indicates that his father Thomas Lyon was still alive.

1806, Thomas Lyon was a Lieutenant Colonel.

1807, Thomas Lyon was Lieutenant Colonel, an unidentified Daniel Lyon a Second Lieutenant and Daniel Lyon Surgeon.

1809, Thomas Lyon Lieutenant Colonel, Daniel Lyon Captain.

1810, Thomas Lyon Lieutenant Colonel and Samuel Lyon Ensign.

!811, Thomas Lyon Lieutenant Colonel.

1811, Daniel Lyon Surgeon was deceased.[95]

Thomas Lyon belonged to the Masonic Eastern Light Lodge.

Eunice Bennett was born on 21 Jan 1751 at Fairfield, Fairfield County, CT. She died before 1801 at Chenango County, NY.[96]

Known children of Colonel Thomas [II] Lyon and Eunice Bennett were as follows:

26.   i.   Thomas Lyon III was born say 1785. He died on 3 Sep 1837.[97]

This is the Thomas Lyon, Jr. who made the court deposition concerning Capt. Thomas Lyon's death in 1813. It is not positively known which of the first two wives of Thomas Lyon was his mother. Thomas Lyon was an ensign in the NY 16th Infantry on 6 Jul 1813. That is the same Company that his father had commanded at the time of his death.

He was a 2nd Lt in 16th U. S. Infantry, Captain M. Greenwood's Company on 15 Aug 1813 and resigned 6 Nov 1814.[98] He retired from the service on 30 Nov 1814.[99]

+ 27.   ii.   Rose Linda Lyon was born circa 1784. She married Amariah Coburn, son of Nathaniel Coburn, in 1802. She died in 1855.

Known children of Colonel Thomas [II] Lyon include:

28.   i.   Sterry Lyon[100] married Elizabeth (--?--).[101]

On 21 Jul 1834 Sterry Lyon of Washington County, MI acquired 1/2 of the NE quarter of section 20 in Howell Township, Livingston County, MI. There were several Gregory's abutting Sterry's land.

---

[94]Ernest Cruikshank, *The First American Frontier* (Reprinted Arno Press, 1971),Book 1, Volume 1, page 18.

[95]Military Minutes of the Council of Appointments of the State of New York.

[96]Lynda McGinnis, *Christoffersen Family Chart*.

[97]Solinda Christoffersen phone and written material.

[98]Heitman F. B., *Historical Register of the US Army* (Washington, DC: pub., 1890), page 650.

[99]U. S. Archives Military Records Group 94, Lt Thomas Lyon III, 1814.

[100]Milton Charboneau, *Early Land Owners & Settlers of Livingston County Michigan 1826 to 1870's*.

[101]Ibid., page 473.

Nancy and Charles S Gregory of Washtenaw County acquired the west 1/2 of the NE and SE quarter of section 20 respectively on 20 Jun 1835 making them Sterry's next door neighbor.

On 28 Sep 1835 Morgan Lyon of Chenango County NY acquired the NE quarter of section 18 in the same township. Sections 18 and 20 are catty-cornered to each other so Sterry's and Morgan's lots would be about 3/4 miles apart with the Gregory lots between.

Based on these land purchases and location it is assumed that Sterry Lyon is a child of Thomas.[102]

29.   ii.   Nancy Lyon was born in 1780.[103] She married Robert Hazard.[104]

       Nancy is said to be a daughter of Col Thomas Lyon.[105]

       Robert Hazard was born on 6 Oct 1779 at Southington, Hartford County, CT. He died in 1807 at Chenango County, NY.[106]

30.   iii.   Rufas Lyon was born on 15 Jun 1796 at Oxford, Chenango County, NY.[107]

       Rufus selected his uncle Alexander as his guardian after his father's death.

Eunice Crandall (Widow) died between 1801 and 1802; Thomas Lyon and his wife Eunice signed a deed on 23 Oct 1801. On 30 Mar 1802 Thomas appeared in court and swore to the deed with no mention of wife Eunice. He married Mercy Brown on 4 Apr 1802 according to her pension application. History of Chenango & Madison County NY 1784-1880, states that he married Widow Crandall in 1798 in town of Preston, NY. The parents of Widow Crandall may have been Moses Bennett and Eunice Hurlburt.[108]

There were no known children of Colonel Thomas [II] Lyon and Eunice Crandall (Widow).

Mercy Brown was born in 1774 at RI.[109] She died on 31 Oct 1862 at Guilford Center, Chenango County, NY. She was buried at Mt Hope Cemetery, Norwich, Chenango County, NY.

Known children of Colonel Thomas [II] Lyon and Mercy Brown were as follows:

+ 31.   i.   Betsey Lyon was born on 10 Feb 1803 at Oxford, Chenango County, NY. She married George Knapp, son of George Knapp and Mary Rathbun, circa 1825. She died on 27 Jan 1884 at Guilford Center, Chenango County, NY, at age 80. She was buried at Mt Hope Cemetery, Norwich, Chenango County, NY.

+ 32.   ii.   Morgan Lyon was born on 16 Oct 1810 at Norwich, Chenango County, NY. He married Mary Purple, daughter of Isham Purple and Phoebe Rogers, circa 1835 at Norwich, Chenango County, NY. He married Louisa Purple, daughter of Isham Purple and Phoebe Rogers, circa 1850 at Norwich, Chenango County, NY. He died on 1 Apr 1893 at Vergennes, Kent County, MI, at age 82. He was buried at Foxes Cemetery, Lowell, Kent County, MI.

+ 33.   iii.   William Brown Lyon was born on 5 Jun 1812 at Chenango County, NY. He married Nancy Cahoon on 5 Jan 1834 at Norwich, Chenango County, NY. He married Caroline Smith on 13 Mar 1856. He died on 29 Jan 1897 at Cedar Springs, Kent County, MI, at age 84. He was buried at Roth Coons Cemetery, Lowell, Kent County, MI.

34.   iv.   Mary Lyon.[110]

+ 35.   v.   Lucinda Lyon married Charles H Newton.

---

[102]Everts & Abbott, *History of Livingston County Michigan* (1880).

[103]Tiffany, *Revolutionary War Veterans, Chenango*.

[104]Chenango County, NY, Land Records, Book P, page 45.

[105]Tiffany, *Revolutionary War Veterans, Chenango*.

[106]Ibid.

[107]Robert J Howard, *Extracts of Chenango County Guardianship Records*, Page 35. Refers to Chenango Guardianship Records Book A page 55.

[108]Smith, *History of Chenango and Madison Counties 1784-1880*.

[109]Nelson Tiffany, *DAR Revolutionary War Veterans Records, Chenango County, NY* (Chenango County, NY).

[110]Solinda Christoffersen phone and written material.

7. Dr. Daniel Lyon (*Thomas, John*)[111] was born before 1767 at RI.[112] He married Elizabeth Noble, daughter of Ephriam Noble, circa 1792.[113] He died in 1811 at the Owego River, Tioga County, NY; The probate records of Dr Daniel Lyon include a testimony by Thomas Lyon Jr [III] that says, "that he this deponent was in a boat on the Owego River near the mouth thereof with Daniel Lyon late of the town of Oxford and that the said boat was upset and the said Daniel Lyon drowned and that Elizabeth Lyon is widow of the said deceased."

This testimony is in agreement with the entry in the *Military Minutes of the Council of Appointments of the State of New York, Council of Appointments, Military, 1783-1821* which state in 1811 that he then was deceased and replaced by the Surgeons Mate Levi Farr. The last Military Records entry where he was alive is 1809.[114,115]

A Daniel Lyon was listed as an Ensign in the Saratoga County Militia in 1796 at Saratoga County, NY.[116] Daniel was listed in the 1810 census living between Alexander Lyon and Moses Bennett. He and his wife were in the age group 26-45. There were 4 boys and 3 girls in house also in 1810 at Oxford, Chenango County, NY.[117]

Elizabeth Noble was born in 1775. She died in 1852 at Bradford County, PA. She was buried at Monroeton Cemetery, Monroeton, Bradford County, PA.[118]

Known children of Dr. Daniel Lyon and Elizabeth Noble all born at Oxford, Chenango County, NY, were as follows:

+ 36.   i.   Captain Daniel Lyon was born on 22 Sep 1794. He married Elizabeth Lewis say 1820 at Chenango County, NY. He died in 1849.
+ 37.   ii.   Truxton Lyon was born in 1796. He married Olive Lewis, daughter of Benjamin Lewis, say 1819. He married Harriet (--?--) say 1832. He died on 15 Nov 1862.
   38.   iii.   Randolph Lyon. In 1821 Randolph wasn't listed as one of the sellers of his father's portion of lot 55 in Chenango County. It is said that he had gone to Canada where he became a musician.[119,120]
   39.   iv.   Marcus Lyon died before 1821; In 1821 Marcus wasn't listed as one of the sellers of his father's portion of lot 55 in Chenango County and is presumed to be deceased by then.[121]
   40.   v.   Sally Lyon[122] married Sherman Havins before 1821. She died after 31 Aug 1821.
     Sherman Havins and his wife Sally sold their portion of her father's land to William Bennett on 31 Aug 1821.[123]
   41.   vi.   Laura Lyon[124] married (--?--) Ross.
+ 42.   vii.   Cynthia Lyon was born in 1806. She married Isaac Huyck, son of William Huyck and Margaret Westbrook. She died on 14 Oct 1892.

8. Alexander Lyon (*Thomas, John*)[125] was born on 21 Apr 1776 at Sandgate, Bennington County, VT; Cyclopedia of Chautauqua County NY, in an autobiography written by his son Charles, says Alexander was born in Chenango County NY in 1776. This cannot be true as Chenango County was closed to settlement until

[111]Perry, *The Fitch Gazetteer*, page 241.
[112]William's Papers, Box 5, folder 10.
[113]Clement F. Heverly, *Pioneer and Patriot Families of Bradford County, PA 1770-1800* (Towanda, PA: Bradford Star Print, 1913), Volume 2, page 401.
[114]Probate Records, Chenango County, NY, Letters of Administration Volume A, page 15.
[115]Military Minutes of the Council of Appointments of the State of New York, Volume 2, page 1278.
[116]Ibid., Volume 1, page 350.
[117]United States 1810 Census, Oxford, Chenango County, NY.
[118]Tombstone, Monroeton Cemetery.
[119]Chenango County, NY, Land Records, Volume 54, page 9.
[120]C F Heverly, *History of Monroe Township and Borough 1779-1885* (Towanda, PA: Journal Printing Company, 1885).
[121]Chenango County, NY, Land Records, Volume 54, page 9.
[122]Heverly, *Pioneer and Patriot Families of Bradford County, PA 1770-1800*.
[123]Chenango County, NY, Land Records, Volume 54, page 9.
[124]Heverly, *Pioneer and Patriot Families of Bradford County, PA 1770-1800*.
[125]Chenango County, NY, Land Records, Volume G, page 459.

1789. In 1776 his parents owned property in both Sandgate VT and Salem NY. Further, in the 1850 census Alexander said he was born in VT.[126,127] He married Olive Van Berger, daughter of John Van Berger and Hannah Flowers, circa 1797 at Chenango County, NY.[128] He died on 20 Feb 1851 at Hector, Tompkins County, NY, at age 74.[129]

Alexander died intestate and his estate was administered on 29 Mar 1851 in Tompkins County, NY. The administration mentions widow Olive; heirs Sophia wife of Amos Westcott, Ozro Lyon, James Lyon, Alvah Lyon, Rosanna wife of Walter Lumis, John Lyon, Charles Lyon, Alanson Lyon, Ruth Lewis (deceased) and Benjamin Lyon (deceased). Ruth Lewis left children Simeon, Charles, John, Almira, Artemesia and Thomas O: Benjamin Lyon left wife Martha now wife on Isaac Adams and children Maria, Olive, Luther, Eseck, Alanzo, Delia, Lydia and Madison.[130] The Biography and History of Chautauqua County, New York says that Alexander had 13 children, some of whom were born in Oxford, Chenango County and that Alexander moved to Tompkins County in 1825.[131] Alexander Lyon is listed in the 1850 Hector, Tompkins County, NY census. In 1854 Schuyler County was created and included part of Tompkins County which put Hector into Schuyler County.[132]

Olive Van Berger[133] was born on 8 Nov 1778 at West Springfield, Hampden County, MA. She died on 3 Sep 1853 at Tompkins County, NY, at age 74.

Known children of Alexander Lyon and Olive Van Berger were as follows:

+ 43. i. James Lyon was born on 22 Nov 1796 at Oxford, Chenango County, NY. He married Aseneath Smith. He married Johanna (--?--) before 1850. He died on 20 Apr 1856 at Marshall County, IN, at age 59. He was buried at Burr Oak Cemetery, Culver, Marshall County, IN.

+ 44. ii. Roxylena Lyon was born on 7 Mar 1798 at Oxford, Chenango County, NY. She married Walter Simmons. She died on 19 Dec 1892 at Chautauqua County, NY, at age 94. She was buried at Fluvanna Cemetery, Ellicott, Chautauqua County, NY.

  45. iii. Esick Lyon was born on 13 Dec 1799 at Oxford, Chenango County, NY. He married Maria Davis.[134] He died circa 1841 at Busti, Chautauqua County, NY.

He left a will on 22 Mar 1841; proven 22 Mar 1841. Mentions wife Maria, father Alexander, siblings James Lyon, Rosa S Simmons, Alvah Lyon, Martha P Lewis, John Lyon, Benjamin Lyon, Ozro Lyon, Sophia N Westcott, Charles Lyon and Alanson Lyon.[135]

Maria Davis[136] died after 22 Mar 1841.

+ 46. iv. Alvah Lyon was born circa 1803 at Oxford, Chenango County, NY. He married Wealtha (--?--) circa 1824. He died after 1880 at Hamilton County, OH.

+ 47. v. Martha P. Lyon was born circa 1805 at NY. She married Simeon Rathbun Lewis, son of James Lewis and Olive Rathbun. She died between 1841 and 1851.

+ 48. vi. John Lyon was born in 1806 at Oxford, Chenango County, NY. He married Ann Frances Wescott circa 1830. He married Rebecca Chapin, daughter of Roderick Chapin and Hepsipah Norton, circa 1842. He died on 25 Dec 1893 at Newark, Licking County, OH. He was buried at Cedar Hill Cemetery, Newark, Licking County, OH.

[126]United States 1850 Census, Hector, Tompkins County, NY.

[127]Obed Edson, *Biography and Portrait Cyclopedia of Chautauqua County, New York*. Also known as *Biography and History of Chautauqua County* (Philadelphia PA: John Graham, 1891), page 36.

[128]Letter Lynda K. McGinnis to Guy Wallis, 5 Dec 1997.

[129]Helen F Lewis, *New York Finger Lake Pioneer Families*, page 217.

[130]Lewis, *New York Finger Lake Pioneer Families*.

[131]Edson, *Biography and History of Chautauqua County*, page 36.

[132]United States 1850 Census, Hector, Tompkins County, NY.

[133]Edson, *Biography and History of Chautauqua County*.

[134]Ted Thomas Lyons, *William Lyon of Roxbury, MA and Some of his Descendants* (Belton, MO: Lyon's Families Association of America, 1997), page 70.

[135]Chautauqua County NY, Will book 1 1830-1843, Will book I 1830-1843, page 359.

[136]Lyons, *William Lyon of Roxbury, MA and Some of his Descendants*, page 70.

+ 49. vii. Benjamin Lyon was born on 8 Mar 1808 at Oxford, Chenango County, NY. He married Mary Ann Mathews circa 1840. He died between 22 Mar 1841 and 1845.

+ 50. viii. Ozro Lyon was born on 16 Apr 1810 at Oxford, Chenango County, NY. He married Emeline Williams on 23 Oct 1830. He died on 25 Sep 1891 at Warren County, PA, at age 81. He was buried at Foster Cemetery, Lander, Warren County, PA.

   51. ix. Francisco Lyon was born circa 1812 at Oxford, Chenango County, NY. He died young by drowning.[137]

+ 52. x. Sophia Ann Lyon was born on 20 Jun 1814 at Oxford, Chenango County, NY. She married Amos Westcott. She died on 20 Jun 1893 at NY at age 79. She was buried at Seneca Union Cemetery, Valois, Schuyler County, NY.

   53. xi. Alexander Lyon was born circa 1816 at Oxford, Chenango County, NY. He died young by drowning.[138]

+ 54. xii. Charles J Lyon was born on 12 Feb 1819 at Oxford, Chenango County, NY. He married Hester Ann Chapin, daughter of Roderick Chapin and Sarah Clough, on 11 Sep 1839 at Tompkins County, NY. He died on 11 Feb 1895 at Jamestown, Chautauqua County, NY, at age 75.

+ 55. xiii. Alanson Lyon was born on 26 May 1822 at Oxford, Chenango County, NY. He married Barbara Ann Norton. He died on 18 Apr 1889 at Allegheny County, PA, at age 66.

+**9.** Anna B. ~~Lyon~~ *Bennett* (*Thomas, John*) was born say 1780 at Sandgate, Bennington County, VT. She married Daniel Gregory, son of Jachin Gregory, circa 1794.[139] She married (--?--) Tanner after 1804.[140] She died on 27 Oct 1824.[141]

There are no primary sources to link Anna B to her assumed parents of Thomas Lyon [I] and Huldah Burlingame. The linkage is based on that assumption in "Ancestors and Descendants of Henry Gregory" and Daniel Gregory's will being witnessed by Samuel and Alexander Lyon and Thomas Lyon Jr [II] being the executor.

Daniel Gregory was baptized on 17 Nov 1765 at Wilton, Fairfield County, CT.[142] He died circa Jan 1804 at Chenango County, NY. He left a will on 5 Sep 1803 at Oxford, Chenango County, NY; probated on 3 Feb 1804. Will mentions wife Anna, sons Asa and Daniel, daughter Polly, brother Jakin. Thomas Lyon Jr. [II] and Uri Tracy were named as executors. Samuel Gregory, Samuel and Alexander Lyon signed as witnesses.[143]

Known children of Anna B. Lyon and Daniel Gregory all born at Oxford, Chenango County, NY, were as follows:

   56. i. Asa Gregory was born on 30 Aug 1795.[144] He married Arenal Spencer.[145]

        Arenal Spencer was born on 4 Mar 1799.[146]

   57. ii. Polly Gregory was born on 1 Jan 1797. She married Ezra Huntley. She died on 26 Dec 1828 at Chenango County, NY, at age 31.[147] She was buried at Saint Andrews Cemetery, New Berlin, Chenango County, NY.[148]

---

[137]Ibid.

[138]Ibid.

[139]Grant Gregory, *Ancestors and Descendants of Henry Gregory* (Rutland, VT: Tuttle Publishing Co, 1938), page 124.

[140]Ibid., page 125.

[141]Ibid., page 124.

[142]Gregory, *Ancestors and Descendants of Henry Gregory*.

[143]Guy Wallis, *Notes from the files of the Surrogate Court of Chenango County, NY* (1995), Liber A, page 38.

[144]Gregory, *Ancestors and Descendants of Henry Gregory*, page 125.

[145]RootsWeb WorldConnect Project, Kent database.

[146]Ibid.

[147]Gregory, *Ancestors and Descendants of Henry Gregory*, page 125.

[148]Find A Grave.

Ezra Huntley[149] was born on 1 Jan 1777. He died on 12 Dec 1857 at age 80. He was buried at Saint Andrews Cemetery, New Berlin, Chenango County, NY.[150]

58. iii. Daniel Gregory was born on 26 Nov 1799.[151] He married Charlotte H (--?--). He died between 1870 and 1880.[152]

59. iv. John Gregory was born on 9 May 1802. He died on 9 Jul 1802 at Oxford, Chenango County, NY.[153]

60. v. Anna Gregory was born on 22 Mar 1804. She married Reuben Rounds circa 1823. She married (--?--) Clark circa 1851. She died on 14 Nov 1887 at Warren County, PA, at age 83.[154] She was buried at Union Grove Cemetery, Lander, Warren County, PA.[155]

Reuben Rounds was born on 14 Mar 1796. He died on 25 May 1850 at Warren County, PA, at age 54.[156] He was buried at Union Grove Cemetery, Lander, Warren County, PA.[157]

There were no known children of Anna B. Lyon and (--?--) Tanner.

[149]Gregory, *Ancestors and Descendants of Henry Gregory*.
[150]Find A Grave.
[151]Gregory, *Ancestors and Descendants of Henry Gregory*, page 125.
[152]United States 1880 Census, Carthage, Jasper County, MO.
[153]Gregory, *Ancestors and Descendants of Henry Gregory*, page 125.
[154]Ibid.
[155]Find A Grave.
[156]Tombstone.
[157]Find A Grave.

Generation Four

15. Daniel Lyon (*Samuel, Thomas, John*)[158] was born say 1785. He married Asenath Cook.

Daniel Lyon Jr, farmer, bought land from Samuel and Olive Lyon of Oxford, farmer. In 1810 Daniel Jr and wife Asenath sold the land back to Samuel Lyon at Oxford, Chenango County, NY.[159] This is probably the Daniel Lyon numerated in the 1810 Census living between James Bennet and Ephraim Nobles, four residence from his father Samuel.[160]

Asenath Cook[161] was born on 8 Sep 1786. She died in 1828.[162]

Known children of Daniel Lyon and Asenath Cook were:

+ 61.   i.   Miranda Lyon was born circa 1806 at NY. She married Adijah Dewey Chittenden. She died in 1869. She was buried at Riverside Cemetery, Whitney Point, Broome County, NY.

16. Elizabeth Lyon (*Samuel, Thomas, John*)[163] was born on 7 Dec 1786. She married Ira Burlingame, son of Lt Israel Burlingame and Eunice Crandall, circa 1803 at Chenango County, NY.[164] She died on 4 Jul 1864 at Franklinville, Carraraugus County, NY, at age 77.[165] She was buried at Cadiz Cemetery, Franklinville, Cattaraugus County, NY.[166]

She was also known as Betsey Lyon.

Ira Burlingame was born on 5 Nov 1778 at Weathersfield, Windsor County, VT.[167] He died on 29 Nov 1846 at Franklinville, Cattaraugus County, NY, at age 68.[168] He was buried at Cadiz Cemetery, Franklinville, Cattaraugus County, NY.[169]

Known children of Elizabeth Lyon and Ira Burlingame were as follows:

62.   i.   Almira Burlingame was born on 20 Jan 1805 at Oxford, Chenango County, NY. She married Artemus Haynes.[170]

63.   ii.   Selah Burlingame was born on 14 Nov 1806 at Norwich, Chenango County, NY.[171] He married Hannah Maria McClure on 27 Dec 1836.[172] He died on 18 Aug 1862 at age 55.[173] He was buried at Cadiz Cemetery, Franklinville, Cattaraugus County, NY.[174]

Hannah Maria McClure was born circa 1816.[175] She died on 10 Dec 1866.[176] She was buried at Cadiz Cemetery, Franklinville, Cattaraugus County, NY.[177]

---

[158]Lyon, *Lyon Memorial, NY Families*, page 321.
[159]Chenango County, NY, Land Records, Volume L, page 159 and Volume N, page 525.
[160]United States 1810 Census, Oxford, Chenango County, NY.
[161]Chenango County, NY, Land Records, Volume N, page 525.
[162]RootsWeb WorldConnect Project, Kate's database.
[163]Lyon, *Lyon Memorial, NY Families*, page 322.
[164]Ibid.
[165]John W Ladwig, *Rickertson Burlingame* 1997.
[166]Cattaraugus County, NY Cemeteries, 1930.
[167]Art Reierson, *Burlingame Family*.
[168]Tombstone.
[169]Find A Grave.
[170]Reierson, *Burlingame Family*, page 50.
[171]Ibid.
[172]Tombstone.
[173]Reierson, *Burlingame Family*, page 50.
[174]Cattaraugus County, NY Cemeteries.
[175]Find A Grave.
[176]Tombstone.
[177]Cattaraugus County, NY Cemeteries.

64. iii. Philo Burlingame was born on 18 Jan 1809 at Franklinville, Cattaraugus County, NY.[178] He married Sally McClure.

65. iv. LeRoy Burlingame was born on 15 Jan 1811 at NY. He married Deborah Washburn in 1833.[179]

Deborah Washburn died in 1867 at Cattaraugus County, NY.[180] She was buried at Cadiz Cemetery, Cadiz, Cattaraugus County, NY.[181]

66. v. Caroline Burlingame was born on 21 Sep 1813 at Willet, Cortland County, NY. She married Hiram McClure in 1826.[182]

Caroline McClure of Alleghany NY attended the 1883 Lyon reunion and was said to be a descendant of Elizabeth Lyon Burlingame.[183]

67. vi. Sophronia Burlingame was born on 14 Jan 1816 at Oxford, Chenango County, NY. She married Samuel Searle, son of Isaac Searle and Martha Hotchkiss. She died on 25 Jul 1857 at age 41.[184]

Samuel Searle was born in 1812. He died in 1865.

68. vii. Ira Lewellen Burlingame was born on 5 May 1818 at Oxford, Chenango County, NY. He married Paulin Washburn. He died in 1856.[185]

69. viii. John Burlingame was born on 23 Jul 1820 at Oxford, Chenango County, NY. He married Arvilla Searle, daughter of Isaac Searle and Martha Hotchkiss, on 5 Nov 1846.[186] He died on 26 Feb 1887 at age 66. He was buried at Mount Prospect Cemetery, Franklinville, Cattaraugus County, NY.[187]

Arvilla Searle[188] was born on 16 Apr 1825. She died on 9 Mar 1903 at Cattaraugus County, NY, at age 77. She was buried at Mount Prospect Cemetery, Franklinville, Cattaraugus County, NY.[189]

70. ix. Platt Burlingame was born on 22 Sep 1823 at Franklinville, Cattaraugus County, NY.[190] He married Lucy Searle, daughter of Isaac Searle and Martha Hotchkiss, say 1842.[191] He married Lucina Thomas say 1856.[192] He died on 2 Sep 1868 at age 44.[193] He was buried at Mount Morris Cemetery, Mount Morris, Livingston County, NY.[194]

Lucy Searle was born on 8 Dec 1822 at NY. She died on 7 Oct 1854 at Cattaraugus County, NY, at age 31.[195] She was buried at Mount Prospest Cemetery, Franklinveil, Cattaraugus County, NY.[196]

[178]Reierson, *Burlingame Family*, page 50.
[179]Ibid.
[180]Tombstone.
[181]Find A Grave.
[182]Reierson, *Burlingame Family*, page 50.
[183]*Lyon Reunion of 1883*.
[184]Reierson, *Burlingame Family*, page 50.
[185]Ibid.
[186]Ibid.
[187]Find A Grave.
[188]Broderbund, *World Family Tree*, Volume 6.
[189]Find A Grave.
[190]Reierson, *Burlingame Family*, page 50.
[191]United States 1850 Census, Burton, Cattaraugus County, NY.
[192]United States 1860 Census, Mount Morris, Livingston County, NY.
[193]Tombstone.
[194]Find A Grave.
[195]Tombstone.
[196]Find A Grave.

Lucina Thomas was born in 1832 at NY. She died on 20 Feb 1910.[197] She was buried at Mount Morris City Cemetery, Mont Morris, Livingston County, NY.[198]

71.   x.   Elizabeth Burlingame was born on 3 May 1826 at Franklinville, Cattaraugus County, NY. She married DeWitt Scott. She died in 1900 at Corry, PA.[199]

72.   xi.   Artemus Haynes Burlingame was born on 6 Jan 1830. He married Lousia Rogers. He died on 12 Jan 1903 at age 73.[200]

Lousia Rogers was born in May 1832. She died on 3 Apr 1925 at age 92.

73.   xii.   Cathrine Cordlia Burlingame was born on 21 May 1832 at Franklinville, Cattaraugus County, NY. She married Homer Jones.[201]

17. Samuel Lyon (*Samuel, Thomas, John*)[202] was born circa 1789. He married (--?--) Betsey circa 1815. He died on 2 May 1867.[203] He was buried at North Norwich Cemetery, North Norwich, Chenango County, NY.[204]

He was shoemaker in 1860.

(--?--) Betsey was born circa 1792 at NY.[205] She was also known as Eddy.

Known children of Samuel Lyon and (--?--) Betsey all born at NY were as follows:

+ 74.   i.   Anna Augusta Lyon was born circa 1816. She married Cuyler PerLee circa 1842. She died on 6 Jun 1891.

75.   ii.   Catherine Lyon was born circa 1828.[206]

+ 76.   iii.   Theron Lyon was born circa 1829. He married Mary (--?--) say 1858. He died on 10 Mar 1877.

+ 77.   iv.   Thomas Lyon was born circa 1830. He married Mary (--?--).

+ 78.   v.   Darius E Lyon was born circa 1831. He married Mary Ann (--?--) circa 1858. He married Frankie Balcom on 19 Jan 1874 at Sherburne, Chenango County, NY. He died in 1892.

+ 79.   vi.   Janette M Lyon was born circa 1832. She married Charles S Waters circa 1857. She died on 28 Oct 1895.

80.   vii.   Richard Lyon was born circa 1833.
            He was printer.[207]

18. Mary Lyon (*Samuel, Thomas, John*)[208] was born circa 1794 at NY.[209] She married Samuel Pollard, son of James Pollard and Mercy Barlett.[210]

She was also known as Polly Lyon.

Samuel Pollard[211] was born in Jun 1791 at Woodstock, Windsor County, VT.[212] He died on 3 Oct 1871 at Nanticoke, Broome County, NY, at age 80. He was buried at Nanticoke Cemetery, Nanticoke, Broome County, NY.[213]

[197]Tombstone.

[198]Find A Grave.

[199]Reierson, *Burlingame Family*, page 50.

[200]Ibid.

[201]Ibid.

[202]Lyon, *Lyon Memorial, NY Families*, page 322.

[203]Tombstone.

[204]Find A Grave.

[205]United States 1860 Census, North Norwich, Chenango County, NY.

[206]United States 1850 Census, North Norwich, Chenango County, NY.

[207]Ibid., Norwich, Chenango County, NY.

[208]Lyon, *Lyon Memorial, NY Families*, page 322.

[209]United States 1850 Census, Nanticoke, Broome County, NY.

[210]Maurice J Pollard, *History of the Pollard Family in America, The* (Dover, NH: self published, 1964), Volume 2, page 130.

[211]RootsWeb WorldConnect Project, Sally's database.

Known children of Mary Lyon and Samuel Pollard all born at NY were as follows:

81. i. Olive Pollard was born on 28 Aug 1825. She married Charles C Smith. She died on 16 Nov 1891 at NY at age 66.[214] She was buried at Nanticoke Cemetery, Nanticoke, Broome County, NY.[215]

Attended the 1883 Lyon reunion as a descendant of Polly Lyon Pollard.[216]

Charles C Smith was born on 28 Apr 1822 at NY. He died on 6 Nov 1891 at NY at age 69.[217] He was buried at Nanticoke Cemetery, Nanticoke, Broome County, NY.[218]

82. ii. Ronaldo Pollard was born circa 1827. He married Frances Cynthia Smith. He died on 26 Aug 1908 at Berea, Cuyahoga County, OH. He was buried at Woodville Cemetery, Middlebury Heights, Cuyahoga County, OH.[219]

Attended the 1883 Lyon reunion as a descendant of Polly Lyon Pollard.[220]

Frances Cynthia Smith was born on 21 Aug 1837 at NY. She died on 22 Jul 1911 at Berea, Cuyahoga County, NY, at age 73.[221]

83. iii. Harriet Pollard was born on 21 Mar 1830. She married Nathan H Cary. She died on 18 Feb 1855 at Nanticoke, Broome County, NY, at age 24.[222] She was buried at Nanticoke Cemetery, Nanticoke, Broome County, NY.[223]

Attended the 1883 Lyon reunion as a descendant of Polly Lyon Pollard.[224]

Nathan H Cary was born circa 1824 at NY.[225]

84. iv. Noah Pollard was born circa 1832.[226]

85. v. Lydia Pollard was born in 1834. She married Oliver Clark Ferguson circa 1855.[227] She died in 1913 at NY. She was buried in 1914 at Floral Park Cemetery, Johnson City, Broome County, NY.[228]

Oliver Clark Ferguson was born in 1829 at NY. He died in 1902 at NY.[229] He was buried at Floral Park Cemetery, Johnson City, Broome County, NY.[230]

86. vi. Julia Pollard[231] was born circa 1838.[232]

19. Sally Lyon (*Samuel, Thomas, John*)[233] was born circa 1795 at NY. She married Greene Rathbun, son of Greene Rathbun and Sarah Nichols, in 1818.[234]

Greene Rathbun was born circa 1790 at RI. He died on 5 Jan 1851 at Chenango County, NY.[235]

---

[212]US Army Register of Enlistments 1798-1914.
[213]Find A Grave.
[214]Tombstone.
[215]Find A Grave.
[216]*1883 Lyon Reunion.*
[217]Tombstone.
[218]Find A Grave.
[219]Ibid.
[220]*1883 Lyon Reunion.*
[221]Find A Grave.
[222]Tombstone.
[223]Find A Grave.
[224]*1883 Lyon Reunion.*
[225]United States 1850 Census, Nanticoke, Broome County, NY.
[226]Ibid.
[227]United States 1900 Census, Binghamton, Broome County, NY.
[228]Find A Grave.
[229]Tombstone.
[230]Find A Grave.
[231]United States 1850 Census, Nanticoke, Broome County, NY.
[232]United States 1860 Census, Nanticoke, Broome County, NY.
[233]Lyon, *Lyon Memorial, NY Families*, page 321.
[234]RootsWeb WorldConnect Project, T Dowling database.
[235]Ibid.

Known children of Sally Lyon and Greene Rathbun were as follows:

87.   i.   Mary Rathbun was born in 1824 at NY. She married Curtis Chatfield. She died on 8 Jan 1894 at NY. She was buried at Taylor Cemetery, Taylor, Cortland County, NY.[236]

Attended the 1883 Lyon reunion as a descendant of Sally Lyon Rathbun.[237]

Curtis Chatfield was born circa 1824 at New Woodstock, Onondaga County, NY. He died on 12 Jan 1900 at New Woodstock, Onondaga County, NY.[238]

88.   ii.   Lydia Rathbun[239] was born circa 1826 at NY.

89.   iii.   Henry Rathbun[240] was born circa 1828 at NY.

90.   iv.   Randall Robert Rathbun was born circa 1832 at NY. He married Olive H Richards on 23 Dec 1858 at Cincinnatus, Cortland County, NY.[241]

Olive H Richards[242] was born in 1836 at NY. She died in 1901 at NY.[243] She was buried at Cincinnatus Cemetery, Cincinnatus, Cortland County, NY.[244] Attended the 1883 Lyon reunion as a descendant of Sally Lyon Rathbun.[245]

91.   v.   Daniel Rathbun[246] was born circa 1836 at NY.

92.   vi.   John Edgar Rathbun[247] was born circa 1838 at NY. He married Delette Wire at NY. He died in 1912 at NY.[248] He was buried at Cincinnatus Cemetery, Cincinnatus, Cortland County, NY.[249]

Delette Wire was born in 1846 at NY. She died in 1911.[250] She was buried at Cincinnatus Cemetery, Cincinnatus, Cortland County, NY.[251]

93.   vii.   Francis Rathbun[252] was born circa 1843.

20. Huldah Lyon (*Samuel, Thomas, John*)[253] was born in 1796 at NY. She married Charles Smith.[254]

Charles Smith was born circa 1781 at RI.[255]

Known children of Huldah Lyon and Charles Smith all born at NY were as follows:

94.   i.   Almon Smith[256] was born circa 1822.

95.   ii.   Charles Smith[257] was born circa 1825.

96.   iii.   Nathan Smith[258] was born circa 1827.

97.   iv.   Susan Smith[259] was born circa 1830.

---

[236]Find A Grave.

[237]*1883 Lyon Reunion*.

[238]Find A Grave.

[239]United States 1850 Census, Pitcher, Chenango County, NY.

[240]Ibid.

[241]RootsWeb WorldConnect Project, T Dowling database.

[242]Ibid.

[243]Tombstone.

[244]Find A Grave.

[245]*1883 Lyon Reunion*.

[246]United States 1850 Census, Pitcher, Chenango County, NY.

[247]Ibid.

[248]Tombstone.

[249]Find A Grave.

[250]Tombstone.

[251]Find A Grave.

[252]United States 1850 Census, Pitcher, Chenango County, NY.

[253]Lyon, *Lyon Memorial, NY Families*, page 321.

[254]Ibid.

[255]United States 1850 Census, Nanticoke, Broome County, NY.

[256]Ibid.

[257]Ibid.

[258]Ibid.

[259]Ibid.

98.   v.   Martin Smith[260] was born circa 1833.

21. George Rowley Lyon (*Samuel, Thomas, John*) was born on 16 Aug 1800. He married Susanne Lyon, daughter of David Lyon and Charity Wilson, on 28 Dec 1822.[261] He died on 19 Jul 1887 at age 86.[262] He was buried at Sylvan Lawn Cemetery, Greene, Chenango County, NY.[263]

George learned the blacksmith trade from James R Glover and in 1822 moved to Greene where he began the Lyon Iron Works. Attended the 1883 Lyon reunion.[264]

Susanne Lyon was born on 30 May 1803.[265] She died on 29 Mar 1877 at age 73.[266] She was buried at Sylvan Lawn Cemetery, Greene, Chenango County, NY.[267] Susanne Lyon is a descendent of Thomas Lyon of Rye, New York. and not a descendant of William Lyon of Roxbury MA.[268]

Known children of George Rowley Lyon and Susanne Lyon were as follows:

+ 99.   i.   Henry A Lyon was born on 22 Nov 1826 at NY. He married Elvira H Dyer, daughter of John Dyer and Harriet Shaw. He died on 2 Dec 1908 at Greene, Chenango County, NY, at age 82. He was buried at Sylvan Lawn Cemetery, Greene, Chenango County, NY.

+ 100. ii. Anne Eliza Lyon was born in Aug 1829 at NY. She married Judson B Babcock circa 1855. She married Isaac B Perlee in 1888. She died in 1912. She was buried at Sylvan Lawn Cemetery, Greene, Chenango County, NY.

+ 101. iii. George Milton Lyon was born on 15 Feb 1832. He married Eliza C Lewis. He died on 28 Oct 1865 at age 33. He was buried at Sylvan Lawn Cemetery, Greene, Chenango County, NY.

   102. iv. Mary Alice Lyon[269] was born on 11 May 1839. She died in May 1841.[270] She was buried at Sylvan Lawn Cemetery, Greene, Chenango County, NY.[271]

+ 103. v.   Alice Susan Lyon was born on 14 Sep 1842 at NY. She married Anson Burdette Holcomb in 1870. She died on 9 Feb 1896 at age 53. She was buried at Sylvan Lawn Cemetery, Greene, Chenango County, NY.

22. Lucina Lyon (*Samuel, Thomas, John*)[272] was born on 1 Apr 1803 at NY. She married John Pollard, son of James Pollard and Mercy Barlett, circa 1825.[273] She died on 25 Mar 1881 at Vernon County, WI, at age 77.[274] She was buried at Liberty Pole Cemetery, Viroqua, Vernon County, WI.[275]

She was also known as Lucy Lyon.

John Pollard was born circa 1797 at VT.[276] He died on 21 Feb 1864 at Nanticoke, Broome County, NY.[277] He was buried at Nanticoke Cemetery, Nanticoke, Broome County, NY.[278] He was farmer.

Known children of Lucina Lyon and John Pollard were as follows:

---

[260]Ibid.

[261]Lyon, *Lyon Memorial, NY Families*, page 322.

[262]Tombstone, Sylvan Lawn Cemetery, Greene, Chenango County, NY.

[263]Find A Grave.

[264]*1883 Lyon Reunion*.

[265]Lyon, *Lyon Memorial, NY Families*, page 164.

[266]*Chenango American Newspaper*.

[267]Find A Grave.

[268]Lyon, *Lyon Memorial, NY Families*, page 109.

[269]Ibid., page 164.

[270]Tombstone.

[271]Find A Grave.

[272]United States 1850 Census, Newark, Tioga County, NY.

[273]Pollard, *History of the Pollard Family in America*, Volume 2, page 130.

[274]Tombstone.

[275]Find A Grave.

[276]United States 1850 Census, Newark, Tioga County, NY.

[277]Tombstone.

[278]Find A Grave.

104. i. Lavina M Pollard was born on 29 Mar 1826 at NY.[279] She married Hiram Owen.[280] She died on 30 Oct 1898 at age 72.[281] She was buried at Liberty Pole Cemetery, Viroqua, Vernon County, NY.[282]

Hiram Owen was born on 14 May 1827 at NY. He died on 21 Mar 1893 at age 65.[283] He was buried at Liberty Pole Cemetery, Viroqua, Vernon County, WI.[284]

105. ii. George Pollard was born circa 1828 at NY.[285]
He was farmer.

106. iii. Sabrina Pollard was born circa 1834 at NY.[286]

107. iv. William Pollard was born circa 1836 at NY.[287]

108. v. Lucinda Pollard[288] was born on 27 Mar 1839 at NY. She married Henry C Gosling.[289] She died on 7 Apr 1901 at WI at age 62.[290] She was buried at Liberty Pole Cemetery, Viroqua, Vernon County, WI.[291]

Henry C Gosling was born on 8 May 1844. He died on 4 Feb 1916 at age 71. He was buried at Liberty Pole Cemetery, Viroqua, Vernon County, WI.[292]

109. vi. Seneca Pollard[293] was born on 27 Sep 1841 at Newark Valley, Tioga County, NY.[294] He married Amanda A Ballard circa 1866. He died on 27 May 1928 at Palatine, Cook County, IL, at age 86.[295] He was buried at Viroqua Cemetery, Viroqua, Vernon County, WI.[296]

Amanda A Ballard was born on 18 Nov 1845 at Nanticoke, Broome County, NY.[297] She died on 16 Jan 1931 at Palatine, Cook County, IL, at age 85; Tombstone gives death as 18 Nov 1931.[298] She was buried at Viroqua Cemetery, Viroqua, Vernon County, WI.[299]

110. vii. Ira Jerome Pollard[300] was born on 27 Mar 1844 at Newark Valley, Tioga County, NY.[301] He married Parintha A Cody on 31 Dec 1866. He died in Jan 1915 at age 70. He was buried at Ketchumville Cemetery, Newark Valley, Tioga County, NY.[302]
Attended the 1883 Lyon reunion as a descendant of Lucy Lyon Pollard.[303]
Parintha A Cody was born on 31 Dec 1866 at NY. She died in 1938. She was buried at Ketchumville Cemetery, Newark Valley, Tioga County, NY.[304]

111. viii. Ellen Pollard was born circa 1846 at NY.[305]

---

[279]Tombstone.
[280]United States 1850 Census, Southport, Chemung County, NY.
[281]Tombstone.
[282]Find A Grave.
[283]Tombstone.
[284]Find A Grave.
[285]United States 1850 Census, Newark, Tioga County, NY.
[286]Ibid.
[287]Ibid.
[288]Ibid.
[289]Find A Grave.
[290]Tombstone.
[291]Find A Grave.
[292]Ibid.
[293]United States 1850 Census, Newark, Tioga County, NY.
[294]New York Civil War Records.
[295]Death Records, Illinois.
[296]Find A Grave.
[297]Death Records, Illinois.
[298]Tombstone.
[299]Find A Grave.
[300]United States 1850 Census, Newark, Tioga County, NY.
[301]New York Civil War Records.
[302]Find A Grave.
[303]1883 Lyon Reunion.
[304]Find A Grave.

112.   ix.   Eugene Pollard was born circa 1849 at NY.[306]

24. Lovisa Lyon (*Samuel, Thomas, John*) was born on 14 Aug 1806. She married William T Smith circa 1832.[307] She died on 9 Oct 1884 at age 78.[308] She was buried at Sylvan Lawn Cemetery, Greene, Chenango County, NY.[309]

She was also known as Louisa Lyon. She was also known as Louis Lyon. Attended the 1883 Lyon reunion.[310]

William T Smith was born on 20 Feb 1801 at RI. He died on 28 Feb 1870 at age 69.[311] He was buried at Sylvan Lawn Cemetery, Greene, Chenango County, NY.[312]

Known children of Lovisa Lyon and William T Smith all born at NY were as follows:

113.   i.   Mary E Smith was born circa 1833. She married Joseph McCray.[313]
          Attended the 1883 Lyon reunion as a descendant of Louisa Lyon Smith.[314]
          Joseph McCray was born circa 1824 at NY. He died before 1870.[315]
114.   ii.   George S Smith was born circa 1834.[316]
115.   iii. Juliete Smith was born circa 1836.[317] She married Moses N Tubbs. She died on 17 Jul 1889 at NY.[318] She was buried at Hope Cemetery, Newark Valley, Tioga County, NY.[319]
          Attended the 1883 Lyon reunion as a descendant of Louisa Lyon Smith.[320]
          Moses N Tubbs was born in 1832 at PA. He died on 18 Dec 1919. He was buried at Hope Cemetery, Newark Valley, Tioga County, NY.[321]
116.   iv.   William A Smith was born circa 1842.[322]
          Attended the 1883 Lyon reunion as a descendant of Louisa Lyon Smith.[323]

27. Rose Linda Lyon (*Thomas, Thomas, John*) was born circa 1784. She married Amariah Coburn, son of Nathaniel Coburn, in 1802. She died in 1852; Her death is reported in the Sun Prairie, Dane, WI, due to smallpox.[324]

Known children of Rose Linda Lyon and Amariah Coburn were as follows:

117.   i.   Esick L Coburn was born on 19 Nov 1803 at Chenango County, NY. He married Hannah R Jewel on 10 Oct 1826. He married Phoebe Smith, daughter of Gable Smith and Abigale (--?--), say 1844.
          He was farmer.[325]
          Hannah R Jewel was born on 22 May 1803. She died circa 1843.[326]

[305]United States 1850 Census, Newark, Tioga County, NY.
[306]Ibid.
[307]Lyon, *Lyon Memorial, NY Families*, page 322.
[308]Tombstone, Sylvan Lawn Cemetery, Greene, Chenango County, NY.
[309]Find A Grave.
[310]*1883 Lyon Reunion.*
[311]Tombstone, Sylvan Lawn Cemetery, Greene, Chenango County, NY.
[312]Find A Grave.
[313]United States 1860 Census, Smithville, Chenango County, NY.
[314]*1883 Lyon Reunion.*
[315]United States 1860 Census, Smithville, Chenango County, NY.
[316]United States 1850 Census, Smithville, Chenango County, NY.
[317]Ibid.
[318]Tombstone.
[319]Find A Grave.
[320]*1883 Lyon Reunion.*
[321]Find A Grave.
[322]United States 1850 Census, Smithville, Chenango County, NY.
[323]*1883 Lyon Reunion.*
[324]Solinda Christoffersen phone and written material.
[325]*History of Crawford County Pennsylvania* (Chicago, IL: Warner, Beers & Co, 1885), page 929.
[326]Ibid.

Phoebe Smith was born circa 1820 at Crawford County, PA.[327]

118.   ii. Sally Coburn[328] was born in 1804 at Guilford, Chenango County, NY.[329] She married Newel Knight on 7 Jun 1825. She died on 15 Sep 1834 at Turnhanis Landing, MO.[330]

Newel Knight was born on 13 Sep 1800 at Marlborough, Windham County, VT. He died on 11 Jan 1847 at NE at age 46.[331]

119.   iii. Emily Coburn was born in 1813.[332] She married (--?--) Austin.

31. **Betsey Lyon** (*Thomas, Thomas, John*) was born on 10 Feb 1803 at Oxford, Chenango County, NY.[333] She married George Knapp, son of George Knapp and Mary Rathbun, circa 1825. She died on 27 Jan 1884 at Guilford Center, Chenango County, NY, at age 80; Cause of death listed on death certificate was Paralysis. She was buried at Mt Hope Cemetery, Norwich, Chenango County, NY.

A memorial of Mrs Betsey Lyon was given at a Lyon reunion by her lifetime acquaintance, Mrs Daniel Wagner. "Seeing a notice of the death of Mrs George Knapp, of Guilford, last week greatly saddened me, as we had been life-long friends, she being but one month older than myself. We became acquainted in June 1822, when we were but twenty years of age. On visiting an uncle three or four miles east of this village, I found Betsey Lyon boarding there, she being the teacher of their district school to whom I was introduced. She told me she was the oldest child of Col. Lyon, who was killed at the battle of York, Canada in the War of 1812, by the same explosion of the mine secretly laid by the British, that killed General Pike, our commander while taking possession of their batteries. Betsey was then in the twelfth year of her age, and had one sister and two little brothers. Their mother was left on a small new farm, in the north-east quarter of this town. Betsey soon after came to this village," (in a different handwriting, Norwich probably) "to live in the family of Joseph Fenton, one of our first prominent merchants, that she might have a chance to attend the village schools and get an education. The last year before her marriage she taught in this village in a school house on West Main Street, near where her daughter Mrs Mandeville now lives and boarded with Thomas Stee--who married her Aunt. The art to which my life had then become devoted soon led me to the cities and enabled me to form the acquaintance of ladies of wealth & culture but during my long life I have never seen one that I thought surpassed Betsey Lyon in all the best and highest attributes of Woman.[334]" Betsey joined the Guilford Congregational Church on 7 Jul 1833 three years before she and George bought their land in Guilford.

George Knapp was born on 12 May 1802 at Exeter, Washington County, RI.[335] He died on 2 Jul 1878 at Guilford Center, Chenango County, NY, at age 76.[336] He was buried at Mt Hope Cemetery, Norwich, Chenango County, NY. The Chenango County land records show that George Knapp bought 2 parcels of land in Guilford on 2 Apr 1836 totaling 115 acres. The 1850 census says he was a farmer with $2500 and the 1855 New York census says he owned his own land and had a frame house valued at $300. Listed as residing in the home with him were his wife Betsey, mother-in-law Mercy Lyon, and children Thomas G., Charles W., Frances L., Henry A., and Joseph S.

Known children of Betsey Lyon and George Knapp were as follows:

120.   i. Mary Elizabeth Knapp was born on 28 Dec 1826 at Oxford, Chenango County, NY. She married Danforth R Cushman on 18 Jan 1876. She died on 23 Feb 1887 at age 60. She was buried at Norwich, Chenango County, NY.

[327]Ibid., page 929.

[328]Joseph Smith Papers.

[329]Ibid.

[330]Ibid.

[331]Lynda McGinnis, *Christoffersen Family Chart*.

[332]Solinda Christoffersen phone and written material.

[333]Death Certificate, Betsey Knapp, 31 Jan 1884.

[334]Notes from the files of the Chenango County NY Historian.

[335]Alfred Averill, Dr. Knapp, *Knapp Family, Aaron Knapp of Taunton, MA in 1638 and Some of his Descendants*. Winter Park, FL: unpublished, 1961), page 40.

[336]*Surrogate Court Records, Chenango County, NY*, Chenango County Surrogate Records file 3612A.

Teacher in 1860.[337] Attended the 1883 Lyon reunion as a descendant of Betsey Lyon Knapp at Chenango County, NY.[338]

Danforth R Cushman was born circa 1808. He died on 30 May 1893.

121.   ii.   Mercy Jane Knapp was born on 2 Feb 1831 at Oxford, Chenango County, NY. She married William Garret Mandeville on 4 Jan 1857 at Guilford Center, Chenango County, NY. She died on 13 Jun 1907 at Norwich, Chenango County, NY, at age 76. She was buried on 16 Jun 1907 at Mt Hope Cemetery, Norwich, Chenango County, NY.[339]

Mercy Jane's given name is listed as Jane M. in the court petition filed following her father's death but as Mercy Jane in the Aaron Knapp Genealogy, the church marriage records and in the papers of Mrs John B. Meola.[340] Attended the 1883 Lyon reunion as a descendant of Betsey Lyon Knapp at Chenango County, NY.[341]

William Garret Mandeville was born on 20 Apr 1826 at Caroline Center, Caroline, Tompkins County, NY. He died on 4 Nov 1897 at age 71. He was buried on 6 Nov 1897 at Mt Hope Cemetery, Norwich, Chenango County, NY. William left Caroline, Tompkins Co NY and went first to Ithaca and then to Norwich and engaged in business as a hatter.

122.   iii.   George Thomas Knapp was born on 15 Jan 1833 at Oxford, Chenango County, NY.[342] He married Lavina King Webb on 19 Oct 1859. He died on 29 Mar 1891 at Fisher, Champaign County, IL, at age 58; One source says George died at Houstonville, IL rather than Fisher. Houstonville is a small settlement near Fisher. He was buried at Riverview Cemetery Saybrook, McLean County, IL.

The 1880 census shows George Thomas Knapp to be living in Cheneys Grove Township (Saybrook), McLean County, IL.

Lavina King Webb was born on 13 Nov 1830 at New Berlin, Chenango County, NY.[343] She died on 10 Jan 1906 at age 75. She was buried at Riverview Cemetery Saybrook, McLean County, IL.[344]

123.   iv.   Judge Charles William Knapp[345] was born on 8 Sep 1834 at Oxford, Chenango County, NY. He married Rebecca Mary Peabody on 25 Dec 1860. He died on 16 Jul 1902 at Rocky Ford, Otero County, CO, at age 67; Cause of death given in Rocky Ford Gazette, 20 Jun 1902, page 4 was "stroke of paralysis."[346] He was buried circa 19 Jul 1902 at Rocky Ford, Otero County, CO.

In the 1860 Pera, Champaign, IL census, Charles was listed as a merchant with $100 in real estate and $700 in cash. Living with him were James Lyon (born in MI) and Joseph McMurray, his future law partner. In the 1870 census he was living in Saybrook, McLean County, IL and listed as being in the insurance business with $3600 in real estate and $850 in cash. In the 1874 McLean County Atlas he advertised as a police magistrate, justice of the peace, real estate, insurance and loan collecting agent.

All the children were born there (1863-1878) and attended grade school in Saybrook. The four older girls finished high school and Harriet, Olive, and Jane attended Illinois Normal School. They then moved to Johnson, KS in 1885 and managed the St. Elmo Hotel and Livery Stable. Charles W. Knapp was one of the first councilmen in Johnson and was admitted to the bar to practice law on 17 Dec 1890. About 1894, the Knapp family sold the

---

[337]United States 1860 Census, Guilford, Chenango County, NY.

[338]1883 Lyon Reunion.

[339]Guy Wallis, Chenango County NY Notes (5 Aug 1996).

[340]Notes from files the files of the Chenango County NY Historian.

[341]1883 Lyon Reunion.

[342]Tombstone, Riverview Cemetery, Saybrook, McLean County, IL.

[343]Col Wm. King, Hezekiah King & his Descendants (1895), extract in Chenango County Historians Office.

[344]Tombstone, Riverview Cemetery, Saybrook, McLean County, IL.

[345]Knapp, Knapp Family, Aaron Knapp of Taunton, MA.

[346]Obituary of C. W. Knapp, (Rocky Ford, Otero County, CO: Rocky Ford Enterprise, 20 Jun 1902); Colorado Historical Society.

St Elmo Hotel and moved to Rocky Ford, Otero, CO, where they purchased a small acreage south of town. Charles W. Knapp and Ambrose B. Wallis had a law office together in Rocky Ford for several years. The 1880 census gives the family address as Jefferson St, Saybrook City, McLean County IL.[347]

Rebecca Mary Peabody[348] was born on 23 Nov 1843 at Switzerland County, IN. She died on 27 Jun 1914 at Waukegan, Lake County, IL, at age 70.[349] She was buried on 22 Jul 1914 at Rosehill Cemetery, Chicago, Cook County, IL.[350] Cause of death listed as natural causes due to old age with no contributory causes. Her death certificate states that she was buried at Oakwood, Waukegan, Lake Co, IL. The interment record at Rosehill shows she was buried there at a later date. Following the death of her husband, Rebecca lived with her daughters, Bertha Bell and Harriet in Rocky Ford, CO. After the birth of Robert LaFord Wallis in Nov 1902 who was sickly, Rebecca went to live with her daughter, Jane who lived in Waukegan, Lake County, IL. Her death certificate indicates she was there by Jan 1904.

There are several reports that Rebecca's health was poor. Joseph Morrow says that she was crippled with arthritis and restricted to a chair and foot stool.

124.   v.   David H. Knapp was born on 27 Jan 1836 at Oxford, Chenango County, NY. He married Mary Ann Collins in 1860. He died on 25 Jun 1912 at age 76. He was buried on 29 Jun 1912 at Mt Hope Cemetery, Norwich, Chenango County, NY.

David was listed as an attorney and counselor, justice of peace and life insurance agent located over T. Rogers & Son's Clothing Store in Norwich, NY in the 1869/70 Chenango County directory. He still resided in Chenango Co as late as Feb 1879. Notes from the Chenango county historian state that he later lived in New York City.[351]

Mary Ann Collins was born on 25 Nov 1839. She died on 19 Sep 1912 at age 72.[352] She was buried on 21 Sep 1912.[353]

125.   vi.   Sarah Knapp was born on 1 Jan 1838 at Guilford Center, Chenango County, NY. She married John A. Clark on 1 Nov 1860 at Sidney, Delaware County, NY.

Occupation listed as a teacher in the 1860 Chenango census.

126.   vii.   Frances L. Knapp was born on 1 Apr 1840 at Guilford Center, Chenango County, NY. She married Truman Cable at Afton, Chenango County, NY.

Teacher.[354]

127. viii.   Henry M. Knapp was born in 1844 at Guilford Center, Chenango County, NY.

Henry was living in Chenango Co, NY in Feb 1879 but later moved to Milwaukee, WI.[355]

128.   ix.   Joseph S. Knapp was born in 1847 at Guilford Center, Chenango County, NY. He married Mary Aims at St Paul, Ramsey County, MN. He died after 1922 at St Paul, Ramsey County, MN.

Mary Aims. Name may have been Aime.

32. Morgan Lyon (*Thomas, Thomas, John*) was born on 16 Oct 1810 at Norwich, Chenango County, NY. He married Mary Purple, daughter of Isham Purple and Phoebe Rogers, circa 1835 at Norwich, Chenango

[347]United States 1880 Census, Saybrook, McLean County, IL.

[348]Selim Howard Peabody, *Peabody Genealogy* (Boston, MA: Charles H. Pope, 1909).

[349]Death Certificate, # 6329, Lake County, IL.

[350]Tombstone, Section 117, Lot 6, #35.

[351]Notes from files the files of the Chenango County NY Historian.

[352]Wallis, *Chenango County NY Notes*.

[353]Ibid.

[354]United States 1860 Census, Guilford, Chenango County, NY.

[355]Notes from files the files of the Chenango County NY Historian.

County, NY.[356] He married Louisa Purple, daughter of Isham Purple and Phoebe Rogers, circa 1850 at Norwich, Chenango County, NY; Morgan and Louisa separated about 1865 but remained married.[357] He died on 1 Apr 1893 at Vergennes, Kent County, MI, at age 82.[358] He was buried at Foxes Cemetery, Lowell, Kent County, MI.[359]

On 28 Sep 1835 Morgan Lyon of Chenango County NY acquired the NE quarter of section 18 Howell Township, Livingston County, MI in 1835.[360] Morgan Lyon moved to Kent Co, Michigan in 1837 and settled near Grand Rapids. In the 1870 and 1880 census Morgan was living with Fern Edmonds who was said to be a widowed niece. In the 1910 census she, Fern Edmonds, was living with Orson and Nancy Snow and said to be single and a sister-in-law. In 1920 she was living with James A and Lizza J Brownell and said to be single and a sister-in-law.

Mary Purple[361] was born on 9 Jun 1812 at CT. She died on 6 Aug 1848 at Vergennes, Kent County, MI, at age 36.[362] She was buried at Foxes Cemetery, Lowell, Kent County, MI.[363]

Known children of Morgan Lyon and Mary Purple were as follows:

+ 129.   i.   Matilda H Lyon was born on 6 Aug 1835 at NY. She married John H Ryder, son of Benjamin Ryder and Charity Hicks, circa 1855. She died on 14 Sep 1877 at Kent County, MI, at age 42. She was buried at Foxes Cemetery, Lowell, Kent County, MI.

+ 130.   ii. James A Lyon was born on 21 Jul 1838 at Lowell, Kent County, MI. He married Emma Fuller on 25 Dec 1866 at Ada, Kent County, MI. He died on 18 May 1904 at Lowell, Kent County, MI, at age 65. He was buried at Oakwood Cemetery, Lowell, Kent County, MI.

+ 131.   iii. Emily Lyon was born in Jun 1845 at Kent County, MI. She married Hiram B Aldrich, son of Henry Aldrich, on 5 Feb 1864. She and Hiram B Aldrich were divorced in 1881 at Kent County, MI. She married Helmus Hendricks, son of Abram Hendricks and Hannah (--?--), circa 1882. She died on 9 Jul 1918 at MI at age 73. She was buried at Oak Hill Cemetery, Grand Rapids, Kent County, MI.

  132.   iv. Thomas J Lyon was born say 1845 at Kent County, MI. He died say 1845.[364] He was buried at Foxes Cemetery, Lowell, Kent County, MI.[365]

Louisa Purple[366] was born on 13 Nov 1823 at Chenango County, NY. She died on 6 Aug 1913 at Kent County, MI, at age 89.[367] She was buried at Foxes Cemetery, Lowell, Kent County, MI.[368] Louise was a sister of Morgan's first wife Mary.

Starting with the 1870 census she was living alone in Lowell but said she was married. Morgan was living with Fern Edmonds said to be his house keeper.

Known children of Morgan Lyon and Louisa Purple were:

+ 133.   i.   Mary E Lyon was born on 15 Aug 1850 at Vergennes, Kent County, MI. She married Orren Omar Adams on 6 Feb 1871. She died on 26 Sep 1924 at Chicago, Cook County, IL, at age 74. She was buried at Foxes Cemetery, Lowell, Kent County, MI.

[356]James Lowry, *Morgan Lyon, Forgotten Pioneer a Historical and Genealogical Biography* (self published, 2006).
[357]Ibid., page 49.
[358]Tombstone.
[359]Find A Grave.
[360]Everts & Abbott, *History of Livingston County Michigan*.
[361]Lowry, *Morgan Lyon Biography*, page 19.
[362]Tombstone.
[363]Find A Grave.
[364]Tombstone.
[365]Find A Grave.
[366]Lowry, *Morgan Lyon Biography*, page 19.
[367]Tombstone.
[368]Find A Grave.

33. William Brown Lyon (*Thomas, Thomas, John*) was born on 5 Jun 1812 at Chenango County, NY. He married Nancy Cahoon on 5 Jan 1834 at Norwich, Chenango County, NY. He married Caroline Smith on 13 Mar 1856. He died on 29 Jan 1897 at Cedar Springs, Kent County, MI, at age 84.[369] He was buried at Roth Coons Cemetery, Lowell, Kent County, MI.[370]

William B Lyon, his wife and children Betsey, Henry and George settled near farm of his brother-in-law and sister the Newtons in 1839.[371]

Nancy Cahoon was born on 25 Dec 1812.[372] She died on 2 Jan 1856 at Lowell, Kent County, MI, at age 43.[373]

Known children of William Brown Lyon and Nancy Cahoon were as follows:

+ 134.   i.   Henry W Lyon was born on 22 Mar 1835 at NY. He married Jane (--?--).
+ 135.   ii.   Betsey Lyon was born on 30 Aug 1836 at Chenango County, NY. She married Emmett H Merritt.
  136.   iii.   George Rufus Lyon was born on 7 May 1838 at Chenango County, NY.[374] He died in Nov 1862 at age 24.[375] He was buried at Cave Hill National Cemetery, Louisville, Jefferson County, KT.[376]
  137.   iv.   William A. Lyon was born on 4 Mar 1841 at Lowell, Kent County, MI. He married Lavina Elpha Oakes, daughter of (--?--) Oakes and Caroline Smith, say 1870. He married Laura (--?--) circa 1898.[377] He married Kate Tery on 9 Jun 1904 at Lee, Allegan, MI.[378]

     Lavina Elpha Oakes[379] was born circa 1848 at MI.[380]
     Laura (--?--) was born in Jun 1848 at MI.[381]
+ 138.   v.   Nelson Thomas Lyon was born on 20 Aug 1843 at Lowell, Kent County, MI. He married Mary Morgan circa 1865. He died on 18 Mar 1872 at Lowell, Kent County, MI, at age 28.
+ 139.   vi.   Richard Brown Lyon was born on 14 Jan 1846 at Lowell, Kent County, MI. He married Adelaide Martha Brown, daughter of William H. Brown, before 1868. He married Henrietta Sturgis on 27 Sep 1887 at Coffeyville, Montgomery County, KS. He and Henrietta Sturgis were divorced on 8 Aug 1890 at Neodesha, Wilson County, KS. He married Martha Lockwood circa 1891. He married Alice Matilda Watson on 9 Nov 1904 at Emo, Rainy River District, Ontario, Canada. He died on 4 Jul 1924 at Conneaut, Ashtabula, OH, at age 78.
  140.   vii.   Phebe R Lyon was born on 10 Jul 1849 at Lowell, Kent County, MI.[382] She married (--?--) Canon.[383]

Caroline Smith married (--?--) Oakes circa 1845.[384] She died on 29 Jan 1908.[385]

Known children of William Brown Lyon and Caroline Smith all born at Lowell, Kent County, MI, were as follows:

---

[369]Ancestry Family Trees, Bruce Lyon's U C Lyon Family Tree.
[370]Find A Grave.
[371]Lowry, *Morgan Lyon Biography*, page 26.
[372]*Lyon, Smith, Klump Family Bible*.
[373]Ancestry Family Trees, Bruce Lyon's U C Lyon Family Tree.
[374]Ibid.
[375]*Lyon, Smith, Klump Family Bible*.
[376]Ancestry Family Trees, Bruce Lyon's U C Lyon Family Tree.
[377]United States 1900 Census, Grand Rapids, Kent County, MI.
[378]Ancestry Family Trees, Bruce Lyon's U C Lyon Family Tree.
[379]United States 1850 Census, Vergennes, Kent County, MI.
[380]Ibid.
[381]United States 1900 Census, Grand Rapids, Kent County, MI.
[382]Ancestry Family Trees, Bruce Lyon's U C Lyon Family Tree.
[383]*Lyon, Smith, Klump Family Bible*.
[384]United States 1850 Census, Vergennes, Kent County, MI.
[385]*Lyon, Smith, Klump Family Bible*.

141.   i.   Frederick A Lyon was born on 19 Jan 1857.[386] He died on 15 May 1937 at age 80.[387] He was buried at Garfield Park Cemetery, East Grand Rapids, Kent County, MI.[388]

+ 142.   ii.   Mary A Lyon was born on 18 Oct 1858. She married George H Hall in 1885. She died on 24 Aug 1941 at age 82.

143.   iii.   Dodge G Lyon was born on 16 Nov 1861. He died on 18 Dec 1884 at age 23.[389]

+ 144.   iv.   Ella Lyon was born on 16 Feb 1866. She married Christopher W Klump on 15 Sep 1886. She died on 2 Jun 1949 at age 83.

145.   v.   Emma Lyon was born on 16 Feb 1866.[390] She died on 4 Oct 1872 at Lowell, Kent County, MI, at age 6.[391]

35. Lucinda Lyon (*Thomas, Thomas, John*) married Charles H Newton.[392]

Charles H Newton was born on 25 May 1807 at MA. He died on 16 Oct 1855 at Lowell, Kent County, MI, at age 48.[393] He was buried at Foxes Cemetery, Lowell, Kent County, MI.[394] Charles H Newton was In Vergennes and Howell Townships by about 1837. He was farmer in 1850.[395]

Known children of Lucinda Lyon and Charles H Newton were as follows:

146.   i.   Clark Newton was born circa 1833 at NY.[396]

147.   ii.   Truman C Newton was born circa 1834 at NY.[397]

148.   iii.   Mercy E Newton was born circa 1838 at MI.[398] She married Alphanso Filkins.[399] She married Elberton Kimberley circa 1888.[400]

Alphanso Filkins was born circa 1839 at MI.[401]

149.   iv.   Charles H Newton was born circa 1841 at MI.[402]

150.   v.   Orrin R Newton was born circa 1844 at MI.[403]

36. Captain Daniel Lyon (*Daniel, Thomas, John*) was born on 22 Sep 1794 at Oxford, Chenango County, NY. He married Elizabeth Lewis say 1820 at Chenango County, NY. He died in 1849 at Monroeton, Bradford County, PA.[404] He was buried at Monroeton Cemetery, Monroeton, Bradford County, PA.[405]

Daniel Lyon Jr, farmer, purchased land in Oxford, Chenango County, NY from Samuel Lyon in 1806. If his birth date of 1794 is correct he would have been 11 years old.[406] In 1821 Daniel moved to Monroe in Bradford County PA where he was a millwright and bridge builder. He also was a musician playing the fiddle, fife and flute.

Daniel was commissioned a captain in the military in 1821.[407]

[386]Ancestry Family Trees, Bruce Lyon's U C Lyon Family Tree.
[387]*Lyon, Smith, Klump Family Bible.*
[388]Find A Grave.
[389]*Lyon, Smith, Klump Family Bible.*
[390]Ancestry Family Trees, Bruce Lyon's U C Lyon Family Tree.
[391]*Lyon, Smith, Klump Family Bible.*
[392]Letter Olive Buckley to Mrs Wells, 27 Apr 1931, Chenango Co. Historian.
[393]Tombstone.
[394]Find A Grave.
[395]United States 1850 Census, Vergennes, Kent County, MI.
[396]United States 1880 Census, Otisco, Ionia County, MI.
[397]United States 1850 Census, Vergennes, Kent County, MI.
[398]Ibid.
[399]United States 1880 Census, Otisco, Ionia County, MI.
[400]Lowry, *Morgan Lyon Biography*, page 63.
[401]United States 1880 Census, Otisco, Ionia County, MI.
[402]United States 1850 Census, Vergennes, Kent County, MI.
[403]Ibid.
[404]Tombstone, Monroeton Cemetery.
[405]Find A Grave.
[406]Chenango County, NY, Land Records, Volume L, page 159.
[407]Heverly, *Pioneer and Patriot Families of Bradford County, PA 1770-1800.*

Elizabeth Lewis was born on 17 Oct 1799 at Tioga County, NY.[408] She died in 1852.[409] She was buried at Monroeton Cemetery, Monroeton, Bradford County, PA.[410]

Known children of Captain Daniel Lyon and Elizabeth Lewis were as follows:

151. i. Sophia Lyon was born on 12 Feb 1821 at Monroeton, Bradford County, PA. She married Orlando Nelson Salisbury on 24 Dec 1844.[411] She died on 13 Feb 1846 at Jim Thorpe, Carbon County, PA, at age 25.[412] She was buried at Monroeton Cemetery, Monroeton, Bradford County, PA.[413]

Orlando Nelson Salisbury[414] was born in 1817 at PA. He married Caroline Hoyt say 1850. He died in 1892.[415] He was buried at Clark Cemetery, Beech Creek, Clinton County, PA.[416]

152. ii. Eugenia Lyon was born in 1823 at Bradford County, PA.[417] She married George Smith on 9 Nov 1843.[418] She died on 13 Jan 1854 at Bradford County, PA.[419] She was buried at Monroeton Cemetery, Monroeton, Bradford County, PA.[420]

+ 153. iii. Mary Eliza Lyon was born in 1825 at Bradford County, PA. She married William B. Dodge.

+ 154. iv. Otis P. Lyon was born in 1827 at Bradford County, PA. He married Loretta E Lawrence on 7 Jan 1850.

+ 155. v. Samuel M Lyon was born circa 1829 at PA. He married Eliza Dodge. He died in 1896.

+ 156. vi. Daniel Lewis Lyon was born on 7 Sep 1830 at Monroeton, Bradford County, PA. He married Eleanor Salisbury. He died on 1 Sep 1906 at Clay County, SD, at age 75. He was buried at Bluff View, Vermillion, Clay County, SD.

+ 157. vii. Theodore Burr Lyon was born in 1835 at Bradford County, PA. He married Eliza Northrup. He died on 9 Nov 1895 at Bradford County, PA. He was buried at Monroeton Cemetery, Monroeton, Bradford County, PA.

+ 158. viii. Augusta Lyon was born circa 1841 at PA. She married Orson A. Baldwin.

37. Truxton Lyon (*Daniel, Thomas, John*) was born in 1796 at Oxford, Chenango County, NY.[421] He married Olive Lewis, daughter of Benjamin Lewis, say 1819. He married Harriet (--?--) say 1832.[422] He died on 15 Nov 1862 at Jackson, Madison County, TN.[423]

Truxton moved to Monroe Bradford County Pa in 1821 and engaged in the carding and fulling business. In 1831 Truxton had contracted to build seventeen miles of track for the B&O railroad from the current Ellicott City MD to the current Mt Airy MD. He failed to pay his workers, a labor revolt resulted and he subsequently lost the contract.

In 1848 he was involved in a suit with the state of Ohio involving canal tolls.[424] In 1840 Truxton was living in Adams, Washington County, OH.

---

[408]Ibid.

[409]Tombstone, Monroeton Cemetery.

[410]Find A Grave.

[411]Heverly, *Pioneer and Patriot Families of Bradford County, PA 1770-1800*, page 68.

[412]Tombstone.

[413]Find A Grave.

[414]Heverly, *Pioneer and Patriot Families of Bradford County, PA 1770-1800*.

[415]Find A Grave.

[416]Ibid.

[417]RootsWeb WorldConnect Project, Cheryl database.

[418]Heverly, *Pioneer and Patriot Families of Bradford County, PA 1770-1800*, page 66.

[419]Tombstone.

[420]Find A Grave.

[421]Heverly, *Pioneer and Patriot Families of Bradford County, PA 1770-1800*.

[422]United States 1860 Census, St Francisville, Clark County, MO.

[423]*Newspaper*, Mariette Ohio Register, 5 Dec 1862, page 3 column 1.

[424]Heverly, *Pioneer and Patriot Families of Bradford County, PA 1770-1800*.

He was listed in the 1850 Clark County, MO census with children born after 1833 and owned a female slave born c 1802. Truxton was a representative to the Ohio legislature from Washington and Morgan Counties in 1841.[425] He was contractor of public works in Clark County MO.[426]

Olive Lewis was born in 1798. She married Josiah Haines before 1850.[427] She died on 26 Sep 1893 at Franklindale, Bradford County, PA.

Known children of Truxton Lyon and Olive Lewis were as follows:

+ 159.   i.   Dr. Randolph Lyon was born on 7 May 1820. He married Jerusla (--?--). He died on 2 Jul 1887 at Bradford County, PA, at age 67. He was buried at Franklin Center Christian Cemetery, Franklindale, Bradford County, PA.

+ 160.   ii.   William Lewis Lyon was born on 11 Dec 1821 at Monroeton, Bradford County, PA. He married Helen Lemira Fisher on 25 Apr 1845 at Bradford County, PA. He died on 15 Jul 1887 at Bradford County, PA, at age 65. He was buried at Monroeton Cemetery, Monroeton, Bradford County, PA.

   161.   iii.   Cordelia Lyon was born circa 1823.[428] She married James Lawrence Rockwell, son of Abner C Rockwell and Betsy Gordon, on 15 Sep 1845 at Bradford County, PA.[429] She died on 15 May 1850 at Bradford County, PA.[430] She was buried at Monroeton Cemetery, Monroeton, Bradford County, PA.[431]

James Lawrence Rockwell[432] was born on 15 Feb 1814 at Monroeton, Bradford County, PA.[433] He married Isabella Banks Wilson on 10 Dec 1851. He died on 23 Nov 1875 at Monroeton, Bradford County, PA, at age 61. He was buried at Monroeton Cemetery, Monroeton, Bradford County, PA.[434] He was merchant.

   162.   iv.   Dr James W. Lyon[435] was born circa 1826 at Bradford County, PA.

There was a James W Lyon in the 1870, Hector, Scuyler County NY census .born c 1826 NY. He was a surgeon and dentist, had a housekeeper but no wife or any children named Lyon.[436]

Harriet (--?--) was born circa 1820 at OH.[437]

Known children of Truxton Lyon and Harriet (--?--) were as follows:

   163.   i.   Mary Ann Lyon was born circa 1833 at PA.[438] She married Samuel Spangler on 3 Mar 1853 at Clark County, MO.[439]

   164.   ii.   Daniel Lyon was born circa 1836 at PA.[440]

   165.   iii.   Joseph Lyon was born circa 1837 at OH.[441]

   166.   iv.   Curtis Cass Lyon was born circa 1845 at OH.[442]

[425]Israel Ward LL D Andrews, *Centennial Historical Address before the Citizens of Washington County, 4 Jul 1876* (Cincinnati: Peter G Thompson, 1877), page 77.

[426]United States 1850 Census, Clark County, MO.

[427]Heverly, *Pioneer and Patriot Families of Bradford County, PA 1770-1800*.

[428]Tombstone.

[429]RootsWeb WorldConnect Project, Cheryl database.

[430]Tombstone.

[431]Find A Grave.

[432]Heverly, *Pioneer and Patriot Families of Bradford County, PA 1770-1800*, Volume 2, page 3.

[433]RootsWeb WorldConnect Project, Cheryl database.

[434]Find A Grave.

[435]Heverly, *Pioneer and Patriot Families of Bradford County, PA 1770-1800*.

[436]United States 1870 Census, Hector, Schuyler County, NY.

[437]United States 1860 Census, St Francisville, Clark County, MO.

[438]United States 1850 Census, Clark County, MO.

[439]Marriage Record, Clark County, MO.

[440]United States 1850 Census, Clark County, MO.

[441]Ibid.

[442]Ibid.

167.　　v.　Frank Lyon was born circa 1852 at MO.[443]

42. Cynthia Lyon (*Daniel, Thomas, John*)[444] was born in 1806 at Oxford, Chenango County, NY. She married Isaac Huyck, son of William Huyck and Margaret Westbrook. She died on 14 Oct 1892 at IA.[445] She was buried at West Union Cemetery, West Union, Fayette County, IA.[446]

Isaac Huyck was born in 1801 at PA. He died in 1879 at IA.[447] He was buried at West Union Cemetery, West Union, Fayette County, IA.[448]

Known children of Cynthia Lyon and Isaac Huyck all born at PA were as follows:

168.　　i.　Daniel Huyck was born circa 1826. He married Eliza E (--?--).[449]

Eliza E (--?--) was born circa 1830 at PA.[450]

169.　　ii.　William Huyck was born circa 1831. He married Nancy J (--?--).[451]

Nancy J (--?--) was born circa 1832 at PA.[452]

170.　　iii.　Charles Huyck was born circa 1834.[453]
　　　　　　He was carpenter.

171.　　iv.　Sarah Huyck was born circa 1839.[454]

172.　　v.　Randolph Huyck[455] was born in 1842. He married Amanda (--?--). He died in 1919 at Dakota County, MN.[456] He was buried at Corinthian Cemetery, Farmington, Dakota County, MN.[457]

Amanda (--?--) was born in 1840 at OH. She died in 1921 at Dakota County, MN.[458] She was buried at Corinthian Cemetery, Farmington, Dakota County, MN.[459]

43. James Lyon (*Alexander, Thomas, John*)[460] was born on 22 Nov 1796 at Oxford, Chenango County, NY. He married Aseneath Smith.[461] He married Johanna (--?--) before 1850; My Division, Marshall County, IN.[462] He died on 20 Apr 1856 at Marshall County, IN, at age 59.[463] He was buried at Burr Oak Cemetery, Culver, Marshall County, IN.[464]

He was blacksmith in 1850. He left a will at Marshall County, IN; probated 10 Jan 1857 and 12 May 1857. Mentions wife Joannah and two youngest daughters Achsah Matilda Lyon and Mary Helen Lyon.

[443]United States 1860 Census, St Francisville, Clark County, MO.
[444]Heverly, *Pioneer and Patriot Families of Bradford County, PA 1770-1800*.
[445]Tombstone.
[446]Find A Grave.
[447]Tombstone.
[448]Find A Grave.
[449]United States 1850 Census, Standing Stone, Bradford County, PA.
[450]Ibid.
[451]United States 1880 Census, West Union, Fayette County, IA.
[452]Ibid.
[453]United States 1850 Census, Standing Stone, Bradford County, PA.
[454]Ibid.
[455]Ibid.
[456]Tombstone.
[457]Find A Grave.
[458]Tombstone.
[459]Find A Grave.
[460]Lewis, *New York Finger Lake Pioneer Families*.
[461]RootsWeb WorldConnect Project, Pamela Miller's database.
[462]United States 1850 Census.
[463]Tombstone.
[464]Find A Grave.

The administration of the will lists the living heirs as: James Lyon, Olive Martindale, George O Lyon, John Lyon, Roxy Drake, Catharine Boles, Malinda Marples, Cornelia M Carle, Axa H Lyon, Mary H Lyon. The last three were under 21 years of age.[465]

Aseneath Smith was born circa 1799.[466] She died before 1850 at IN.[467]

Known children of James Lyon and Aseneath Smith were as follows:

173.   i.   John Lyon was born at NY.[468]

+ 174.   ii.   Alexander Lyon was born in 1819 at NY. He married Esther Ann (--?--) say 1842. He married Adeline (--?--) say 1858.

+ 175.   iii.   Olive Lyon was born on 23 Jul 1824 at NY. She married Warren Martindale. She died on 24 Sep 1908 at Chandlers Valley, Warren County, PA, at age 84.

+ 176.   iv.   George Osro Lyon was born in Jan 1826 at Franklinville, Cattaraugus County, NY. He married Mary Ann Rathbun, daughter of Newman Rathbun and Olive Rathbun, on 15 Feb 1847 at Lyndon, Cattaraugus County, NY. He died in 1901 at Chandler's Valley, Warren County, NY. He was buried at Chandlers Valley Cemetery, Chandlers Valley, Warren County, PA.

+ 177.   v.   James Lyon was born circa 1829 at NY. He married Sophia (--?--) on 5 Apr 1846 at La Porte County, IN. He married Elizabeth Taplin on 23 Mar 1868 at Marshall County, IN.

178.   vi.   Johanna Lyon was born circa 1830 at NY. She married Frederick S Lewis.

     In the 1860 Wyoming, Kent County, MI census Frederick S Lewis and his wife Joanna were living with Mary H Lyon born c 1848 in PA.[469]

     Frederick S Lewis was born circa 1824 at NY. He was farm laborer.[470] He may be the Fred Lewis age 45 with wife Joanna age 40 both born in NY living in Washington, DeKalb County, MO.[471]

+ 179.   vii.   Catherine Lyon was born on 4 Jul 1832 at NY. She married Dr Llewellyn Boles on 11 Feb 1849 at Marshall County, IN. She married William Neckander. She died on 13 Nov 1889 at Carbon County, WY, at age 57. She was buried at Trails End Cemetery, Medicine Bow, Carbon County, WY.

180.   viii.   Cornelia Lyon was born after 1835 at NY.[472] She married (--?--) Carle before 1850.[473]

181.   ix.   Roxsylania Lyon[474] was born circa 1836 at NY. She married Joseph Drake on 20 Jun 1852.[475] She was also known as Roxy Lyon.

182.   x.   Achsah Matilda Lyon[476] was born in 1842 at PA.[477] She died on 11 Oct 1863 at Cass County, IN.[478]

183.   xi.   Mary Helen Lyon was born circa 1847 at PA.[479]

     In the 1860 Wyoming, Kent County, MI census Mary H Lyon was living with Frederick S Lewis and his wife Joanna.[480]

---

[465]*Will*, of James Lyon.

[466]RootsWeb WorldConnect Project, Debbi's database.

[467]United States 1850 Census, Marshall County, IN.

[468]*Will*, of James Lyon, Marshall County, IN.

[469]United States 1860 Census, Wyoming, Kent County, MI.

[470]Ibid.

[471]United States 1870 Census, Washington, DeKalb County, MO.

[472]*Will*, of James Lyon, Marshall County, IN.

[473]United States 1850 Census, My Division, Marshall County, IN.

[474]Ibid., Marshall County, IN.

[475]Marshall County, IL Marriage Records, Book B1, page 112.

[476]United States 1850 Census, Marshall County, IN.

[477]Ibid., My Division, Marshall County, IN.

[478]RootsWeb WorldConnect Project, Debbi's database.

[479]United States 1850 Census, Marshall County, IN.

[480]United States 1860 Census, Wyoming, Kent County, MI.

Johanna (--?--) was born circa 1830 at NY.[481] She married (--?--) DeBolt.[482]
There were no known children of James Lyon and Johanna (--?--).

44. Roxylena Lyon (*Alexander, Thomas, John*)[483] was born on 7 Mar 1798 at Oxford, Chenango County, NY. She married Walter Simmons. She died on 19 Dec 1892 at Chautauqua County, NY, at age 94.[484] She was buried at Fluvanna Cemetery, Ellicott, Chautauqua County, NY.[485]

She was also known as Rosa S Lyon.[486]

Walter Simmons was born on 16 Aug 1792 at Columbus, Chenango County, NY. He died on 4 Jul 1856 at Chautauqua County, NY, at age 63.[487] He was buried at Fluvanna Cemetery, Ellicott, Chautauqua County, NY.[488] He was farmer.

Known children of Roxylena Lyon and Walter Simmons were as follows:

- 184. i. Anna Marie Simmons.[489]
- 185. ii. Alexander Simmons[490] was born on 16 Apr 1817 at Jamestown, Chautauqua County, NY. He married Laura Ann Clark. He died on 13 Dec 1893 at Chautauqua County, NY, at age 76. He was buried at Fluvanna Cemetery, Jamestown, Chautauqua County, NY.[491]

  He was farmer.

  Laura Ann Clark was born on 15 Jan 1821. She died on 13 May 1904 at age 83.[492] She was buried at Fluvanna Cemetery, Jamestown, Chautauqua County, NY.[493]
- 186. iii. Otis Simmons[494] was born on 21 Jul 1819 at Jamestown, Chautauqua County, NY. He married Caroline A (--?--).[495] He died on 6 Jun 1893 at Fluvanna Cemetery, Jamestown, Chautauqua County, NY, at age 73. He was buried at Fluvanna Cemetery, Jamestown, Chautauqua County, NY.[496]

  Caroline A (--?--) was born in 1825. She died on 12 Oct 1880.[497] She was buried at Fluvanna Cemetery, Jamestown, Chautauqua County, NY.[498]
- 187. iv. George Simmons was born on 26 Apr 1822 at NY. He married Mary Ann Wetsell. He died on 13 Mar 1879 at age 56.[499]
- 188. v. Emeline Simmons[500] was born on 15 Sep 1825. She married John C Wetsell. She died on 4 Apr 1857 at age 31; Date may be 4 April 1851. She was buried at Fluvanna Cemetery, Jamestown, Chautauqua County, NY.[501]

---

[481]United States 1850 Census.
[482]Probate Records, of James Lyon, Marshall County, IN.
[483]Lewis, *New York Finger Lake Pioneer Families*.
[484]Tombstone.
[485]Find A Grave.
[486]Chautauqua County NY, Will book, Will book 1, page 1830-1841.
[487]Tombstone.
[488]Find A Grave.
[489]RootsWeb WorldConnect Project, Debbi's database.
[490]United States 1850 Census, Ellicott, Chautauqua County, NY.
[491]Find A Grave.
[492]Tombstone.
[493]Find A Grave.
[494]RootsWeb WorldConnect Project, Debbi's database.
[495]Tombstone.
[496]Find A Grave.
[497]Tombstone.
[498]Find A Grave.
[499]RootsWeb WorldConnect Project, Debbi's database.
[500]Ibid.
[501]Find A Grave.

189. vi. Andrew Ambrose Simmons[502] was born on 16 Jan 1827 at Chautauqua County, NY. He married Mary Jane Herrick. He died on 12 Aug 1882 at Chautauqua County, NY, at age 55.[503]

    He was cooper.

    Mary Jane Herrick was born circa 1829. She died in 1909.[504]

190. vii. John Simmons was born on 11 Jul 1832 at Chautauqua County, NY. He married Mary Catherine Wilson. He died on 22 May 1921 at Bemus Point, Chautauqua County, NY, at age 88.[505] He was buried at Fluvanna Cemetery, Bemus Point, Chautauqua County, NY.[506]

    He was farmer.

    Mary Catherine Wilson was born in 1836. She died on 26 Dec 1885 at Ellery Center, Chautauqua County, NY. She was buried at Fluvanna Cemetery, Ellicott, Chautauqua County, NY.[507]

191. viii. Orvin Simmons was born on 3 Nov 1835 at Chautauqua County, NY. He married Sabra O Tracy.[508] He died in 1919.[509] He was buried at Fluvanna Cemetery, Ellicott, Chautauqua County, NY.[510]

    He was farmer.

    Sabra O Tracy was born on 28 Dec 1859 at Chautauqua County, NY. She died on 3 Sep 1927 at Chautauqua County, NY, at age 67.[511] She was buried at Fluvanna Cemetery, Ellicott, Chautauqua County, NY.[512]

192. ix. Clarissa Simmons was born circa 1836 at Chautauqua County, NY.[513]

193. x. Loranda Simmons[514] was born on 19 Nov 1838 at Fluvana, Chautauqua County, NY. She married Joseph Franklin Klock. She married Charles Elmore Hapgood. She died on 21 Oct 1896 at Brocton, Chautauqua County, NY, at age 57.[515] She was buried at fluvanna Cemetery, Ellicot, Chautauqua County, NY.[516]

    Joseph Franklin Klock was born on 1 Dec 1834. He died on 21 Aug 1866 at age 31.[517] He was buried at Fluvanna Cemetery, Ellicott, Chautauqua County, NY.[518] He was farmer.

    Charles Elmore Hapgood was born in 1842. He died on 20 Jul 1904.[519] He was mason.

194. xi. Obed Simmons was born on 26 Feb 1842 at Chautauqua County, NY. He married Mary (--?--).[520] He died on 11 May 1882 at Chautauqua County, NY, at age 40.[521]

    He was farmer.

    Mary (--?--) was born circa 1849 at NY.[522]

---

[502] New York Civil War Records.
[503] Tombstone.
[504] RootsWeb WorldConnect Project, Debbi's database.
[505] Ibid.
[506] Find A Grave.
[507] Ibid.
[508] RootsWeb WorldConnect Project, Debbi's database.
[509] Tombstone.
[510] Find A Grave.
[511] RootsWeb WorldConnect Project, Debbi's database.
[512] Find A Grave.
[513] RootsWeb WorldConnect Project, Debbi's database.
[514] United States 1850 Census, Ellicott, Chautauqua County, NY.
[515] Find A Grave.
[516] Ibid.
[517] Ibid.
[518] Ibid.
[519] Ibid.
[520] United States 1860 Census, Ellery, Chautauqua County, NY.
[521] RootsWeb WorldConnect Project, Debbi's database.
[522] United States 1860 Census, Ellery, Chautauqua County, NY.

195. xii. Lewis Simmons was born on 15 May 1861 at Chautauqua County, NY.[523] He died on 12 Dec 1902 at Bath, Steuben County, NY, at age 41.[524]

He was cooper.

46. Alvah Lyon (*Alexander, Thomas, John*)[525] was born circa 1803 at Oxford, Chenango County, NY. He married Wealtha (--?--) circa 1824.[526] He died after 1880 at Hamilton County, OH.[527]

He was omnibus driver in 1850.

Wealtha (--?--) was born circa 1808 at NY.[528] She died after 1880 at Hamilton County, OH.[529]

Known children of Alvah Lyon and Wealtha (--?--) were as follows:

+ 196. i. Thomas Lyon was born circa 1825 at NY. He married Kesiah (--?--).
+ 197. ii. Benjamin M Lyon was born in Apr 1827 at NY. He married Susan A (--?--).
+ 198. iii. Jeddiah Lyon was born circa 1829. He married Julia A (--?--).
  199. iv. Jane A Lyon was born circa 1831 at NY.[530]
  200. v. William W Lyon was born in Sep 1832 at OH. He married Elle M (--?--) circa 1880.[531]

  He was locomotive engineer.

  Elle M (--?--) was born in May 1855 at OH.[532]
  201. vi. Emaline Lyon was born circa 1833 at OH.[533]
+ 202. vii. Alexander J Lyon was born circa 1836 at OH. He married Nancy Jane (--?--).
+ 203. viii. Clarissa Lyon was born circa 1837 at NY. She married George M Riley.
+ 204. ix. Alva Perry Lyon was born in Oct 1838 at NY. He married Flora M Marsh circa 1866. He died in 1913 at Hamilton County, OH. He was buried at Williams Cemetery, Williams, Hamilton County, IA.
  205. x. Charles D Lyon was born circa 1841 at NY.[534]
+ 206. xi. Walter F Lyon was born circa 1849 at OH. He married Elizabeth Poppe circa 1869. He died on 17 Jul 1910 at North Bend, Hamilton County, OH.

47. Martha P Lyon (*Alexander, Thomas, John*)[535] was born circa 1805 at NY. She married Simeon Rathbun Lewis, son of James Lewis and Olive Rathbun. She died between 1841 and 1851.[536]

Martha P Lewis is mentioned in Esick Lyon's will written in 1841 but she isn't mentioned in the Alexander Lyon probate of 1851. However, Alexander's probate papers do list a deceased daughter Ruth, married to a Lewis. It is presumed that Ruth and Martha P Lewis are the same person.[537,538] She was also known as Ruth Lyon.[539]

Simeon Rathbun Lewis was born on 24 Mar 1801 at Oxford, Chenango County, NY.[540]

Known children of Martha P Lyon and Simeon Rathbun Lewis were as follows:

[523]New York Civil War Records.
[524]RootsWeb WorldConnect Project, Debbi's database.
[525]Lewis, *New York Finger Lake Pioneer Families*.
[526]United States 1850 Census, Spencer, Hamilton County, OH.
[527]United States 1880 Census, Cincinnati, Hamilton County, OH.
[528]United States 1850 Census, Spencer, Hamilton County, OH.
[529]United States 1880 Census, Cincinnati, Hamilton County, OH.
[530]United States 1850 Census, Spencer, Hamilton County, OH.
[531]United States 1900 Census, Cincinnati, Hamilton County, OH.
[532]Ibid.
[533]United States 1850 Census, Spencer, Hamilton County, OH.
[534]Ibid.
[535]Chautauqua County NY, Will book, Will book I 1830-1843, page 359.
[536]Ibid.
[537]Ibid.
[538]Probate Records, 29 Mar 1851, Alexander Lyon, Schuyler County, NY.
[539]Lewis, *New York Finger Lake Pioneer Families*.
[540]J. C. Cooley, *Rathbone Family* (1898), page 245.

207.   i.   Simeon Lewis[541] died after 1851.[542]
208.   ii.   Charles Lewis died after 1851.[543]
209.   iii.   John Lewis died after 1851.[544]
210.   iv.   Almyra Lewis died after 1851.[545]
211.   v.   Artemisa Lewis died after 1851.[546]
212.   vi.   Thomas O Lewis died after 1851.[547]

48. John Lyon (*Alexander, Thomas, John*)[548] was born in 1806 at Oxford, Chenango County, NY. He married Ann Frances Wescott circa 1830. He married Rebecca Chapin, daughter of Roderick Chapin and Hepsipah Norton, circa 1842.[549] He died on 25 Dec 1893 at Newark, Licking County, OH.[550] He was buried at Cedar Hill Cemetery, Newark, Licking County, OH.[551]

He was farmer when living in NY but a carpenter/joiner when living in OH.

Ann Frances Wescott was born circa 1812 at Hampton, Washington County, NY. She died on 29 Sep 1841 at Stillwater, Saratoga County, NY.[552] She was buried at Lake View Cemetery, Jamestown, Chautauqua County, NY.[553]

Known children of John Lyon and Ann Frances Wescott were as follows:

+ 213.   i.   Mary Angeline Lyon was born in May 1830 at NY. She married Alonzo Joel Marsh say 1845. She died in 1919. She was buried at Lake View Cemetery, Jamestown, Chautauqua County, NY.
214.   ii.   John Lyon was born circa 1834 at NY.[554]
215.   iii.   Sarah Lyon was born circa 1837 at NY.[555]
+ 216.   iv.   Minerva Lyon was born circa 1837 at NY. She married Alex B Hastings. She was buried at Lake View Cemetery, Jamestown, Chautauqua County, NY.
217.   v.   John Myron Lyon was born on 6 Jun 1837 at Busti, Chautauqua County, NY.[556] He died on 27 Nov 1882 at Jamestown, Chautauqua County, NY, at age 45.[557] He was buried at Lake View Cemetery, Jamestown, Chautauqua County, NY.[558]

Rebecca Chapin was born on 12 Jan 1812 at Hampton, Washington County, NY. She died on 8 Aug 1899 at age 87.[559] She was buried at Cedar Hill Cemetery, Newark, Licking County, OH.[560] She was also known as Ada Lyon.

Known children of John Lyon and Rebecca Chapin were as follows:

218.   i.   Seth Lyon was born circa 1843 at NY.[561]

---

[541]Lewis, *New York Finger Lake Pioneer Families*.
[542]Ibid.
[543]Ibid.
[544]Ibid.
[545]Ibid.
[546]Ibid.
[547]Ibid.
[548]Ibid.
[549]Lyons, *William Lyon of Roxbury, MA and Some of his Descendants*, page 70.
[550]Death Records, Ohio Volume 2 page 232. FHC film 912555.
[551]Find A Grave.
[552]RootsWeb WorldConnect Project, Debbi's database.
[553]Find A Grave.
[554]United States 1850 Census, Busti, Chautauqua County, NY.
[555]Ibid.
[556]New York Civil War Records.
[557]RootsWeb WorldConnect Project, Debbi's database.
[558]Find A Grave.
[559]RootsWeb WorldConnect Project, Debbi's database.
[560]Find A Grave.
[561]United States 1850 Census, Busti, Chautauqua County, NY.

219. ii. Leonidas J Lyon was born in 1849 at PA.[562] He died on 3 Jun 1893 at Newark, Licking County, OH.[563] He was buried at Cedar Hill Cemetery, Newark, Licking County, OH.[564]

220. iii. Teresia Lyon was born circa 7 Jan 1857 at NY. She married (--?--) Stevens. She died on 30 Sep 1925 at Newark, Licking County, OH.[565]

49. Benjamin Lyon (*Alexander, Thomas, John*) was born on 8 Mar 1808 at Oxford, Chenango County, NY. He married Mary Ann Mathews circa 1840. He died between 22 Mar 1841 and 1845.[566]

Mary Ann Mathews[567] was born circa 1830 at NY. She married Isaac Adams before 1850.[568] She died in Apr 1880 at Watkins, Schuyler County, NY; cause of death at age 47 was consumption.[569] She was also known as Martha.

Known children of Benjamin Lyon and Mary Ann Mathews were as follows:

221. i. Olive Lyon.[570]

222. ii. Luther Lyon.[571]

223. iii. Lydia Lyon.[572]

224. iv. Maria Lyon was born at NY.[573]

+ 225. v. Madison Lyon was born in Oct 1838 at Chautauqua County, NY. He married Sarah (--?--) circa 1862.

226. vi. Eugene Lyon was born on 27 Feb 1840 at Jamestown, Chautauqua County, NY.[574]

227. vii. Esick Lyon was born circa 1841.[575]

+ 228. viii. Alonzo H Lyon was born on 12 Feb 1842 at Jamestown, Chautauqua County, NY. He married Mary J (--?--) say 1865. He married Carrie R (--?--) say 1876.

229. ix. Adelia Lyon was born circa 1845 at NY.[576]
In 1850 Adelia was living with her mother who had married Isaac Adams.

50. Ozro Lyon (*Alexander, Thomas, John*) was born on 16 Apr 1810 at Oxford, Chenango County, NY. He married Emeline Williams on 23 Oct 1830. He died on 25 Sep 1891 at Warren County, PA, at age 81.[577] He was buried at Foster Cemetery, Lander, Warren County, PA.[578]

Emeline Williams was born on 6 Jan 1813 at Ovid, Seneca County, NY. She died on 20 Mar 1879 at age 66.[579] She was buried at Foster Cemetery, Lander, Warren County, PA.[580]

Known children of Ozro Lyon and Emeline Williams were as follows:

+ 230. i. Frank M Lyon was born on 22 Mar 1832. He married Almira Amanda Putnam, daughter of Daniel Putnam and Betsey Barrett. He died on 19 Jul 1863 at PA at age 31. He was buried at Thompson Hill Cemetery, Warren County, PA.

---

[562]Ibid.

[563]Tombstone.

[564]Find A Grave.

[565]Death Records, Ohio.

[566]Chautauqua County NY, Will book, Will book 1, 1830-1841, page 359.

[567]New York Civil War Records., Enlistment records of her sons Alonzo and Eugene Lyon.

[568]Probate Records, 29 Mar 1851, Alexander Lyon, Schuyler County, NY.

[569]United States 1880 Census, Mortality Schedule.

[570]Probate Records, 29 Mar 1851, Alexander Lyon, Schuyler County, NY.

[571]Ibid.

[572]Ibid.

[573]Ibid.

[574]New York Civil War Records.

[575]United States 1850 Census, Hector, Tompkins County, NY.

[576]Ibid.

[577]Tombstone.

[578]Find A Grave.

[579]Lyons, *William Lyon of Roxbury, MA and Some of his Descendants*, page 133.

[580]Find A Grave.

231. ii. Henry C Lyon was born on 21 Apr 1834 at Lodi, Seneca County, NY.[581] He married Abigal Picket.[582] He died on 11 Jan 1865 at Salisbury Prison, NC, at age 30.[583]

+ 232. iii. Olive Lyon was born on 28 Mar 1837 at NY. She married Heman Braley on 15 Nov 1860 at Warren County, PA. She died on 25 Apr 1871 at Farmington, Warren County, PA, at age 34.

+ 233. iv. Charles H Lyon was born on 28 Mar 1839 at NY. He married Mary Jane Thompson on 2 Jan 1867 at Carroll, Cattaraugus County, NY. He died on 2 Mar 1916 at Lander, Warren County, PA, at age 76. He was buried at Foster Cemetery, Lander, Warren County, PA.

+ 234. v. Edward Alanson Lyon was born on 29 Apr 1841 at NY. He married Adeline E Harris on 30 Oct 1866. He married Olive E Leyman on 1 Sep 1920. He died on 9 May 1935 at age 94. He was buried at Pine Hill Cemetery, Falconer, Chautauqua County, NY.

+ 235. vi. Lydia J Lyon was born on 22 Mar 1843 at NY. She married Abram S Thompson on 18 Sep 1864. She died on 20 Apr 1933 at age 90.

+ 236. vii. Emeline Lyon was born on 6 Aug 1845 at NY. She married Alfred M Thompson on 3 Oct 1866. She died on 8 Aug 1918 at age 73.

+ 237. viii. George Washington Lyon was born on 23 Oct 1847 at NY. He married Mary E Beck on 25 Dec 1877. He died on 9 Jan 1914 at age 66. He was buried at Pine Hill Cemetery, Falconer, Chautauqua County, NY.

+ 238. ix. Mary E Lyon was born on 9 Sep 1849 at NY. She married Daniel W Phillips on 25 Dec 1876. She was buried at Foster Cemetery, Lander, Warren County, PA.

+ 239. x. Alexander F Lyon was born on 12 Jul 1852 at NY. He married Elsie A Raymor on 26 Dec 1875. He died on 29 Jul 1945 at age 93. He was buried at Pine Grove Cemetery, Russell, Warren County, PA.

+ 240. xi. Jerome James Lyon was born on 29 Dec 1855 at PA. He married Juliette E Thompson, daughter of Melvin Thompson and Priscilla (--?--), on 4 Jul 1878. He died in 1947 at NY. He was buried at Maple Grove Cemetery, Ashville, Chautauqua County, NY.

+ 241. xii. Alice Permelia Lyon was born on 16 Sep 1857 at PA. She married Leslie W Gates on 18 Mar 1878. She died in 1936 at Warren County, PA. She was buried at Foster Cemetery, Lander, Warren County, PA.

52. Sophia Ann Lyon (*Alexander, Thomas, John*)[584] was born on 20 Jun 1814 at Oxford, Chenango County, NY. She married Amos Westcott.[585] She died on 20 Jun 1893 at NY at age 79.[586] She was buried at Seneca Union Cemetery, Valois, Schuyler County, NY.[587]

Amos Westcott was born on 29 May 1806 at CT. He died on 4 May 1888 at NY at age 81.[588] He was buried at Seneca Union Cemetery, Valois, Schuyler County, NY.[589] He was farmer.

Known children of Sophia Ann Lyon and Amos Westcott all born at NY were as follows:

242. i. William Monroe Westcott was born on 12 Jul 1836.[590] He married Henrietta Lenor Lyon, daughter of Alanson Lyon and Barbara Ann Norton, on 14 Sep 1863. He died on 27 Jun 1922 at age 85.[591]

---

[581]RootsWeb WorldConnect Project, Pamela Miller database.
[582]Ibid.
[583]US Army Death Records.
[584]Lewis, *New York Finger Lake Pioneer Families*.
[585]RootsWeb WorldConnect Project, Pamela Miller database.
[586]Tombstone.
[587]Find A Grave.
[588]Tombstone.
[589]Find A Grave.
[590]United States 1900 Census, Jamestown, Chautauqua County, NY.
[591]Letter, Ronald E Sherry.

Henrietta Lenor Lyon[592] was born on 16 Sep 1843. She died on 25 Apr 1931 at age 87.[593]

243.   ii.   Albert B Westcott was born in 1841.[594]

244.   iii.   Fernando Westcott[595] was born in Jul 1842. He married Mary A (--?--).[596]

Mary A (--?--) was born in Jun 1846 at NY.[597]

245.   iv.   Brunello Westcott was born circa 1846.[598]

246.   v.   Juliette E Westcott was born circa 1848.[599] She married William S Swick.[600]

247.   vi.   Solomon Murlin Westcott was born circa 1850.[601]

248.   vii.   Emily Westcott was born circa 1854.[602]

54.   **Charles J Lyon** (*Alexander, Thomas, John*)[603] was born on 12 Feb 1819 at Oxford, Chenango County, NY. He married Hester Ann Chapin, daughter of Roderick Chapin and Sarah Clough, on 11 Sep 1839 at Tompkins County, NY.[604] He died on 11 Feb 1895 at Jamestown, Chautauqua County, NY, at age 75.[605]

He left a will on 24 Mar 1893 at Chautauqua County, NY; proven 9 Mar 1901. Mentions widow Hester Ann Lyon, sons Charles H Lyon and Fred G Lyon, daughters Sarah D Lyon, Florence T Lyon and Rose Lyon. Granddaughter Nellie Trotter.[606]

Hester Ann Chapin was born on 25 Jun 1817 at Warsaw, Wyoming County, NY.[607] She died on 31 May 1897 at Jamestown, Chautauqua County, NY, at age 79.[608]

Known children of Charles J Lyon and Hester Ann Chapin were as follows:

249.   i.   Chapin Jehohaz Lyon[609] was born on 3 Aug 1840 at Hector, Schuyler County, NY.[610] He married Ellen Jones circa 1860. He died on 23 Jun 1885 at age 44.[611]

He was machine agent.

Ellen Jones was born circa 1843 at NY.[612] She died on 29 May 1881 at Chautauqua County, NY. She left a will on 21 May 1880 at Ellicott, Chautauqua County, NY; proven 13 May 1881. Mentions Husband Chapin J Lyon, father Ebenezer Jones, sister Addie Jones.[613]

+ 250.   ii.   Septimus Alexander Lyon was born on 16 May 1846 at NY. He married Charlotte Ann Howard on 18 May 1864. He died on 30 Oct 1890 at Saint Charles, Madison County, IA, at age 44. He was buried at Saint Charles Cemetery, Saint Charles, Madison County, IA.

251.   iii.   Sarah Delphine Lyon was born on 7 Apr 1854.[614] She died on 28 Feb 1941 at Chautauqua County, NY, at age 86.[615]

[592]United States 1860 Census, Jamestown, Chautauqua County, NY.

[593]Letter, Ronald E Sherry.

[594]United States 1860 Census, Hector Schuyler County, NY.

[595]Ibid.

[596]United States 1900 Census, Hector, Schuyler County, NY.

[597]Ibid.

[598]United States 1860 Census, Hector Schuyler County, NY.

[599]Ibid.

[600]Tombstone.

[601]United States 1860 Census, Hector Schuyler County, NY.

[602]Ibid.

[603]Lewis, *New York Finger Lake Pioneer Families*.

[604]Edson, *Biography and History of Chautauqua County*, page 39.

[605]RootsWeb WorldConnect Project, Pamela Miller database.

[606]*Will*, Chautauqua County, NY.

[607]Edson, *Biography and History of Chautauqua County*.

[608]RootsWeb WorldConnect Project, Pamela Miller database.

[609]Edson, *Biography and History of Chautauqua County*.

[610]New York Civil War Records.

[611]RootsWeb WorldConnect Project, Pamela Miller database.

[612]United States 1880 Census, Jamestown, Chautauqua County, NY.

[613]*Will*, Chautauqua County, NY.

[614]United States 1900 Census, Jamestown, Chautauqua County, NY.

She was kept a boarding house.

55. Alanson Lyon (*Alexander, Thomas, John*) was born on 26 May 1822 at Oxford, Chenango County, NY. He married Barbara Ann Norton. He died on 18 Apr 1889 at Allegheny County, PA, at age 66.[616]

Barbara Ann Norton was born in Oct 1824 at NY. She died on 10 May 1904 at age 79.[617]
Known children of Alanson Lyon and Barbara Ann Norton were:
+ 252.   i.   Henrietta Lenor Lyon was born on 16 Sep 1843. She married William Monroe Westcott, son of Amos Westcott and Sophia Ann Lyon, on 14 Sep 1863. She died on 25 Apr 1931 at age 87.

[615]Lois M Barris, *Genealogical Information Reported in Dunkirk NY Newspapers*, 3 Mar 1941.
[616]RootsWeb WorldConnect Project, Pamela Miller database.
[617]Ibid.

Generation Five

61. Miranda Lyon (*Daniel, Samuel, Thomas, John*) was born circa 1806 at NY.[618] She married Adijah Dewey Chittenden. She died in 1869.[619] She was buried at Riverside Cemetery, Whitney Point, Broome County, NY.[620]

Attended the 1883 Lyon reunion as a descendant of Daniel Lyon.[621]

Adijah Dewey Chittenden was born in 1805 at NY. He died in 1904.[622] He was buried at Riverside Cemetery, Whitney Point, Broome County, NY.[623] He was blacksmith.

Known children of Miranda Lyon and Adijah Dewey Chittenden all born at Greene, Chenango County, NY, were as follows:

    253.   i.   Dr Daniel Jairus Chittenden was born in Nov 1832.[624] He married Elizabeth G (--?--).[625]

                Elizabeth G (--?--) was born in Jun 1834 at NY.[626]

    254.   ii.   Leroy Cook Chittenden[627] was born on 26 May 1837.[628] He married Sarah Jenine (--?--). He died in 1871.[629] He was buried at Riverside Cemetery, Whitney Point, Broome County, NY.[630]

                Sarah Jenine (--?--) was born in 1840 at NY. She died in 1915. She was buried at Riverside Cemetery, Whitney Point, Broome County, NY.[631]

    255.   iii.   Dr Joseph H Chittenden[632] was born in 1839. He married De Ette Smith. He died in 1909. He was buried at Spring Forest Cemetery, Binghamton, Broome County, NY.[633]

                He was also known as James H Chittenden. Attended the 1883 Lyon reunion as a descendant of Daniel [of Samuel] Lyon.[634]

                De Ette Smith was born in 1840. She died in 1929.[635] She was also known as Helen D Smith.

    256.   iv.   William Augustus Chittenden[636] was born on 4 Mar 1842.[637] He married Josephine M Prentice.[638] He died on 8 Jul 1886 at Chicago, Cook County, IL, at age 44.[639] He was buried at Spring Forest Cemetery, Binghamton, Broome County, NY.[640]

---

[618]United States 1850 Census, Triangle, Broome County, NY.

[619]Tombstone.

[620]Find A Grave.

[621]*1883 Lyon Reunion.*

[622]Tombstone.

[623]Find A Grave.

[624]United States 1850 Census, Triangle, Broome County, NY.

[625]United States 1900 Census, Addison, Steuben County, NY.

[626]Ibid.

[627]United States 1850 Census, Triangle, Broome County, NY.

[628]New York Civil War Records.

[629]Tombstone.

[630]Find A Grave.

[631]Ibid.

[632]United States 1850 Census, Triangle, Broome County, NY.

[633]Find A Grave.

[634]*1883 Lyon Reunion.*

[635]Tombstone.

[636]United States 1850 Census, Triangle, Broome County, NY.

[637]New York Civil War Records.

[638]United States 1880 Census, Binghamton, Broome County, NY.

[639]Death Records, Cook County, IL.

[640]Find A Grave.

He was insurance agent. Attended the 1883 Lyon reunion as a descendant of Daniel [of Samuel] Lyon.[641]

Josephine M Prentice[642] was born in 1850 at NY. She died in 1926.[643] She was buried at Spring Forest Cemetery, Binghamton, Broome County, NY.[644]

74. Anna Augusta Lyon (*Samuel, Samuel, Thomas, John*) was born circa 1816 at NY.[645] She married Cuyler PerLee circa 1842.[646] She died on 6 Jun 1891 at NY.[647] She was buried at North Norwich Cemetery, North Norwich, Chenango County, NY.[648]

Attended the 1883 Lyon reunion as a descendant of Samuel Lyon Jr.[649]

Cuyler PerLee was born circa 1812 at NY.[650] He died on 8 Apr 1872 at NY. He was buried at North Norwich Cemetery, North Norwich, Chenango County, NY.[651] He was farmer.

Known children of Anna Augusta Lyon and Cuyler PerLee all born at NY were as follows:

257.   i.   Frederick PerLee was born circa 1844.[652] He died after 1865.[653]

258.   ii.   Elizabeth PerLee[654] was born circa 1846. She died on 23 Sep 1898 at NY.[655] She was buried at North Norwich Cemetery, North Norwich, Chenango County, NY.[656]

259.   iii.   Lillie PerLee was born circa 1848.[657]

Attended the 1883 Lyon reunion as a descendant of Samuel Lyon Jr.[658]

260.   iv.   Henry PerLee was born circa 1852.[659] He died on 2 Jan 1934.[660] He was buried at NY.[661] He was farmer.

261.   v.   Paul PerLee was born circa 1853.[662] He married Sarah J (--?--) circa 1907.[663] He died on 23 Apr 1930.[664] He was buried at North Norwich Cemetery, North Norwich, Chenango County, NY.[665]

He was farmer.

Sarah J (--?--) was born circa 1869 at England, UK.[666]

76. Theron Lyon (*Samuel, Samuel, Thomas, John*) was born circa 1829 at NY.[667] He married Mary (--?--) say 1858.[668] He died on 10 Mar 1877.[669] He was buried at North Norwich Cemetery, North Norwich, Chenango County, NY.[670]

---

[641]*1883 Lyon Reunion.*
[642]United States 1880 Census, Binghamton, Broome County, NY.
[643]Tombstone.
[644]Find A Grave.
[645]United States 1880 Census, North Norwich, Chenango County, NY.
[646]United States 1850 Census, North Norwich, Chenango County, NY.
[647]Tombstone.
[648]Find A Grave.
[649]*1883 Lyon Reunion.*
[650]United States 1850 Census, North Norwich, Chenango County, NY.
[651]Find A Grave.
[652]United States 1850 Census, North Norwich, Chenango County, NY.
[653]New York Civil War Records.
[654]United States 1850 Census, North Norwich, Chenango County, NY.
[655]Tombstone.
[656]Find A Grave.
[657]United States 1880 Census, North Norwich, Chenango County, NY.
[658]*1883 Lyon Reunion.*
[659]United States 1880 Census, North Norwich, Chenango County, NY.
[660]Tombstone.
[661]Find A Grave.
[662]United States 1880 Census, North Norwich, Chenango County, NY.
[663]United States 1930 Census, North Norwich, Chenango County, NY.
[664]Tombstone.
[665]Find A Grave.
[666]New York State 1915 Census, North Norwich, Chenango County, NY.
[667]United States 1850 Census, North Norwich, Chenango County, NY.

He was farmer.

Mary (--?--) was born circa 1838 at NY.[671] She died on 27 Jul 1915.[672] She was buried at North Norwich Cemetery, North Norwich, Chenango County, NY.[673]

Known children of Theron Lyon and Mary (--?--) were:

+ 262.   i.   Edward Lyon was born in Dec 1860 at NY. He married Carrie E (--?--) circa 1881.

77. Thomas Lyon (*Samuel, Samuel, Thomas, John*)[674] was born circa 1830 at NY. He married Mary (--?--).[675]

He was farmer in 1860.

Mary (--?--) was born circa 1838 at NY.[676]

Known children of Thomas Lyon and Mary (--?--) were:

263.   i.   Edward Lyon was born circa 1860 at Chenango County, NY.[677]

78. Darius E Lyon (*Samuel, Samuel, Thomas, John*) was born circa 1831 at NY. He married Mary Ann (--?--) circa 1858.[678] He married Frankie Balcom on 19 Jan 1874 at Sherburne, Chenango County, NY.[679] He died in 1892 at Rock County, WI. He was buried at Grove Cemetery, Footville, Rock County, WI.[680]

He was shoemaker in 1860.

Mary Ann (--?--) was born circa 1831 at NY.[681] She died before 1870.[682]

Known children of Darius E Lyon and Mary Ann (--?--) were as follows:

264.   i.   Marvin D Lyon[683] was born on 13 Jul 1859 at Chenango County, NY. He married Minnie Schultz. He died on 28 Sep 1908 at Jefferson County, WI, at age 49.[684] He was buried at Rock Lake Cemetery, Jefferson County, WI.[685]

    Minnie Schultz was born on 4 Nov 1864. She died on 9 Jul 1936 at Jefferson County, WI, at age 71.[686] She was buried at Rock Lake Cemetery, Jefferson County, WI.[687]

265.   ii.   Charles Lyon was born circa 1864 at NY.[688]

Frankie Balcom was born circa 1842 at NY.[689]

Known children of Darius E Lyon and Frankie Balcom were:

---

[668] United States 1870 Census, Preston, Chenango County, NY.

[669] Tombstone.

[670] Find A Grave.

[671] United States 1870 Census, Preston, Chenango County, NY.

[672] Tombstone.

[673] Find A Grave.

[674] United States 1860 Census, North Norwich, Chenango County, NY.

[675] Ibid.

[676] Ibid.

[677] Ibid.

[678] Ibid.

[679] *Newspaper*, Sherburne, NY.

[680] Find A Grave.

[681] United States 1860 Census, North Norwich, Chenango County, NY.

[682] United States 1870 Census, Sherburne, Chenango County, NY.

[683] United States 1860 Census, North Norwich, Chenango County, NY.

[684] Tombstone.

[685] Find A Grave.

[686] Tombstone.

[687] Find A Grave.

[688] United States 1880 Census, Columbus Center, Chenango County, NY.

[689] Ibid.

266.   i.   Freeman Lyon[690] was born on 31 Oct 1875 at NY.[691] He married Lulu Belle (--?--) circa 1901.[692]

           He was butcher.[693]

79.   Janette M Lyon (*Samuel, Samuel, Thomas, John*) was born circa 1832 at NY; Tombstone indicates birth c Feb 1836.[694] She married Charles S Waters circa 1857.[695] She died on 28 Oct 1895.[696] She was buried at North Norwich Cemetery, North Norwich, Chenango County, NY.[697]

     She was also known as Mary Jeanette Waters. Attended the 1883 Lyon reunion as a descendant of Samuel Lyon Jr.[698]

     Charles S Waters was born circa 1833 at NY.[699] He died on 5 Sep 1889.[700] He was buried at North Norwich Cemetery, North Norwich, Chenango County, NY.[701]

     Known children of Janette M Lyon and Charles S Waters all born at NY were as follows:

267.   i.   Theodore S Waters was born circa 1859.[702]

           Attended the 1883 Lyon reunion as a descendant of Samuel Lyon Jr.[703]

268.   ii.   William O Waters was born circa 1862.[704]

           Attended the 1883 Lyon reunion as a descendant of Samuel Lyon Jr.[705]

269.   iii.   Charles H Waters was born circa 1869.[706]

99.   Henry A Lyon (*George, Samuel, Thomas, John*)[707] was born on 22 Nov 1826 at NY. He married Elvira H Dyer, daughter of John Dyer and Harriet Shaw.[708] He died on 2 Dec 1908 at Greene, Chenango County, NY, at age 82.[709] He was buried at Sylvan Lawn Cemetery, Greene, Chenango County, NY.[710]

     Attended the 1883 Lyon reunion as a descendant of George R Lyon.[711] He was president of an Iron Works in 1900.

     Elvira H Dyer was born in Mar 1830 at Willet, Cortland County, NY. She died on 25 May 1909 at Greene, Chenango County, NY, at age 79.[712] She was buried at Sylvan Lawn Cemetery, Greene, Chenango County, NY.[713]

     Known children of Henry A Lyon and Elvira H Dyer were as follows:

+ 270.   i.   Harriet A Lyon was born circa 1852 at NY. She married Edward A Barnard. She died after 1912.

[690]Ibid.

[691]World War I Draft Records.

[692]United States 1910 Census, Edgerton, Rock County, WI.

[693]World War I Draft Records.

[694]United States 1850 Census, North Norwich, Chenango County, NY.

[695]United States 1880 Census, Sherburne, Chenango County, NY.

[696]Tombstone.

[697]Find A Grave.

[698]*1883 Lyon Reunion.*

[699]United States 1880 Census, Sherburne, Chenango County, NY.

[700]Tombstone.

[701]Find A Grave.

[702]United States 1880 Census, Sherburne, Chenango County, NY.

[703]*1883 Lyon Reunion.*

[704]United States 1880 Census, Sherburne, Chenango County, NY.

[705]*1883 Lyon Reunion.*

[706]United States 1880 Census, Sherburne, Chenango County, NY.

[707]Lyon, *Lyon Memorial, NY Families*, page 164.

[708]Probate Records, Chenango County, Settlements Book #10, page 381, 383.

[709]Tombstone, Sylvan Lawn Cemetery, Greene, Chenango County, NY.

[710]Ibid.

[711]*1883 Lyon Reunion.*

[712]Tombstone, Sylvan Lawn Cemetery, Greene, Chenango County, NY.

[713]Find A Grave.

+ 271.   ii.   Susan A Lyon was born in 1853 at NY. She married John Dempster Eaton in 1893. She died in 1932. She was buried at Sylvan Lawn Cemetery, Greene, Chenango County, NY.

272.   iii.   Walter Dyer Lyon[714] was born on 22 Oct 1867 at Greene, Chenango County, NY.[715] He died in 1937. He was buried at Sylvan Lawn Cemetery, Greene, Chenango County, NY.[716]

Attended the 1883 Lyon reunion as a descendant of George R Lyon.[717] He was secretary of an Iron Works in 1900.

100.   Anne Eliza Lyon (*George, Samuel, Thomas, John*)[718] was born in Aug 1829 at NY. She married Judson B Babcock circa 1855.[719] She married Isaac B Perlee in 1888.[720] She died in 1912.[721] She was buried at Sylvan Lawn Cemetery, Greene, Chenango County, NY.[722]

Attended the 1883 Lyon reunion in Chenango County NY in 1883.[723]

Judson B Babcock was born circa 1827 at NY.[724] He died before 1870; In 1870 Ann was living with her father and Judson was not in the census.[725] He was jeweler.

Known children of Anne Eliza Lyon and Judson B Babcock were:

273.   i.   Nellie Babcock was born circa 1856 at NY.[726]

Isaac B Perlee[727] was born on 7 May 1833 at NY. He died on 5 Mar 1901 at age 67.[728] He was buried at North Norwich Cemetery, North Norwich, Chenango County, NY.[729]

There were no known children of Anne Eliza Lyon and Isaac B Perlee.

101.   George Milton Lyon (*George, Samuel, Thomas, John*) was born on 15 Feb 1832. He married Eliza C Lewis.[730] He died on 28 Oct 1865 at age 33.[731] He was buried at Sylvan Lawn Cemetery, Greene, Chenango County, NY.[732]

Eliza C Lewis was born circa 1834 at NY.[733]

Known children of George Milton Lyon and Eliza C Lewis all born at NY were as follows:

274.   i.   Lewis Lyon was born circa 1856.[734]

275.   ii.   William R Lyon was born circa 1857.[735]

He was farmer. Attended the 1883 Lyon reunion as a descendant of George R Lyon.[736]

276.   iii.   Mary Lyon was born circa 1859.[737]

[714]Probate Records, Chenango County, Settlements Book #10, page 381, 383.
[715]United States 1900 Census, Greene, Chenango County, NY.
[716]Tombstone, Sylvan Lawn Cemetery, Greene, Chenango County, NY.
[717]*1883 Lyon Reunion*.
[718]Lyon, *Lyon Memorial, NY Families*, page 164.
[719]United States 1860 Census, Greene, Chenango County, NY.
[720]United States 1900 Census, Greene, Chenango County, NY.
[721]Tombstone.
[722]Find A Grave.
[723]*1883 Lyon Reunion*.
[724]United States 1860 Census, Greene, Chenango County, NY.
[725]United States 1870 Census, Greene, Chenango County, NY.
[726]United States 1860 Census, Greene, Chenango County, NY.
[727]RootsWeb WorldConnect Project, Debbi's database.
[728]Tombstone.
[729]Find A Grave.
[730]Lyon, *Lyon Memorial, NY Families*, page 164.
[731]Tombstone, Sylvan Lawn Cemetery, Greene, Chenango County, NY.
[732]Find A Grave.
[733]Lyon, *Lyon Memorial, NY Families*, page 164.
[734]United States 1860 Census, Greene, Chenango County, NY.
[735]Ibid.
[736]*1883 Lyon Reunion*.
[737]United States 1860 Census, Greene, Chenango County, NY.

277.   iv.   Francis H Lyon was born circa 1872.[738]

103.   Alice Susan Lyon (*George, Samuel, Thomas, John*) was born on 14 Sep 1842 at NY. She married Anson Burdette Holcomb in 1870.[739] She died on 9 Feb 1896 at age 53.[740] She was buried at Sylvan Lawn Cemetery, Greene, Chenango County, NY.[741]
Attended the 1883 Lyon reunion as a descendant of George R Lyon.[742]

Anson Burdette Holcomb[743] was born in 1841 at NY. He died in 1905.[744] He was buried at Sylvan Lawn Cemetery, Greene, Chenango County, NY.[745] He was book keeper.
   Known children of Alice Susan Lyon and Anson Burdette Holcomb both born at NY were as follows:
278.   i.   Anna B Holcomb was born circa 1871.[746] She died in 1906.[747] She was buried at Sylvan Lawn Cemetery, Greene, Chenango County, NY.[748]
279.   ii.   Olive L Holcomb was born circa 1873.[749]
         Attended the 1883 Lyon reunion as a descendant of George R Lyon.[750]

129.   Matilda H Lyon (*Morgan, Thomas, Thomas, John*)[751] was born on 6 Aug 1835 at NY. She married John H Ryder, son of Benjamin Ryder and Charity Hicks, circa 1855.[752] She died on 14 Sep 1877 at Kent County, MI, at age 42.[753] She was buried at Foxes Cemetery, Lowell, Kent County, MI.[754]

John H Ryder[755] was born on 22 Sep 1831 at Canada. He died on 15 Jan 1894 at Grand Rapids, Kent County, MI, at age 62.[756]
   Known children of Matilda H Lyon and John H Ryder all born at MI were as follows:
280.   i.   Frank W Ryder was born on 1 Mar 1856.[757] He married Anna Reusser, daughter of Samuel Reusser and Rosina Roth, on 24 May 1894 at Lowell, Kent County, MI. He died on 14 Nov 1912 at Lowell, Kent County, MI, at age 56.[758]

         Anna Reusser[759] was born on 20 Apr 1877 at Thun, Bern Canton, Switzerland.[760] She died on 20 Aug 1962 at Grand Rapids, Kent County, MI, at age 85.[761]
281.   ii.   Frederick B Ryder was born circa 1858.[762] He died on 5 Feb 1887 at Midland County, MI.[763]

[738]United States 1880 Census, Fenton, Broome County, NY.
[739]Lyon, *Lyon Memorial, NY Families*, page 164.
[740]RootsWeb WorldConnect Project, Debbi's database.
[741]Find A Grave.
[742]*1883 Lyon Reunion*.
[743]United States 1880 Census, Greene, Chenango County, NY.
[744]Tombstone.
[745]Find A Grave.
[746]United States 1880 Census, Greene, Chenango County, NY.
[747]Tombstone.
[748]Find A Grave.
[749]United States 1880 Census, Greene, Chenango County, NY.
[750]*1883 Lyon Reunion*.
[751]United States 1850 Census, Vergennes, Kent County, MI.
[752]Lowry, *Morgan Lyon Biography*, page 36.
[753]Tombstone.
[754]Find A Grave.
[755]Lowry, *Morgan Lyon Biography*, page 36.
[756]Ibid., page 71.
[757]Ibid., page 36.
[758]Ibid., page 72.
[759]Ibid., page 79.
[760]Ibid.
[761]Ibid.
[762]United States 1860 Census, Vergennes, Kent County, MI.
[763]Lowry, *Morgan Lyon Biography*, page 77.

282. iii. George Ryder was born on 15 Sep 1860.[764] He died on 10 Jul 1878 at age 17.[765] He was buried at Foxes Cemetery, Lowell, Kent County, MI.[766]

283. iv. Mary Louise Ryder[767] was born on 10 Mar 1866. She married Frederick B March. She married (--?--) Roulo say 1887. She died on 31 Oct 1953 at Los Angeles, Los Angeles County, CA, at age 87.[768]

Frederick B March was born in Feb 1869 at MN. He died before 17 Apr 1930.[769]

284. v. Jay B Ryder was born circa 1875.[770] He married Helen A (--?--) circa 1902.[771] He died on 25 Feb 1917 at Omaha, Douglas County, NE.[772]

Helen A (--?--) was born circa 1875 at Hamburg, Hamburg County, Germany.[773]

130. James A Lyon (*Morgan, Thomas, Thomas, John*)[774] was born on 21 Jul 1838 at Lowell, Kent County, MI; Said to have been born in an Indian wigwam. He married Emma Fuller on 25 Dec 1866 at Ada, Kent County, MI.[775] He died on 18 May 1904 at Lowell, Kent County, MI, at age 65.[776] He was buried at Oakwood Cemetery, Lowell, Kent County, MI.[777]

A James Lyon, a teacher, born in Michigan was living with Charles William Knapp in Champaign, IL in the 1860 census.

Emma Fuller was born on 9 Mar 1847 at Rochester, Monroe County, NY. She died on 23 Oct 1892 at Grand Rapids, Kent County, MI, at age 45.[778] She was buried at Oakwood Cemetery, Lowell, Kent County, MI.[779]

Known children of James A Lyon and Emma Fuller were as follows:

285. i. Sarah C Lyon was born on 27 Nov 1867 at Kent County, MI.[780] He died on 6 Nov 1947 at South Bend, St Joseph's County, IN, at age 79.

286. ii. Sanford W Lyon was born in Jan 1870 at Independence, Buchanan County, IA. He died circa 1880.[781]

+ 287. iii. Bertha Lyon was born on 20 Dec 1871 at Independence, Buchanan County, IA. She married Tracy F Hawley circa 1901. She died on 24 Mar 1944 at Alameda, Alameda County, CA, at age 72.

+ 288. iv. Martha L Lyon was born circa 1874 at Independence, Buchanan County, IA. She married Russell Fred Thompson, son of Jacob Thompson and Caroline (--?--). She died in 1954 at Pinellas County, FL.

131. Emily Lyon (*Morgan, Thomas, Thomas, John*)[782] was born in Jun 1845 at Kent County, MI. She married Hiram B Aldrich, son of Henry Aldrich, on 5 Feb 1864. She and Hiram B Aldrich were divorced in 1881

---

[764]Ibid., page 36.
[765]Tombstone.
[766]Find A Grave.
[767]United States 1880 Census, Lowell, Kent County, MI.
[768]Lowry, *Morgan Lyon Biography*, page 77.
[769]Ibid.
[770]United States 1880 Census, Lowell, Kent County, MI.
[771]United States 1910 Census, Omaha, Douglas County, NE.
[772]Lowry, *Morgan Lyon Biography*, page 77.
[773]United States 1910 Census, Omaha, Douglas County, NE.
[774]United States 1850 Census, Vergennes, Kent County, MI.
[775]Lowry, *Morgan Lyon Biography*, page 50.
[776]Michigan Death Records.
[777]Lowry, *Morgan Lyon Biography*, page 71.
[778]Ibid., page 61.
[779]Ibid.
[780]Ibid., page 50.
[781]Ibid., page 51.

at Kent County, MI. She married Helmus Hendricks, son of Abram Hendricks and Hannah (--?--), circa 1882. She died on 9 Jul 1918 at MI at age 73. She was buried at Oak Hill Cemetery, Grand Rapids, Kent County, MI.[783]

Hiram B Aldrich was born in Sep 1838 at MI. He died on 28 Jan 1907 at Lowell, Kent County, MI, at age 68.[784]

Known children of Emily Lyon and Hiram B Aldrich were as follows:

289.   i.   Lillian D Aldrich was born in 1866 at MI. She married Duke Van Dyke. She died on 18 Dec 1920 at Los Angeles, Los Angeles County, CA. She was buried at Oak Hill Cemetery, Grand Rapids, Kent County, MI.[785]

Duke Van Dyke was born circa 1852 at Netherlands. He died on 23 Apr 1914 at Rochester, Olmsted County, MN. He was buried at Oak Hill Cemetery, Grand Rapids, Kent County, MI.[786]

290.   ii.   Charles H Aldrich was born on 5 Jan 1869 at Vergennes, Kent County, MI. He died in Oct 1941 at age 72.[787]

Helmus Hendricks[788] was born in 1838. He died in 1926.[789] He was buried at Oak Hill Cemetery, Grand Rapids, Kent County, MI.[790]

There were no known children of Emily Lyon and Helmus Hendricks.

133. Mary E Lyon (*Morgan, Thomas, Thomas, John*)[791] was born on 15 Aug 1850 at Vergennes, Kent County, MI. She married Orren Omar Adams on 6 Feb 1871.[792] She died on 26 Sep 1924 at Chicago, Cook County, IL, at age 74.[793] She was buried at Foxes Cemetery, Lowell, Kent County, MI.[794]

Orren Omar Adams was born on 28 Jul 1839 at Greene County, NY.[795] He died on 21 Jul 1909 at Lowell, Kent County, MI, at age 69.[796] He was buried at Foxes Cemetery, Lowell, Kent County, MI.[797] He was farmer and mason.

Known children of Mary E Lyon and Orren Omar Adams were:

291.   i.   Cora Louise Adams[798] was born on 7 Oct 1873 at Campbell, Ionia County, MI. She married John F Krum on 26 Apr 1891. She died on 2 Nov 1910 at Grand Rapids, Kent County, MI, at age 37.[799] She was buried at Foxes Cemetery, Lowell, Kent County, MI.[800]

John F Krum was born circa 1872 at MI. He was farmer in 1910.[801]

[782]United States 1850 Census, Vergennes, Kent County, MI.
[783]Lowry, *Morgan Lyon Biography*, page 71.
[784]Ibid., page 78.
[785]Ibid., page 73.
[786]Ibid.
[787]Ibid.
[788]Ibid., page 78.
[789]Tombstone.
[790]Find A Grave.
[791]United States 1860 Census, Vergennes, Kent County, MI.
[792]United States 1910 Census, Vergennes, Kent County, MI.
[793]Tombstone.
[794]Find A Grave.
[795]Passport Application.
[796]Michigan Death Records.
[797]Find A Grave.
[798]United States 1900 Census, Lowell, Kent County, MI.
[799]Lowry, *Morgan Lyon Biography*, page 79.
[800]Find A Grave.
[801]United States 1910 Census, Vergennes, Kent County, MI.

134. Henry W Lyon (*William, Thomas, Thomas, John*) was born on 22 Mar 1835 at NY.[802] He married Jane (--?--).[803]

Jane (--?--) was born circa 1831 at Chenango County, NY.[804]
Known children of Henry W Lyon and Jane (--?--) were:
292.   i.   Lucetta Lyon was born circa 1849.[805]

135. Betsey Lyon (*William, Thomas, Thomas, John*) was born on 30 Aug 1836 at Chenango County, NY. She married Emmett H Merritt.[806]

Known children of Betsey Lyon and Emmett H Merritt were:
293.   i.   George Merritt was born circa 1856 at MI.[807]

138. Nelson Thomas Lyon (*William, Thomas, Thomas, John*) was born on 20 Aug 1843 at Lowell, Kent County, MI.[808] He married Mary Morgan circa 1865. He died on 18 Mar 1872 at Lowell, Kent County, MI, at age 28; Cause of death was smallpox.[809]

Mary Morgan was born circa 1848 at NY.[810] She married (--?--) Provost say 1873.[811]
Known children of Nelson Thomas Lyon and Mary Morgan were as follows:
294.   i.   Edward B Lyon was born circa 1865 at NY.[812]
295.   ii. Ida Lyon was born circa 1869 at MI.[813]
+ 296.   iii. L B Lyon was born on 17 Dec 1870 at MI. He married Lillian LeClair, daughter of Daniel LeClair and Betsey Parker, on 5 May 1889 at Lowell, Keny County, MI. He married Emma Louise Tank in Oct 1929. He died on 30 Nov 1958 at age 87. He was buried at Lake View Cemetery, Ludington, Mason County, MI.
297.   iv. Elsie Lyon was born circa Jun 1872. She died on 17 Sep 1872.[814]

139. Richard Brown Lyon (*William, Thomas, Thomas, John*) was born on 14 Jan 1846 at Lowell, Kent County, MI. He married Adelaide Martha Brown, daughter of William H. Brown, before 1868. He married Henrietta Sturgis on 27 Sep 1887 at Coffeyville, Montgomery County, KS. He and Henrietta Sturgis were divorced on 8 Aug 1890 at Neodesha, Wilson County, KS. He married Martha Lockwood circa 1891. He married Alice Matilda Watson on 9 Nov 1904 at Emo, Rainy River District, Ontario, Canada. He died on 4 Jul 1924 at Conneaut, Ashtabula, OH, at age 78.[815]

Adelaide Martha Brown[816] was born circa 1842 at NY.[817] She died on 10 Sep 1882 at Evart, Osceola County, MI. She was buried at Evart, Osceola County, MI.[818]

---

[802] Ancestry Family Trees, Bruce Lyon's U C Lyon Family Tree.
[803] New York State 1855 Census.
[804] Ibid.
[805] Ibid.
[806] Ancestry Family Trees, Bruce Lyon's U C Lyon Family Tree.
[807] United States 1870 Census, Saranac, Ionia County, MI.
[808] Ancestry Family Trees, Bruce Lyon's U C Lyon Family Tree.
[809] Lowry, *Morgan Lyon Biography*, page 52.
[810] United States 1870 Census, Lowell, Kent County, MI.
[811] United States 1880 Census, Big Rapids, Mecosta County, MI.
[812] United States 1870 Census, Lowell, Kent County, MI.
[813] Ibid.
[814] Lowry, *Morgan Lyon Biography*, page 52.
[815] Ancestry Family Trees, Bruce Lyon's U C Lyon Family Tree.
[816] Letter Olive Buckley to Mrs Wells.
[817] United States 1870 Census, Lowell, Kent County, MI.

Known children of Richard Brown Lyon and Adelaide Martha Brown were as follows:

+ 298.   i.   Charles William Lyon was born circa 1868 at Bowne, Kent County, MI. He married Bertha Mae McDonald on 25 Dec 1893 at New London, Waupaca County, WI.

  299.   ii.   Joseph Birtie Lyon was born in 1870 at MI. He died in 1880.[819]

  300.   iii.   Ray Richard Lyon was born on 16 Mar 1876 at Evart, Osceola County, MI. He married May Eva Smith on 15 Jul 1916.[820]

      He was also known as Ray Richard Lyon.

      May Eva Smith was born circa 1889 at OH.[821]

  301.   iv.   Floyd B Lyon was born on 10 May 1876. He married Ada T Greer in 1892 at Neodesha, Wilson County, KA. He died on 26 Apr 1894 at Neodesha, Wilson County, KA, at age 17.[822]

  302.   v.   Grace Lyon was born in Apr 1881 at Evart, Osceola County, MI. She married Harry O'Neil.[823]

Harry O'Neil was born in 1880.[824]

Henrietta Sturgis[825] died at Coffeeville, Montgomery County, KS.
There were no known children of Richard Brown Lyon and Henrietta Sturgis.

Martha Lockwood was born on 15 Jun 1869 at Riverton, Floyd County, IA.[826] She married Isaac Welty circa 1900.[827] She died on 16 Dec 1936 at Gooding County, ID, at age 67.[828]

Known children of Richard Brown Lyon and Martha Lockwood were as follows:

  303.   i.   Clifford Lyon was born in 1891. He died in 1896.[829]

+ 304.   ii.   Ulysses Clair Lyon was born on 1 Apr 1893 at Kabetogama County, MN. He married Flora Hesser on 18 Mar 1917 at Glencoe, Payne County, OK. He died on 14 Sep 1968 at Sacramento, Sacramento County, CA, at age 75. He was buried at Sunset Memorial Park, Sacramento, Sacramento County, CA.

  305.   iii.   Violet E Lyon was born on 9 Dec 1895 at Lake of the Woods, Lake of the Woods County, MN. She died on 20 Nov 1993 at age 97.[830]

There were no known children of Richard Brown Lyon and Alice Matilda Watson.

142. Mary A Lyon (*William, Thomas, Thomas, John*) was born on 18 Oct 1858 at Lowell, Kent County, MI. She married George H Hall in 1885. She died on 24 Aug 1941 at age 82.[831]

George H Hall[832] was born in Sep 1888 at Canada.[833]
Known children of Mary A Lyon and George H Hall were:

  306.   i.   Earnest Hall was born in Sep 1888 at MI.[834] He married Lillian W (--?--).[835]

---

[818] Ancestry Family Trees, Bruce Lyon's U C Lyon Family Tree.
[819] Ibid.
[820] Ibid.
[821] Ibid.
[822] Ibid.
[823] Ibid.
[824] Ibid., Bruce Lyon's UC Lyon Family Tree.
[825] Ibid., Bruce Lyon's U C Lyon Family Tree.
[826] Ibid.
[827] United States 1910 Census, Ada County, ID.
[828] Idaho Death Records.
[829] Ancestry Family Trees, Bruce Lyon's U C Lyon Family Tree.
[830] Ibid.
[831] Ibid.
[832] Ibid., Bruce Lyon's UC Lyon Family Tree.
[833] United States 1900 Census, Solon, Kent County, MI.
[834] Ibid.
[835] United States 1940 Census, Grand Rapids, Kent County, MI.

Lillian W (--?--) was born circa 1888 at MI.[836]

144. Ella Lyon (*William, Thomas, Thomas, John*) was born on 16 Feb 1866 at Lowell, Kent County, MI. She married Christopher W Klump on 15 Sep 1886. She died on 2 Jun 1949 at age 83. She was buried at Oakwood Cemetery, Lowell, Kent County, MI.[837]

Christopher W Klump was born in Nov 1860 at MI.[838] He died in 1943.[839] He was buried at Oakwood Cemetery, Lowell, Kent County, MI.[840]

Known children of Ella Lyon and Christopher W Klump both born at MI were as follows:
- 307.   i.   Rena Klump was born in Sep 1888.[841]
- 308.   ii.   Clifford Klump was born in Oct 1890.[842] He died in Nov 1975 at age 85.[843] He was buried at Oakwood Cemetery, Lowell, Kent County, MI.[844]

153. Mary Eliza Lyon (*Daniel, Daniel, Thomas, John*) was born in 1825 at Bradford County, PA.[845] She married William B. Dodge.[846]

Attended the 1883 Lyon reunion as a descendant of Daniel Lyon, MD.[847]

Known children of Mary Eliza Lyon and William B. Dodge both born at Bradford County, PA, were as follows:
- 309.   i.   William Henry Dodge was born in Aug 1850. He married Helen F (--?--).[848]

  Helen F (--?--) was born in Mar 1852.[849]
- 310.   ii.   Ella E Dodge was born circa 1858.[850]

154. Otis P. Lyon (*Daniel, Daniel, Thomas, John*) was born in 1827 at Bradford County, PA.[851] He married Loretta E Lawrence on 7 Jan 1850.[852]

Known children of Otis P. Lyon and Loretta E Lawrence all born at PA were as follows:
- 311.   i.   Sophia Lyon was born circa 1851.[853] She married (--?--) Sheldon.[854]
- 312.   ii.   Frances E Lyon was born circa 1853.[855] She married (--?--) Carrigan.[856]

  (--?--) Carrigan died before 1880.[857]

---

[836]Ibid.
[837]Find A Grave.
[838]United States 1900 Census, Lowell, Kent County, MI.
[839]Ancestry Family Trees, Bruce Lyon's U C Lyon Family Tree.
[840]Find A Grave.
[841]United States 1900 Census, Lowell, Kent County, MI.
[842]Ibid.
[843]Tombstone.
[844]Find A Grave.
[845]RootsWeb WorldConnect Project, Cheryl database.
[846]Heverly, *Pioneer and Patriot Families of Bradford County, PA 1770-1800*.
[847]*1883 Lyon Reunion*.
[848]United States 1900 Census, Towanda, Bradford County, PA.
[849]Ibid.
[850]United States 1860 Census, Towanda, Bradford County, PA.
[851]RootsWeb WorldConnect Project, Cheryl database.
[852]Heverly, *Pioneer and Patriot Families of Bradford County, PA 1770-1800*, page 79.
[853]United States 1870 Census, Cairo, Alexander County, IL.
[854]United States 1880 Census, Saint Lewis, Saint Lewis, MO.
[855]United States 1870 Census, Cairo, Alexander County, IL.
[856]United States 1880 Census, Saint Lewis, Saint Lewis, MO.
[857]Ibid.

313.   iii.   Belle L Lyon was born circa 1859.[858]

155. Samuel M Lyon (*Daniel, Daniel, Thomas, John*)[859] was born circa 1829 at PA. He married Eliza Dodge.[860] He died in 1896.[861]

Eliza Dodge was born in Sep 1829 at NY.[862] She died on 12 Sep 1930 at Bradford County, PA.[863]
Known children of Samuel M Lyon and Eliza Dodge all born at PA were as follows:
314.   i.   Emma Lyon was born circa 1853.[864]
315.   ii.   Clara Lyon was born circa 1859.[865] She died on 17 Jun 1930 at Bradford County, PA.[866]
316.   iii.   Fred Lyon was born circa 1864.[867] He died on 13 Apr 1930 at Bradford County, PA.[868]

156. Daniel Lewis Lyon (*Daniel, Daniel, Thomas, John*) was born on 7 Sep 1830 at Monroeton, Bradford County, PA. He married Eleanor Salisbury.[869] He died on 1 Sep 1906 at Clay County, SD, at age 75.[870] He was buried at Bluff View, Vermillion, Clay County, SD.[871]
He was carriage maker.

Eleanor Salisbury[872] was born on 30 Oct 1836 at PA. She died on 25 Jul 1909 at Madison, Madison County, NE, at age 72.[873] She was buried at Bluff View, Vermillion, Clay County, SD.[874]
Known children of Daniel Lewis Lyon and Eleanor Salisbury were as follows:
+ 317.   i.   Dr May Eugenia Lyon was born on 9 May 1861 at Tipton, Cedar County, IA. She married Dr Alonzo Achinson Cotton, son of Luzerne Cotton and Mary A Dwigans, on 17 Sep 1886 at Newton, Jasper County, IA. She died on 6 Oct 1936 at Detroit, Wayne County, MI, at age 75.
+ 318.   ii.   Gertrude Augusta Lyon was born on 11 Oct 1866 at Blue Grass, Scott County, IA. She married Dr Edward Nathan Smart. She died on 16 Jun 1940 at Norfolk, Madison County, NE, at age 73.

157. Theodore Burr Lyon (*Daniel, Daniel, Thomas, John*) was born in 1835 at Bradford County, PA. He married Eliza Northrup.[875] He died on 9 Nov 1895 at Bradford County, PA.[876] He was buried at Monroeton Cemetery, Monroeton, Bradford County, PA.[877]

Eliza Northrup was born on 23 Apr 1838 at Bradford County, PA. She died on 11 Jan 1914 at Bradford County, PA, at age 75.[878] She was buried at Monroeton Cemetery, Monroeton, Bradford County, PA.[879]

---

[858]United States 1870 Census, Cairo, Alexander County, IL.
[859]Heverly, *Pioneer and Patriot Families of Bradford County, PA 1770-1800*.
[860]United States 1870 Census, Monroe, Bradford County, PA.
[861]RootsWeb WorldConnect Project, Cheryl database.
[862]United States 1900 Census, Monroe, Bradford County, PA.
[863]Robert G Fray, *Bradford County, PA Area Deaths* (Allentown, PA: Robert G Fray, 2000), page 28.
[864]United States 1870 Census, Monroe, Bradford County, PA.
[865]Ibid.
[866]Fray, *Bradford County, PA Area Deaths*, page 22.
[867]United States 1870 Census, Monroe, Bradford County, PA.
[868]Fray, *Bradford County, PA Area Deaths*, page 17.
[869]Heverly, *Pioneer and Patriot Families of Bradford County, PA 1770-1800*.
[870]Tombstone.
[871]Find A Grave.
[872]Heverly, *Pioneer and Patriot Families of Bradford County, PA 1770-1800*.
[873]Tombstone.
[874]Find A Grave.
[875]Heverly, *Pioneer and Patriot Families of Bradford County, PA 1770-1800*.
[876]RootsWeb WorldConnect Project, Cheryl database.
[877]Find A Grave.
[878]RootsWeb WorldConnect Project, Cheryl database.
[879]Find A Grave.

Known children of Theodore Burr Lyon and Eliza Northrup were as follows:

319.   i.   Eugenia Lyon was born circa 1857 at PA.[880]

320.   ii.   Daniel P Lyon was born in 1858. He married Matilda J (--?--). He died in 1911. He was buried at Monroeton Cemetery, Monroeton, Bradford County, PA.[881]

He was blacksmith.

Matilda J (--?--) was born in 1874. She died in 1940. She was buried at Monroeton Cemetery, Monroeton, Bradford County, PA.[882]

158. Augusta Lyon (*Daniel, Daniel, Thomas, John*) was born circa 1841 at PA.[883] She married Orson A. Baldwin.

Attended the 1883 Lyon reunion as a descendant of Daniel Lyon, MD.[884]

Known children of Augusta Lyon and Orson A. Baldwin were:

321.   i.   George L Baldwin was born circa 1872 at PA.[885]

Attended the 1883 Lyon reunion as a descendant of Daniel Lyon, MD.[886]

159. Dr. Randolph Lyon (*Truxton, Daniel, Thomas, John*) was born on 7 May 1820.[887] He married Jerusla (--?--). He died on 2 Jul 1887 at Bradford County, PA, at age 67.[888] He was buried at Franklin Center Christian Cemetery, Franklindale, Bradford County, PA.[889]

Jerusla (--?--) was born on 11 May 1828 at NY. She died on 2 Apr 1881 at Bradford County, PA, at age 52; cause of death was consumption. She was buried at Franklin Center Christian Cemetery, Franklindale, Bradford County, PA.[890]

Known children of Dr. Randolph Lyon and Jerusla (--?--) were as follows:

322.   i.   David Lyon was born circa 1851 at PA.[891]

+ 323.   ii.   Eugene Lyon was born in Mar 1852 at PA. He married Lettie (--?--) circa 1880.

+ 324.   iii.   Watson Lyon was born in 1855 at Bradford County, PA. He married Sarah (--?--) say 1875. He married Alma L (--?--) circa 1888. He died in 1908 at Bradford County, PA. He was buried at Franklin Center Christian Cemetery, Franklindale, Bradford County, PA.

325.   iv.   Henry E Lyon was born circa 1858.[892]

160. William Lewis Lyon (*Truxton, Daniel, Thomas, John*)[893] was born on 11 Dec 1821 at Monroeton, Bradford County, PA.[894] He married Helen Lemira Fisher on 25 Apr 1845 at Bradford County, PA. He died on 15 Jul 1887 at Bradford County, PA, at age 65. He was buried at Monroeton Cemetery, Monroeton, Bradford County, PA.[895]

He was farmer.

---

[880]United States 1870 Census, Monroe, Bradford County, PA.

[881]Find A Grave.

[882]Ibid.

[883]United States 1850 Census, Monroe, Bradford County, PA.

[884]*1883 Lyon Reunion.*

[885]United States 1880 Census, Towanda, Bradford County, PA.

[886]*1883 Lyon Reunion.*

[887]Tombstone.

[888]Ibid.

[889]Find A Grave.

[890]Ibid.

[891]United States 1860 Census, Franklin, Bradford County, PA.

[892]Ibid.

[893]Heverly, *Pioneer and Patriot Families of Bradford County, PA 1770-1800.*

[894]Tombstone.

[895]Find A Grave.

Helen Lemira Fisher was born on 9 Nov 1822 at Monroeton, Bradford County, PA. She died on 22 Apr 1905 at Bradford County, PA, at age 82.[896] She was buried at Monroeton Cemetery, Monroeton, Bradford County, PA.[897]

Known children of William Lewis Lyon and Helen Lemira Fisher all born at Bradford County, PA, were as follows:

+ 326. i.   Locke L Lyon was born on 9 Oct 1845. He married Sarah A Bowman. He died on 6 Oct 1907 at age 61.
+ 327. ii. Frank Fisher Lyon was born circa 1847. He married Mary DeVoe circa 1879. He died in 1916.
+ 328. iii. Cordelia E Lyon was born on 27 Oct 1848. She married Levi Stevens (--?--) say 1870 at PA. She died on 25 May 1939 at age 90.
  329. iv. John Randolph Lyon was born on 16 Jun 1850. He married Gyonda (--?--).[898] He died on 23 Mar 1881 at age 30.[899] He was buried at Monroeton Cemetery, Monroeton, Bradford County, PA.[900]

Gyonda (--?--) was born circa 1851 at NJ.[901]

+ 330. v.   Charles Fred Lyon was born in Feb 1852. He married Melessia M (--?--) circa 1876. He died in 1926.
+ 331. vi. Bell L Lyon was born in 1854. She married William Cole in 1877. She died in 1927.
+ 332. vii. W Walter Lyon was born in Jan 1856. He died in 1940.
  333. viii. James Waldo Lyon was born on 31 Jan 1856. He died on 15 Apr 1880 at age 24.[902] He was buried at Monroeton Cemetery, Monroeton, Bradford County, PA.[903]
  334. ix. Lelia Lyon was born in 1860.[904] She died in 1939.[905] She was buried at Monroeton Cemetery, Monroeton, Bradford County, PA.[906]
              She was also known as Lea Lyon.
  335. x.   D Nettie Lyon[907] was born in Aug 1864. She died in 1936.[908] She was buried at Monroeton Cemetery, Monroeton, Bradford County, PA.[909]

174. Alexander Lyon (*James, Alexander, Thomas, John*) was born in 1819 at NY.[910] He married Esther Ann (--?--) say 1842.[911] He married Adeline (--?--) say 1858.[912]

He was farmer. In 1850 Alexander was living alongside his parents. They were family 857 and he 858. He was farmer in 1850.[913]

Esther Ann (--?--) was born on 11 May 1818 at NY. She died on 17 Aug 1856 at Marshall County, IN, at age 38. She was buried at Burr Oak Cemetery, Culver, Marshall County, IN.[914]

---

[896]Tombstone.
[897]Find A Grave.
[898]United States 1880 Census, Albany, Bradford County, PA.
[899]Tombstone.
[900]Find A Grave.
[901]United States 1880 Census, Albany, Bradford County, PA.
[902]Tombstone.
[903]Ibid.
[904]United States 1870 Census, Franklin, Bradford County, PA.
[905]Tombstone.
[906]Find A Grave.
[907]United States 1870 Census, Franklin, Bradford County, PA.
[908]Tombstone.
[909]Find A Grave.
[910]United States 1850 Census, Marshall County, IN.
[911]Ibid.
[912]United States 1860 Census, Union, Marshall County, IN.
[913]United States 1850 Census, Marshall County, IN.
[914]Letter, April Robbins to Lynda McGinnis, 18 Jul 1999.

Known children of Alexander Lyon and Esther Ann (--?--) were as follows:

336.   i.   Fernando Lyon was born circa 1843 at NY.[915]

337.   ii.   Charles Lyon was born circa 1846 at PA.[916]

Adeline (--?--) was born circa 1842 at NY.[917]

Known children of Alexander Lyon and Adeline (--?--) both born at IN were as follows:

338.   i.   Henry Lyon was born circa 1859.[918]

339.   ii.   Aaron Lyon was born on 4 Jun 1861. He died on 29 Jan 1862. He was buried at Burr Oak Cemetery, Culver, Marshall County, IN.[919]

175. Olive Lyon (*James, Alexander, Thomas, John*)[920] was born on 23 Jul 1824 at NY. She married Warren Martindale.[921] She died on 24 Sep 1908 at Chandlers Valley, Warren County, PA, at age 84.[922]

In the 1900 census Olive said that she was a widow and had had 1 child and that that child was still living. The William Martindale living with her in 1850 is probably a child of her husband by a previous marriage. George O Lyon said she was his sister.[923] She was also known as Olive Lyon.

Warren Martindale was born circa 1812 at VT.[924]

Known children of Olive Lyon and Warren Martindale were:

340.   i.   Frances Martindale was born circa 1853 at NY.[925] She married (--?--) Wells.[926] She was also known as Frank Martindale.

176. George Osro Lyon (*James, Alexander, Thomas, John*)[927] was born in Jan 1826 at Franklinville, Cattaraugus County, NY.[928] He married Mary Ann Rathbun, daughter of Newman Rathbun and Olive Rathbun, on 15 Feb 1847 at Lyndon, Cattaraugus County, NY.[929] He died in 1901 at Chandler's Valley, Warren County, NY.[930] He was buried at Chandlers Valley Cemetery, Chandlers Valley, Warren County, PA.[931]

He was farmer in 1850, carpenter in 1860.

Mary Ann Rathbun was born on 27 Jun 1817 at Norwich, Chenango County, NY.[932] She died in 1905.[933] She was buried at Chandlers Valley, Chandlers Valley, Warren County, PA.[934]

Known children of George Osro Lyon and Mary Ann Rathbun were as follows:

341.   i.   Oren Victoria Lyon was born on 11 Feb 1850 at Lyndon, Cattaraugus County, NY. She married Leslie Graham.[935]

---

[915] United States 1850 Census, Marshall County, IN.

[916] Ibid.

[917] United States 1860 Census, Union, Marshall County, IN.

[918] Ibid.

[919] Letter, April Robbins to Lynda McGinnis, 18 Jul 1999.

[920] *Will*, of James Lyon, Marshall County, IN.

[921] United States 1850 Census, Farmersville, Cattaraugus County, NY.

[922] RootsWeb WorldConnect Project, Debbi's database.

[923] United States 1900 Census, Sugar Grove, Warren County, PA.

[924] United States 1850 Census, Farmersville, Cattaraugus County, NY.

[925] United States 1870 Census, Little Valley, Cattaraugus County, NY.

[926] United States 1880 Census, Sugar Grove, Warren County, PA.

[927] *Will*, of James Lyon, Marshall County, IN.

[928] United States 1900 Census, Sugar Grove, Warren County, PA.

[929] Cooley, *Rathbone Family*, page 246.

[930] Tombstone.

[931] Find A Grave.

[932] Cooley, *Rathbone Family*, page 246.

[933] Tombstone.

[934] Find A Grave.

[935] Cooley, *Rathbone Family*, page 246.

342. ii. Orlina Paulina Lyon was born on 10 Jun 1853 at Sugar Grove, Warren County, PA.[936] She died; Orlina is not in any census and assumed to have died young.

343. iii. Sylvia Lyon was born in Jul 1854 at PA. She married (--?--) Jones circa 1874.[937]

344. iv. Elizabeth Jane Lyon was born on 12 Jul 1854 at Sugar Grove, Warren County, PA. She married Jas. Doylnson.[938] She married (--?--) White.[939] She died in 1934.[940] She was buried at Chandlers Valley Cemetery, Chandlers Valley, Warren County, PA.[941]

+ 345. v. George Osro Lyon Jr was born on 21 Dec 1857 at Franklinville, Cattaraugus County, NY. He married Ella Madison on 5 Nov 1885. He died in 1929. He was buried at Chandlers Valley, Chandlers Valley, Warren County, PA.

346. vi. John William Lyon was born on 26 Oct 1860 at Uniontown, Marshall County, IN.[942]

347. vii. Erastus Eugene Lyon was born on 17 May 1862 at Uniontown, Marshall County, IN. He married Katherine Wagner.[943]

Katherine Wagner was born on 11 Apr 1888. She died on 7 Dec 1949 at Chautauqua County, NY, at age 61.[944] She was also known as Hattie Wagner.

177. James Lyon (*James, Alexander, Thomas, John*) was born circa 1829 at NY. He married Sophia (--?--) on 5 Apr 1846 at La Porte County, IN.[945] He married Elizabeth Taplin on 23 Mar 1868 at Marshall County, IN.[946]

He was mechanic in 1860. He was wagon maker in 1870.

Sophia (--?--) was born circa 1815 at NY.[947]

Known children of James Lyon and Sophia (--?--) both born at IN were as follows:

+ 348. i. Ellen M Lyon was born circa 1847. She married Daniel N Dressler on 22 Feb 1866 at Marshall County, IN. She died in 1899.

349. ii. Harriet E Lyon[948] was born in 1848.[949] She married Charles J Swezey on 4 Jul 1865 at Marshall County, IN; Marriage apparently end in divorce after 1880.[950]

Harriette Swezey was living with her nephew Edgar J Dressler in Binghamton, NY in 1930.[951]

Charles J Swezey was born circa 1839 at NY.[952] He married Maximelia M Osborn say 1900. He died in 1907 at NY.[953] He was buried at Rock Stream Cemetery, Starkey, Yates County, NY.[954]

There were no known children of James Lyon and Elizabeth Taplin.

---

[936]Ibid.

[937]United States 1900 Census, Sugar Grove, Warren County, PA.

[938]Cooley, *Rathbone Family*, page 246.

[939]Tombstone.

[940]Ibid.

[941]Find A Grave.

[942]Cooley, *Rathbone Family*, page 246.

[943]Ibid.

[944]Barris, *Genealogical Information Reported in Dunkirk NY Newspapers*, 8 Dec 1949.

[945]United States 1860 Census, Union, Marshall County, IN.

[946]Marshall County, IL Marriage Records, Book B, page 561.

[947]United States 1860 Census, Union, Marshall County, IN.

[948]Ibid.

[949]Tombstone.

[950]Marshall County, IL Marriage Records, Book B, page 226.

[951]United States 1930 Census, Binghamton, Broome County, NY.

[952]United States 1870 Census, Penn, St Joseph County, IN.

[953]Tombstone.

[954]Find A Grave.

179. Catherine Lyon (*James, Alexander, Thomas, John*)[955] was born on 4 Jul 1832 at NY. She married Dr Llewellyn Boles on 11 Feb 1849 at Marshall County, IN.[956] She married William Neckander. She died on 13 Nov 1889 at Carbon County, WY, at age 57.[957] She was buried at Trails End Cemetery, Medicine Bow, Carbon County, WY.[958]

Dr Llewellyn Boles[959] was born circa 1814 at OH.[960] He married Sarah Simmonds on 15 Sep 1836 at Marion County, IN.[961] He was physician.

Known children of Catherine Lyon and Dr Llewellyn Boles were as follows:

350. i.   Henry Boles was born between 1849 and 1854.[962]
351. ii. William Boles was born circa 1856 at IN.[963]
352. iii. Wheeler Boles was born circa 1857 at IN.[964] He married Lillie Beasey on 20 May 1878 at Cass County, IN.[965] He died in 1924.[966] He was buried at Trails End Cemetery, Medicine Bow, Carbon County, WY.[967]

He was also known as Amzi Wheeler Boles.

353. iv. Lilian Boles was born circa 1858 at IN.[968]
354. v.   Emma Boles was born circa 1859 at IN.[969]
355. vi. Lucy Boles was born circa 1860 at MO.[970]
356. vii. Douglass Boles was born circa 1862 at MO.[971]
357. viii. Frank Boles was born circa 1863 at MO.[972]
358. ix. Grant Boles was born circa 1865 at MO.[973]
359. x.   James Boles was born circa 1867 at KS.[974]
360. xi. Jonathan Boles was born circa 1871 at KS.[975]

William Neckander was born circa 1833 at Sweden.[976]
There were no known children of Catherine Lyon and William Neckander.

196. Thomas Lyon (*Alvah, Alexander, Thomas, John*) was born circa 1825 at NY. He married Kesiah (--?--).[977]

Kesiah (--?--) was born in 1831 at OH.[978]
Known children of Thomas Lyon and Kesiah (--?--) all born at OH were as follows:

---

[955]*Will*, of James Lyon.
[956]Marriage Record, Marshall County, Indiana.
[957]Tombstone.
[958]Find A Grave.
[959]Marriage Record, Marshall County, Indiana.
[960]United States 1870 Census, Medina, Jefferson County, KS.
[961]Marriage Record, Marion County, Indiana.
[962]Letter, April Robbins to Lynda McGinnis, 18 Jul 1999.
[963]United States 1870 Census, Medina, Jefferson County, KS.
[964]Ibid.
[965]Marriage Record, Indiana Marriages.
[966]Tombstone.
[967]Find A Grave.
[968]United States 1880 Census, Burrows, Carrol County, IN.
[969]United States 1870 Census, Medina, Jefferson County, KS.
[970]Ibid.
[971]Ibid.
[972]Ibid.
[973]Ibid.
[974]Ibid.
[975]United States 1880 Census, Harrison, Cass County, Indiana.
[976]Ibid.
[977]Ibid., Cincinnati, Hamilton County, OH.
[978]Ibid.

361. i. Judiah A Lyon was born circa 1853.[979]
362. ii. Charles W Lyon was born circa 1855.[980]
363. iii. Elijah Lyon[981] was born in Apr 1857. He married Anna M Butke.[982] He died on 23 Aug 1926 at age 69. He was buried at Vine Street Hill Cemetery, Cincinnati, Hamilton County, OH.[983]

Anna M Butke was born in May 1860 at OH.[984] She died on 20 Mar 1918 at age 57. She was buried at Vine Street Hill Cemetery, Cincinnati, Hamilton County, OH.[985]

364. iv. Thomas Calvin Lyon[986] was born in Jan 1860. He married Matilda (--?--).[987]

Matilda (--?--) was born in Mar 1876 at OH.[988]

197. Benjamin M Lyon (*Alvah, Alexander, Thomas, John*) was born in Apr 1827 at NY.[989] He married Susan A (--?--).[990]

He was stationary engineer in 1900.

Susan A (--?--) was born circa 1834 at NY.[991]
Known children of Benjamin M Lyon and Susan A (--?--) all born at OH were as follows:

365. i. Henry F Lyon was born circa 1854.[992]
+ 366. ii. Erwin E Lyon was born on 10 Sep 1858. He married Kate Hersch circa 1886. He died on 20 Jan 1917 at age 58.
+ 367. iii. Wesley M Lyon was born on 8 Sep 1866. He married Annie S (--?--) circa 1887. He died on 6 Jul 1928 at age 61.
368. iv. Alvah S Lyon was born in Jul 1869.[993]
He was fireman on railroad in 1900.
369. v. George W Lyon was born in Oct 1872.[994]
He was brakeman on railroad in 1900.

198. Jeddiah Lyon (*Alvah, Alexander, Thomas, John*) was born circa 1829. He married Julia A (--?--).[995]

Julia A (--?--) was born circa 1832 at OH.[996]
Known children of Jeddiah Lyon and Julia A (--?--) all born at OH were as follows:

370. i. William Lyon was born circa 1854.[997]
371. ii. Jennette Lyon was born circa 1857.[998]
372. iii. Unnamed Lyon was born in 1860.[999]

---

[979]United States 1860 Census, Cincinnati, Hamilton County, OH.
[980]Ibid.
[981]United States 1880 Census, Cincinnati, Hamilton County, OH.
[982]United States 1900 Census, Cincinnati, Hamilton County, OH.
[983]Find A Grave.
[984]United States 1900 Census, Cincinnati, Hamilton County, OH.
[985]Find A Grave.
[986]United States 1880 Census, Cincinnati, Hamilton County, OH.
[987]United States 1900 Census, Cincinnati, Hamilton County, OH.
[988]Ibid.
[989]Ibid.
[990]United States 1860 Census, Spencer, Hamilton County, OH.
[991]Ibid.
[992]Ibid.
[993]United States 1900 Census, Cincinnati, Hamilton County, OH.
[994]Ibid.
[995]United States 1860 Census, Spencer, Hamilton County, OH.
[996]Ibid.
[997]Ibid.
[998]Ibid.

202. Alexander J Lyon (*Alvah, Alexander, Thomas, John*) was born circa 1836 at OH. He married Nancy Jane (--?--).[1000]

Nancy Jane (--?--) was born circa 1840 at OH.[1001]
Known children of Alexander J Lyon and Nancy Jane (--?--) were:
373.   i.   Theodore Lyon was born circa 1859 at OH.[1002]

203. Clarissa Lyon (*Alvah, Alexander, Thomas, John*) was born circa 1837 at NY. She married George M Riley.[1003]

George M Riley was born circa 1832 at Ireland. He was street car driver in 1860.[1004]
Known children of Clarissa Lyon and George M Riley were:
374.   i.   Mary J Riley was born circa 1859 at OH.[1005]

204. Alva Perry Lyon (*Alvah, Alexander, Thomas, John*) was born in Oct 1838 at NY. He married Flora M Marsh circa 1866.[1006] He died in 1913 at Hamilton County, OH.[1007] He was buried at Williams Cemetery, Williams, Hamilton County, IA.[1008]
He was farmer. He was also known as Edward P Lyon.

Flora M Marsh was born in 1838 at IN. She died in 1927.[1009] She was buried at Williams Cemetery, Williams, Hamilton County, IN.[1010]
Known children of Alva Perry Lyon and Flora M Marsh were:
375.   i.   Elbert Percy Lyon was born on 10 Oct 1877 at Hamilton County, IA.[1011] He died on 4 Sep 1961 at IA at age 83.[1012] He was buried at Williams Cemetery, Williams, Hamilton County, IA.[1013]
He was farmer.

206. Walter F Lyon (*Alvah, Alexander, Thomas, John*) was born circa 1849 at OH.[1014] He married Elizabeth Poppe circa 1869.[1015] He died on 17 Jul 1910 at North Bend, Hamilton County, OH.[1016]
He was railroad brakeman.

Elizabeth Poppe[1017] was born on 11 Dec 1853 at OH. She died on 15 Sep 1912 at OH at age 58.[1018] She was buried at Vine Street Hill Cemetery, Cincinnati, Hamilton County, OH.[1019]

---

[999]Ibid.
[1000]Ibid., Cincinnati, Hamilton County, OH.
[1001]Ibid.
[1002]Ibid.
[1003]Ibid., Spencer, Hamilton County, OH.
[1004]Ibid.
[1005]Ibid.
[1006]United States 1900 Census, Williams, Hamilton County, IA.
[1007]Tombstone.
[1008]Find A Grave.
[1009]Tombstone.
[1010]Find A Grave.
[1011]World War I Draft Records.
[1012]Tombstone.
[1013]Find A Grave.
[1014]United States 1850 Census, Spencer, Hamilton County, OH.
[1015]United States 1900 Census, Mill Creek, Hamilton County, NY.
[1016]Death Records, Ohio.
[1017]United States 1900 Census, Mill Creek, Hamilton County, NY.
[1018]Tombstone.

Known children of Walter F Lyon and Elizabeth Poppe all born at OH were as follows:

376.   i.   Mary Lyon was born circa 1872.[1020]

377.   ii.   William Lyon was born circa 1878.[1021]

378.   iii.   Pearl Lyon[1022] was born on 2 Oct 1880. She died on 16 Feb 1949 at age 68.[1023] She was buried at Vine Street Hill Cemetery, Cincinnati, Hamilton County, OH.[1024]

379.   iv.   Clarence Lyon was born in Dec 1883.[1025]

213. Mary Angeline Lyon (*John, Alexander, Thomas, John*)[1026] was born in May 1830 at NY. She married Alonzo Joel Marsh say 1845.[1027] She died in 1919.[1028] She was buried at Lake View Cemetery, Jamestown, Chautauqua County, NY.[1029]

The Marsh family apparently removed to Washington DC sometime between 1870 and 1880. Angeline was still there through 1910.[1030] She was also known as Mary Lyon.

Alonzo Joel Marsh was born on 26 May 1824 at Chautauqua County, NY. He died on 2 Jan 1892 at age 67.[1031] He was buried at Lake View Cemetery, Jamestown, Chautauqua County, NY; Captain Marsh was apparently first buried at Myrtle Cemetery, Clark, Chautauqua County, New York. His body may have been moved later to Lake View Cemetery, Jamestown, Chautauqua County, NY. Capt Marsh was in the 49th Regiment, New York Volunteers in 1865. He was lumber dealer in 1870.[1032] He was Clerk in District Government in 1880.

Known children of Mary Angeline Lyon and Alonzo Joel Marsh all born at NY were as follows:

380.   i.   Ellen Marsh was born on 15 Oct 1846. She married Lester Fenn Bunce circa 1868. She died on 5 Dec 1880 at NY at age 34.[1033] She was buried at Thayer Cemetery, Carroll, Chautauqua County, NY.[1034]

Lester Fenn Bunce[1035] married Francis E (--?--).

381.   ii.   Herbert M Marsh was born in 1852.[1036] He died in 1861 at NY.[1037] He was buried at Lake View Cemetery, Jamestown, Chautauqua County, NY.[1038]

382.   iii.   Frances M Marsh was born in May 1854. She married (--?--) Frederick.[1039] She married (--?--) Gregory.[1040]

(--?--) Frederick died before 1900.[1041]
(--?--) Gregory died before 1910.[1042]

[1019]Find A Grave.
[1020]United States 1880 Census, Cincinnati, Hamilton County, OH.
[1021]Ibid.
[1022]United States 1900 Census, Mill Creek, Hamilton County, NY.
[1023]Tombstone.
[1024]Find A Grave.
[1025]United States 1900 Census, Mill Creek, Hamilton County, NY.
[1026]United States 1860 Census, Dunkirk, Chautauqua, NY.
[1027]Tombstone.
[1028]Ibid.
[1029]Find A Grave.
[1030]United States 1910 Census, Washington, DC.
[1031]Tombstone.
[1032]United States 1870 Census, Ellicott, Chautauqua County, NY.
[1033]Tombstone.
[1034]Find A Grave.
[1035]United States 1900 Census, Carroll, Chautauqua County, NY.
[1036]United States 1860 Census, Jamestown, Chautauqua County, NY.
[1037]Tombstone.
[1038]Find A Grave.
[1039]United States 1900 Census, Washington, DC.
[1040]United States 1910 Census, Washington, DC.
[1041]United States 1900 Census, Washington, DC.

383.   iv.   Nina Lionne Marsh was born circa 1859. She died in 1878 at NY.[1043] She was buried at Lake View Cemetery, Jamestown, Chautauqua County, NY.[1044]

384.   v.   Alonzo Jay Marsh[1045] was born on 2 Jan 1864. He married Martha B (--?--) in 1900. He was engineer.

Martha B (--?--) was born in Sep 1876 at PA.[1046] She was also known as Beaulah.[1047]

216. Minerva Lyon (*John, Alexander, Thomas, John*) was born circa 1837 at NY; Tombstone gives birth as 1835.[1048] She married Alex B Hastings.[1049] She was buried at Lake View Cemetery, Jamestown, Chautauqua County, NY.[1050]

She was dressmaker. She was also known as Sarah Lyon.

Alex B Hastings was born circa 1838 at PA.[1051] He died before 1880.[1052]

Known children of Minerva Lyon and Alex B Hastings were as follows:

385.   i.   John M Hastings was born circa 1864 at NY.[1053]

386.   ii.   Maude Hastings was born circa 1867 at PA.[1054]

387.   iii.   Vesta Hastings was born in 1870 at PA.[1055]

388.   iv.   Herbert Hastings was born circa 1874 at PA.[1056] He married Grace S (--?--). He died in 1938.[1057] He was buried at Lake View Cemetery, Jamestown, Chautauqua County, NY.[1058]

Grace S (--?--) was born in 1879. She died in 1979.[1059] She was buried at Lake View Cemetery, Jamestown, Chautauqua County, NY.[1060]

225. Madison Lyon (*Benjamin, Alexander, Thomas, John*)[1061] was born in Oct 1838 at Chautauqua County, NY. He married Sarah (--?--) circa 1862.[1062]

In the 1850 census Madison was living with Lewis Bramble and Martha M Bramble who is assumed to be his mother, the widow of Benjamin Lyon.[1063]

Sarah (--?--) was born in Apr 1841 at NY.[1064] In the 1900 census Sarah said she had had three children all of which were deceased.[1065]

Known children of Madison Lyon and Sarah (--?--) both born at NY were as follows:

389.   i.   Frances Lyon was born circa 1866.[1066] He died before 1900.[1067]

[1042]United States 1910 Census, Washington, DC.

[1043]Tombstone.

[1044]Find A Grave.

[1045]United States 1880 Census, Washington DC.

[1046]United States 1900 Census, Washington, DC.

[1047]United States 1910 Census, Orange, Essex County, NJ.

[1048]United States 1850 Census, Busti, Chautauqua County, NY.

[1049]Tombstone.

[1050]Find A Grave.

[1051]United States 1870 Census, Tidioute, Warren County, PA.

[1052]United States 1880 Census, Jamestown, Chautauqua County, NY.

[1053]United States 1870 Census, Tidioute, Warren County, PA.

[1054]Ibid.

[1055]Ibid.

[1056]United States 1880 Census, Jamestown, Chautauqua County, NY.

[1057]Tombstone.

[1058]Find A Grave.

[1059]Tombstone.

[1060]Find A Grave.

[1061]United States 1860 Census, Ramulus, Seneca County, NY.

[1062]United States 1900 Census, Covert, Seneca County, NY.

[1063]United States 1850 Census, Lodi, Seneca County, NY.

[1064]United States 1900 Census, Covert, Seneca County, NY.

[1065]Ibid.

390.   ii.   Henry Lyon was born circa 1867.[1068] He died before 1900.[1069]

228.   Alonzo H Lyon (*Benjamin, Alexander, Thomas, John*) was born on 12 Feb 1842 at Jamestown, Chautauqua County, NY.[1070] He married Mary J (--?--) say 1865.[1071] He married Carrie R (--?--) say 1876.[1072]

In the 1850 census Alonzo was living with his grandparents Alexander Lyon and Olive Van Berger. He was house painter. Alonzo's enlistment papers say he was born in Jamestown on 12 Feb 1842 and that his parents were Benjamin Lyon and Mary Ann Mathews.[1073]

Mary J (--?--) was born circa 1846 at NY.[1074]
Known children of Alonzo H Lyon and Mary J (--?--) were:
391.   i.   William H Lyon was born circa 1868 at NY.[1075]

Carrie R (--?--) was born in Apr 1857 at OH.[1076]
Known children of Alonzo H Lyon and Carrie R (--?--) all born at NY were as follows:
392.   i.   Amelia M Lyon was born circa 1879.[1077]
393.   ii.   Clarence Lyon was born circa 1881.[1078]
394.   iii.   Lena M Lyon was born in Mar 1886.[1079]
395.   iv.   Ineza M Lyon was born in Nov 1888.[1080]
396.   v.   Benjamin H Lyon was born in Jul 1891.[1081]
397.   vi.   Margaret E Lyon was born circa 1903.[1082]

230.   Frank M Lyon (*Ozro, Alexander, Thomas, John*) was born on 22 Mar 1832. He married Almira Amanda Putnam, daughter of Daniel Putnam and Betsey Barrett.[1083] He died on 19 Jul 1863 at PA at age 31.[1084] He was buried at Thompson Hill Cemetery, Warren County, PA.[1085]

He was also known as Frank W, Franklin, Frances and Francisco Lyon. Wounded at Gettysburg 1 July 1863 and died 19 July 1863 on 1 Jul 1863 at Gettysburg, Adams County, PA.[1086]

Almira Amanda Putnam was born on 25 Apr 1837 at Warren, Warren County, PA. She died on 6 Mar 1910 at Admire, Lyon County, KS, at age 72.[1087] She was buried at Ivy Cemetery, Admire, Lyon County, KS.[1088] Almira was living with her eldest brother, Sidney, and her mother in the 1850 Census. She went west to Kansas with her brother and lived with or near him her entire life.

Known children of Frank M Lyon and Almira Amanda Putnam were as follows:

[1066]United States 1870 Census, Covert, Seneca County, NY.
[1067]United States 1900 Census, Covert, Seneca County, NY.
[1068]United States 1870 Census, Covert, Seneca County, NY.
[1069]United States 1900 Census, Covert, Seneca County, NY.
[1070]New York Civil War Records.
[1071]United States 1870 Census, Romulus, Seneca County, NY.
[1072]United States 1900 Census, Ovid, Seneca County, NY.
[1073]New York Civil War Records.
[1074]United States 1870 Census, Romulus, Seneca County, NY.
[1075]Ibid.
[1076]United States 1900 Census, Ovid, Seneca County, NY.
[1077]United States 1880 Census, Covert, Seneca County, NY.
[1078]New York 1892 State Census, Barton, Tioga County.
[1079]United States 1900 Census, Ovid, Seneca County, NY.
[1080]Ibid.
[1081]Ibid.
[1082]United States 1910 Census, Covert, Seneca County, NY.
[1083]RootsWeb WorldConnect Project, Edward database.
[1084]Tombstone.
[1085]Find A Grave.
[1086]Ibid.
[1087]Tombstone.
[1088]Find A Grave.

398.   i.   Earnest Putnam Lyon was born on 31 Oct 1860 at PA. He died on 2 Jun 1862 at age 1. He was buried at Thompson Hill Cemetery, Warren County, PA.[1089]

+ 399.   ii.   Frank Willard Lyon was born on 28 Mar 1862 at Lander, Warren County, PA. He married Mary Catherine Moore on 30 Sep 1883. He died on 22 Aug 1926 at San Juan, Hidalgo County, TX, at age 64. He was buried at Ivy Cemetery, Admire, Lyon County, KS.

232. Olive Lyon (*Ozro, Alexander, Thomas, John*)[1090] was born on 28 Mar 1837 at NY. She married Heman Braley on 15 Nov 1860 at Warren County, PA.[1091] She died on 25 Apr 1871 at Farmington, Warren County, PA, at age 34.

Heman Braley was born on 8 Sep 1834 at PA. He married Amanda Foster circa 1873.[1092] He died on 4 May 1900 at PA at age 65.[1093] He was buried at Foster Cemetery, Lander, Warren County, PA.[1094]

Known children of Olive Lyon and Heman Braley were:

400.   i.   Unnamed Braley was born on 27 Mar 1871 at PA. He died on 29 Mar 1871.[1095] He was buried at Foster Cemetery, Lander, Warren County, PA.[1096]

233. Charles H Lyon (*Ozro, Alexander, Thomas, John*)[1097] was born on 28 Mar 1839 at NY. He married Mary Jane Thompson on 2 Jan 1867 at Carroll, Cattaraugus County, NY. He died on 2 Mar 1916 at Lander, Warren County, PA, at age 76.[1098] He was buried at Foster Cemetery, Lander, Warren County, PA.[1099]

Mary Jane Thompson was born on 11 Oct 1846 at PA. She died on 21 Mar 1928 at PA at age 81.[1100] She was buried at Foster Cemetery, Lander, Warren County, PA.[1101]

Known children of Charles H Lyon and Mary Jane Thompson were as follows:

401.   i.   Clara Augusta Lyon[1102] was born on 4 Jan 1868 at PA. She married Elmer G Wilcox on 10 Oct 1888 at Warren County, PA.[1103] She married Ben Raymond on 17 Mar 1920.[1104] She died on 24 Jun 1958 at age 90.[1105] She was buried at Foster Cemetery, Lander, Warren County, PA.[1106]

Elmer G Wilcox was born on 25 Oct 1850 at NY. He married Belle (--?--) circa 1874.[1107] He died on 27 May 1906 at PA at age 55.[1108] He was buried at Foster Cemetery, Lander, Warren County, PA.[1109]

Ben Raymond[1110] was born on 3 Dec 1867. He died in 1941 at KS.[1111] He was buried at Sharon Springs Cemetery, Sharon Springs, Wallace County, KS.[1112]

[1089]Ibid.
[1090]United States 1860 Census, Framington, Warren County, PA.
[1091]Joan M McRae, *Marriage and Deaths Notices Extracted from Warren County, PA Newspapers* (1982), Volume 1, page 67.
[1092]United States 1880 Census, Farmington, Warren County, PA.
[1093]Tombstone.
[1094]Find A Grave.
[1095]Tombstone.
[1096]Find A Grave.
[1097]United States 1860 Census, Framington, Warren County, PA.
[1098]Tombstone.
[1099]Find A Grave.
[1100]Tombstone.
[1101]Ibid.
[1102]United States 1880 Census, Lander, Warren County, PA.
[1103]Marriage Record, Pennsylvania.
[1104]United States 1920 Census, Warren, Warren County, PA.
[1105]Tombstone.
[1106]Find A Grave.
[1107]United States 1880 Census, Lander, Warren County, PA.
[1108]Tombstone.
[1109]Find A Grave.
[1110]United States 1920 Census, Warren, Warren County, PA.

402. ii. Flora Estelle Lyon[1113] was born circa 1869 at Warren County, PA. She died on 21 Jun 1875 at Warren County, PA.[1114]

403. iii. Ernest W Lyon was born in 1874 at PA. He died in 1876 at PA.[1115]

+ 404. iv. John Melvin Lyon was born on 5 Feb 1875 at PA. He married Kate B Cowles, daughter of Dr Horace Hill Cowles and Cora Fanny Mahan, on 28 May 1902. He died on 12 Feb 1943 at age 68. He was buried at Foster Cemetery, Lander, Warren County, PA.

+ 405. v. Robert Elwood Lyon was born on 2 Dec 1877 at PA. He married Lena Maude Graves on 18 Jul 1904. He married Lucy Angeline Patch on 26 Sep 1931. He died on 13 Mar 1964 at age 86. He was buried at Collins Center Cemetery, Collins Center, Erie County, NY.

+ 406. vi. Stuart Ozro Lyon was born on 5 Feb 1879 at Lander, Warren County, PA. He married Mary Madeline Titus on 13 Aug 1918. He died on 17 Apr 1958 at age 79.

234. Edward Alanson Lyon (*Ozro, Alexander, Thomas, John*)[1116] was born on 29 Apr 1841 at NY. He married Adeline E Harris on 30 Oct 1866.[1117] He married Olive E Leyman on 1 Sep 1920. He died on 9 May 1935 at age 94.[1118] He was buried at Pine Hill Cemetery, Falconer, Chautauqua County, NY.[1119]

Adeline E Harris[1120] was born on 24 Mar 1846 at NY. She died on 8 Feb 1917 at Falconer, Chautauqua County, NY, at age 70.[1121] She was buried at Pine Hill Cemetery, Falconer, Chautauqua County, NY.[1122]

Known children of Edward Alanson Lyon and Adeline E Harris were as follows:

407. i. Flora Maud Lyon[1123] was born on 1 Jun 1866 at PA. She died in 1904. She was buried at Pine Hill Cemetery, Falconer, Chautauqua County, NY.[1124]

408. ii. Jesse M Lyon was born on 4 Mar 1867. He died on 15 Mar 1872 at age 5.[1125] He was buried at Pine Hill Cemetery, Falconer, Chautauqua County, NY.[1126]

409. iii. Morton J Lyon[1127] was born on 5 Sep 1871 at PA. He married Edna R Pratt on 21 Nov 1895; Marriage ended in divorce before 1910. He died on 14 Feb 1931 at age 59.[1128] He was buried at Lake View Cemetery, Jamestown, Chautauqua County, NY.[1129]

Edna R Pratt was born in Jun 1874.[1130]

+ 410. iv. Roy Willard Lyon was born on 6 Dec 1873 at PA. He married Luella B Pritchard on 7 Jan 1897. He married Dolly Farley on 10 Mar 1925. He married Maudel (--?--) say 1942. He died on 7 Feb 1957 at Volusia County, FL, at age 83. He was buried at Hollywood Cemetery, Orange City, Volusia County, FL.

+ 411. v. Belle Gertrude Lyon was born on 14 Sep 1876 at PA. She married Adelbert Reed on 15 Jul 1896. She and Adelbert Reed were divorced before 1910.

[1111]Tombstone.

[1112]Find A Grave.

[1113]Letter, Ronald E Sherry.

[1114]McRae, *Marriage and Deaths Notices Warren County, PA*, Volume 2, page 104.

[1115]Letter, Ronald E Sherry.

[1116]United States 1860 Census, Farmington, Warren County, PA.

[1117]Letter, Ronald E Sherry.

[1118]"Chautauqua Genealogist", Volume 19, #1, page 11.

[1119]Find A Grave.

[1120]United States 1910 Census, Ellicott, Chautauqua County, NY.

[1121]"Chautauqua Genealogist", Volume 19, #1, page 11.

[1122]Find A Grave.

[1123]United States 1900 Census, Ellicott, Chautauqua County, NY.

[1124]Tombstone.

[1125]McRae, *Marriage and Deaths Notices Warren County, PA*, Volume 2, page 54.

[1126]Find A Grave.

[1127]United States 1910 Census, Ellicott, Chautauqua County, NY.

[1128]Letter, Ronald E Sherry.

[1129]Find A Grave.

[1130]United States 1900 Census, Jamestown, Chautauqua County, NY.

412.　vi.　Cora M Lyon[1131] was born on 24 Aug 1878 at PA. She died on 3 Sep 1896 at age 18.[1132]

Olive E Leyman was born on 18 May 1862 at PA.[1133] She died in 1937.[1134] She was buried at Pine Hill Cemetery, Falconer, Chautauqua County, NY.[1135]
There were no known children of Edward Alanson Lyon and Olive E Leyman.

235.　Lydia J Lyon (*Ozro, Alexander, Thomas, John*)[1136] was born on 22 Mar 1843 at NY. She married Abram S Thompson on 18 Sep 1864. She died on 20 Apr 1933 at age 90.[1137]

Abram S Thompson was born on 4 Jul 1844 at PA.[1138]
Known children of Lydia J Lyon and Abram S Thompson were as follows:
413.　i.　Grace M Thompson[1139] was born on 17 Jul 1866 at PA. She married Albert W Hull on 3 Mar 1885.[1140]

Albert W Hull was born on 30 Nov 1862.[1141] He died on 18 Dec 1928 at age 66.[1142]
414.　ii.　Carl E Thompson was born on 13 Oct 1873. He married Lulu Cassady on 7 May 1898.[1143]

Lulu Cassady was born on 25 Jun 1880.[1144]

236.　Emeline Lyon (*Ozro, Alexander, Thomas, John*)[1145] was born on 6 Aug 1845 at NY. She married Alfred M Thompson on 3 Oct 1866. She died on 8 Aug 1918 at age 73.[1146]

Alfred M Thompson was born on 12 Jan 1845 at PA. He died on 27 Dec 1915 at age 70.[1147]
Known children of Emeline Lyon and Alfred M Thompson were:
415.　i.　Minnie May Thompson[1148] was born on 5 Apr 1868 at PA. She married Carl H Cramer on 21 Apr 1887.[1149]

Carl H Cramer was born on 26 Jun 1865.[1150]

237.　George Washington Lyon (*Ozro, Alexander, Thomas, John*)[1151] was born on 23 Oct 1847 at NY. He married Mary E Beck on 25 Dec 1877.[1152] He died on 9 Jan 1914 at age 66.[1153] He was buried at Pine Hill Cemetery, Falconer, Chautauqua County, NY.[1154]

[1131]United States 1880 Census, Farmington, Warren County, PA.
[1132]Letter, Ronald E Sherry.
[1133]"Chautauqua Genealogist", Volume 19, #1, page 11.
[1134]Tombstone.
[1135]Find A Grave.
[1136]United States 1860 Census, Farmington, Warren County, PA.
[1137]Letter, Ronald E Sherry.
[1138]United States 1870 Census, Mead, Warren County, PA.
[1139]Ibid.
[1140]Letter, Ronald E Sherry.
[1141]Ibid.
[1142]Ibid.
[1143]Ibid.
[1144]Ibid.
[1145]United States 1860 Census, Farmington, Warren County, PA.
[1146]Letter, Ronald E Sherry.
[1147]Ibid.
[1148]United States 1880 Census, Farmington, Warren County, PA.
[1149]Letter, Ronald E Sherry.
[1150]Ibid.
[1151]United States 1880 Census, Mead, Warren County, PA.
[1152]Letter, Ronald E Sherry.
[1153]Ibid.

He was farmer.

Mary E Beck[1155] was born on 9 May 1859 at PA. She died on 31 Jan 1922 at age 62.[1156]

Known children of George Washington Lyon and Mary E Beck all born at PA were as follows:

+ 416.   i.   Margaret E Lyon was born on 30 Dec 1879. She married Wayne H Branch on 7 Sep 1904.

   417. ii. Alva G Lyon was born on 5 Jun 1883. She died on 19 Mar 1887 at age 3.[1157]

+ 418. iii. Dennis E Lyon was born on 31 Aug 1889. He married Verna Hartson on 27 Aug 1910. He died in 1966.

+ 419. iv. Bernice B Lyon was born on 13 Jul 1891. She married Harry A Arnold on 3 Dec 1910.

238. Mary E Lyon (*Ozro, Alexander, Thomas, John*)[1158] was born on 9 Sep 1849 at NY. She married Daniel W Phillips on 25 Dec 1876.[1159] She was buried at Foster Cemetery, Lander, Warren County, PA.[1160] She was also known as Marietta E Lyon.[1161]

Daniel W Phillips[1162] was born in May 1848 at PA. He died in 1909 at PA.[1163] He was buried at Foster Cemetery, Lander, Warren County, PA.[1164]

Known children of Mary E Lyon and Daniel W Phillips were:

   420.   i.   Albert Phillips was born in Jun 1882 at PA.[1165]

239. Alexander F Lyon (*Ozro, Alexander, Thomas, John*)[1166] was born on 12 Jul 1852 at NY. He married Elsie A Raymor on 26 Dec 1875. He died on 29 Jul 1945 at age 93.[1167] He was buried at Pine Grove Cemetery, Russell, Warren County, PA.[1168]

He was farmer.

Elsie A Raymor was born on 1 Mar 1859 at PA; Tombstone gives birth as 1860.[1169] She died in 1938.[1170] She was buried at Pine Grove Cemetery, Russell, Warren County, PA.[1171]

Known children of Alexander F Lyon and Elsie A Raymor were as follows:

+ 421.   i.   Leonard W Lyon was born on 27 May 1877 at PA. He married Margaret M Lessler on 18 Feb 1903. He died in 1939. He was buried at Pine Grove Cemetery, Russell, Warren County, PA.

+ 422. ii. William Garfield Lyon was born on 16 Aug 1880. He married Jennie L Toner, daughter of William S Toner and Leona (--?--), on 13 Feb 1907. He died on 13 Jun 1965 at age 84. He was buried at Pine Grove Cemetery, Russell, Warren County, PA.

+ 423. iii. Sherman Henry Lyon was born on 19 Oct 1890 at PA. He married Mildred E Rowland on 18 Jan 1911. He died on 5 Mar 1920 at age 29. He was buried at Pine Grove Cemetery, Russell, Warren County, PA.

[1154]Find A Grave.

[1155]United States 1880 Census, Mead, Warren County, PA.

[1156]Letter, Ronald E Sherry.

[1157]Ibid.

[1158]United States 1860 Census, Farmington, Warren County, PA.

[1159]Letter, Ronald E Sherry.

[1160]Find A Grave.

[1161]United States 1860 Census, Farmington, Warren County, PA.

[1162]Letter, Ronald E Sherry.

[1163]Tombstone.

[1164]Find A Grave.

[1165]United States 1900 Census, Warren, Warren County, PA.

[1166]United States 1860 Census, Farmington, Warren County, PA.

[1167]Tombstone.

[1168]Find A Grave.

[1169]"The Lyon's Tale", Aug-Dec 1995, page 82. Betty Louise Lyon data.

[1170]Tombstone.

[1171]Find A Grave.

240. Jerome James Lyon (*Ozro, Alexander, Thomas, John*) was born on 29 Dec 1855 at PA.[1172] He married Juliette E Thompson, daughter of Melvin Thompson and Priscilla (--?--), on 4 Jul 1878.[1173] He died in 1947 at NY.[1174] He was buried at Maple Grove Cemetery, Ashville, Chautauqua County, NY.[1175]

He was laborer.

Juliette E Thompson was born on 22 Feb 1859 at PA. She died in 1942 at NY.[1176] She was buried at Maple Grove Cemetery, Ashville, Chautauqua County, NY.[1177]

Known children of Jerome James Lyon and Juliette E Thompson were as follows:

+ 424.   i.   Bertha M Lyon was born on 25 Oct 1879 at NY. She married Harmon S King on 8 Aug 1900. She died on 20 Oct 1933 at age 53.

   425.   ii.   Erwin W Lyon was born on 14 Apr 1881. He died on 8 Sep 1881.[1178]

+ 426.   iii.   Nora E Lyon was born on 30 Aug 1883 at NY. She married Earl V Taylor on 21 Dec 1910.

   427.   iv.   Franklin W (--?--) was born on 15 Nov 1885 at NY.[1179] He married Dora Alice Jackson on 28 Jun 1917.[1180] He died in 1963.[1181] He was buried at Maple Grove Cemetery, Ashville, Chautauqua County, NY.[1182]

     He was also known as Frank W Lyon.

     Dora Alice Jackson was born in Feb 1891 at NY. She died on 27 Oct 1918 at NY at age 27.[1183]

+ 428.   v.   Elmer E Lyon was born on 17 Feb 1888 at NY. He married Mabel L Shaut in 1910. He married Mildred I Lind on 26 May 1923. He died on 26 Jul 1943 at age 55. He was buried at Sunset Hill Cemetery, Lakewood, Chautauqua County, NY.

+ 429.   vi.   Willis Charles Lyon was born on 30 Mar 1891 at NY. He married Marguerite Walker on 9 Oct 1915. He died on 24 Sep 1975 at Plant City, Hillsborough County, FL, at age 84.

+ 430.   vii.   Raymond Wallace Lyon was born on 21 Mar 1897 at Gerry, Chautauqua County, NY. He married Nora M Crawford on 31 Mar 1918. He died on 8 Apr 1992 at age 95.

241. Alice Permelia Lyon (*Ozro, Alexander, Thomas, John*)[1184] was born on 16 Sep 1857 at PA. She married Leslie W Gates on 18 Mar 1878.[1185] She died in 1936 at Warren County, PA.[1186] She was buried at Foster Cemetery, Lander, Warren County, PA.[1187]

Leslie W Gates[1188] was born on 18 Jul 1856 at PA. He died on 15 Oct 1915 at age 59.[1189] He was buried at Foster Cemetery, Lander, Warren County, PA.[1190] He was laborer.

Known children of Alice Permelia Lyon and Leslie W Gates were as follows:

[1172]United States 1900 Census, Gerry, Chautauqua County, NY.

[1173]Letter, Ronald E Sherry.

[1174]Tombstone.

[1175]Find A Grave.

[1176]Tombstone.

[1177]Find A Grave.

[1178]"The Lyon's Tale."

[1179]United States 1900 Census, Gerry, Chautauqua County, NY.

[1180]Letter, Ronald E Sherry.

[1181]Tombstone.

[1182]Find A Grave.

[1183]Letter, Ronald E Sherry.

[1184]United States 1880 Census, Mead, Warren County, PA.

[1185]Letter, Ronald E Sherry.

[1186]Tombstone.

[1187]Find A Grave.

[1188]United States 1880 Census, Mead, Warren County, PA.

[1189]Letter, Ronald E Sherry.

[1190]Find A Grave.

431.   i.   George Henry Gates[1191] was born on 25 Sep 1881 at PA. He married Annette May Witz on 8 Mar 1910.[1192] He died on 13 May 1966 at College Place, Walla Walla County, WA, at age 84.[1193] He was buried at Weiler Cemetery, Starbrick, Warren County, PA.[1194]

Annette May Witz was born on 26 Feb 1881 at Warren County, PA. She died on 25 Jul 1956 at TX at age 75. She was buried at Weiler Cemetery, Starbrick, Warren County, PA.[1195]

432.   ii. Lottie E Gates was born on 25 Mar 1886. She died on 9 Mar 1899 at age 12.[1196]

433.   iii. Mildred E Gates[1197] was born on 25 Sep 1893 at PA.[1198] She died in Sep 1979.[1199] She was buried at Foster Cemetery, Lander, Warren County, PA.[1200]

434.   iv. Jessie M Gates was born on 28 Jan 1897 at PA.[1201] She married Elmer J Hagberg on 24 Dec 1915.[1202]

Elmer J Hagberg was born on 10 Mar 1894.[1203]

435.   v.   Merrill Gates[1204] was born on 25 Oct 1898 at PA. He married Flora Reed in 1916. He and Flora Reed were divorced circa 1920. He married Genevieve G Graham on 20 Jan 1922.[1205]

250. Septimus Alexander Lyon (*Charles, Alexander, Thomas, John*)[1206] was born on 16 May 1846 at NY. He married Charlotte Ann Howard on 18 May 1864.[1207] He died on 30 Oct 1890 at Saint Charles, Madison County, IA, at age 44. He was buried at Saint Charles Cemetery, Saint Charles, Madison County, IA.[1208]
He was painter.

Charlotte Ann Howard died in 1884.[1209]
Known children of Septimus Alexander Lyon and Charlotte Ann Howard were as follows:

+ 436.   i.   Helen May Lyon was born on 10 May 1865 at NY. She married Lyman H Trotter circa 1889. She married Albert Davis before 1925. She died on 27 Sep 1940 at age 75. She was buried at Marietta Cemetery, Marietta, Marshall County, IA.

+ 437.   ii. Charles Howard Lyon was born on 23 Oct 1866 at Jamestown, Chautauqua County, NY. He married Minnie Luetta Hartman on 28 Feb 1895 at Saint Charles, Madison County, IA. He died on 5 May 1951 at Coupeville, Island County, WA, at age 84. He was buried at Coupeville, Island County, WA.

438.   iii. Richard J Lyon was born circa 1869 at IA.[1210]

+ 439.   iv. Florence T Lyon was born on 28 Nov 1877 at IA. She married Ray G Simmons. She died on 23 Apr 1921 at NY at age 43. She was buried at Busti Cemetery, Busti, Chautauqua County, NY.

[1191]United States 1900 Census, Warren, Warren County, PA.
[1192]Letter, Ronald E Sherry.
[1193]Death Records, Washington State.
[1194]Find A Grave.
[1195]Ibid.
[1196]Letter, Ronald E Sherry.
[1197]United States 1900 Census, Warren, Warren County, PA.
[1198]Ibid.
[1199]Tombstone.
[1200]Find A Grave.
[1201]United States 1900 Census, Warren, Warren County, PA.
[1202]Letter, Ronald E Sherry.
[1203]Ibid.
[1204]United States 1900 Census, Warren, Warren County, PA.
[1205]Letter, Ronald E Sherry.
[1206]Edson, *Biography and History of Chautauqua County.*
[1207]Letter, Ronald E Sherry.
[1208]Find A Grave.
[1209]"The Lyon's Tale."
[1210]United States 1880 Census, Saint Charles, Madison County, IA.

+ 440. v. Frederick G Lyon was born on 4 Apr 1880 at St Charles, Madison County, IA. He married Mabel Benjamin. He and Mabel Benjamin were divorced before 1915. He married Lulu Ball circa 1915. He died on 4 Mar 1943 at Chautauqua County, NY, at age 62.

+ 441. vi. Rosa Lyon was born on 14 Sep 1883 at IA. She married Henry N Sandberg. She died in 1969. She was buried at Sunset Hill Cemetery, Lakewood, Chautauqua County, NY.

252. Henrietta Lenor Lyon (*Alanson, Alexander, Thomas, John*)[1211] was born on 16 Sep 1843. She married William Monroe Westcott, son of Amos Westcott and Sophia Ann Lyon, on 14 Sep 1863. She died on 25 Apr 1931 at age 87.[1212]

William Monroe Westcott was born on 12 Jul 1836 at NY.[1213] He died on 27 Jun 1922 at age 85.[1214]
Known children of Henrietta Lenor Lyon and William Monroe Westcott all born at NY were as follows:

442. i. Rose Bell Westcott[1215] was born on 28 Aug 1863. She married Oliver P Moyer on 23 Nov 1910. She died on 13 Aug 1924 at age 60.

Oliver P Moyer was born circa 1862 at PA.[1216] He died on 13 Aug 1924.[1217] He was toolmaker.

443. ii. Herman A Westcott was born on 6 Feb 1864. He married Katherine T (--?--). He married Kate Fenton on 19 Oct 1892.[1218] He died on 20 Mar 1929 at age 65.[1219]
He was upholster.
Katherine T (--?--) was born circa 1866 at NY.[1220]
Kate Fenton was born on 24 Jul 1865.[1221] She died on 20 Mar 1929 at age 63.[1222]

444. iii. Flora D Westcott[1223] was born on 23 Apr 1867.[1224] She married Elton B Gardner on 6 Nov 1889.[1225] She died on 13 Aug 1924 at age 57.[1226]

Elton B Gardner[1227] was born on 20 Aug 1865.[1228]

[1211]United States 1860 Census, Jamestown, Chautauqua County, NY.
[1212]Letter, Ronald E Sherry.
[1213]United States 1900 Census, Jamestown, Chautauqua County, NY.
[1214]Letter, Ronald E Sherry.
[1215]United States 1900 Census, Jamestown, Chautauqua County, NY.
[1216]United States 1920 Census, Cattaraugus County, NY.
[1217]"The Lyon's Tale."
[1218]Letter, Ronald E Sherry.
[1219]Ibid.
[1220]United States 1920 Census, Busti, Chautauqua County, NY.
[1221]Letter, Ronald E Sherry.
[1222]"The Lyon's Tale."
[1223]United States 1880 Census, Ellicott, Chautauqua County, NY.
[1224]Letter, Ronald E Sherry.
[1225]Ibid.
[1226]Ibid.
[1227]Ibid.
[1228]Ibid.

Generation Six

262. Edward Lyon (*Theron, Samuel, Samuel, Thomas, John*)[1229] was born in Dec 1860 at NY; North Norwich, Chenango County, NY.[1230] He married Carrie E (--?--) circa 1881.[1231]

Carrie E (--?--)[1232] was born in Aug 1862 at NY.[1233] She died after 1920.[1234]
Known children of Edward Lyon and Carrie E (--?--) were:
445.   i.   Lilla M Lyon[1235] was born in May 1882 at NY.[1236] She married Lynn B Curtis.[1237]

Lynn B Curtis[1238] was born circa 1879 at NY.[1239] He died before 1920.[1240]

270. Harriet A Lyon (*Henry, George, Samuel, Thomas, John*)[1241] was born circa 1852 at NY.[1242] She married Edward A Barnard.[1243] She died after 1912.[1244]
Attended the 1883 Lyon reunion as a descendant of George R Lyon.[1245]

Edward A Barnard was born circa 1853 at NY.[1246]
Known children of Harriet A Lyon and Edward A Barnard were:
446.   i.   Robert H Barnard was born circa 1879 at NY.[1247]

271. Susan A Lyon (*Henry, George, Samuel, Thomas, John*)[1248] was born in 1853 at NY. She married John Dempster Eaton in 1893. She died in 1932.[1249] She was buried at Sylvan Lawn Cemetery, Greene, Chenango County, NY.[1250]
Attended the 1883 Lyon reunion as a descendant of George R Lyon.[1251]

John Dempster Eaton[1252] was born on 25 Oct 1850. He married Martha Burgess in 1880.[1253] He died on 7 Oct 1910 at age 59.[1254] He was buried at Willet Cemetery, Willet, Cortland County, NY.[1255]
Known children of Susan A Lyon and John Dempster Eaton were:

[1229]United States 1870 Census, Preston, Chenango County, NY.
[1230]United States 1900 Census.
[1231]Ibid.
[1232]Ibid.
[1233]Ibid.
[1234]United States 1920 Census, North Norwich, Chenango County, NY.
[1235]United States 1900 Census.
[1236]Ibid.
[1237]United States 1910 Census, North Norwich, Chenango County, NY.
[1238]Ibid.
[1239]Ibid.
[1240]United States 1920 Census, North Norwich, Chenango County, NY.
[1241]Probate Records, Chenango County, Settlements Book #10, page 381, 383.
[1242]United States 1870 Census, Greene, Chenango County, NY.
[1243]Probate Records, Chenango County, Settlements Book #10, pages 381, 383.
[1244]Ibid., Settlements Book #10, page 381, 383.
[1245]*1883 Lyon Reunion.*
[1246]United States 1880 Census, Greene, Chenango County, NY.
[1247]Ibid.
[1248]Probate Records, Chenango County, Settlements Book #10, pages 381, 383.
[1249]Tombstone.
[1250]Find A Grave.
[1251]*1883 Lyon Reunion.*
[1252]Probate Records, Chenango County, Settlements Book #10, pages 381, 383.
[1253]Tombstone.
[1254]Ibid.
[1255]Find A Grave.

447.   i.   Florence Eaton was born in Sep 1897 at NY.[1256]

287.   Bertha Lyon (*James, Morgan, Thomas, Thomas, John*) was born on 20 Dec 1871 at Independence, Buchanan County, IA. She married Tracy F Hawley circa 1901. She died on 24 Mar 1944 at Alameda, Alameda County, CA, at age 72.[1257]

Known children of Bertha Lyon and Tracy F Hawley were:
448.   i.   Jane L Hawley.[1258]

288.   Martha L Lyon (*James, Morgan, Thomas, Thomas, John*) was born circa 1874 at Independence, Buchanan County, IA. She married Russell Fred Thompson, son of Jacob Thompson and Caroline (--?--). She died in 1954 at Pinellas County, FL.[1259]

Russell Fred Thompson was born in 1871 at MI. He died in 1955 at Pinellas County, FL.[1260]
Known children of Martha L Lyon and Russell Fred Thompson both born at IN were as follows:
449.   i.   Dorothy Thompson was born circa 1905.[1261]
450.   ii.   Alice Thompson was born circa 1909.[1262]

296.   L B Lyon (*Nelson, William, Thomas, Thomas, John*) was born on 17 Dec 1870 at MI.[1263] He married Lillian LeClair, daughter of Daniel LeClair and Betsey Parker, on 5 May 1889 at Lowell, Keny County, MI. He married Emma Louise Tank in Oct 1929. He died on 30 Nov 1958 at age 87.[1264] He was buried at Lake View Cemetery, Ludington, Mason County, MI.[1265]
He was fruit farmer.

Lillian LeClair[1266] was born in Feb 1873 at MI. She died on 30 Aug 1927 at MI at age 54.[1267] She was buried at Lake Vier Cemetery, Ludington, Mason County, MI.[1268]
Known children of L B Lyon and Lillian LeClair all born at MI were as follows:
+ 451.   i.   Florence Lyon was born in Feb 1891. She married Lawrence Christensen.
+ 452.   ii.   Morris Nelson Lyon was born on 18 Feb 1898. He married Elida M Houk. He died on 25 Jun 1963 at age 65.
+ 453.   iii.   Horace D Lyon was born circa 1903. He married Helme Gustafson.
+ 454.   iv.   Armand Ronald Lyon was born on 9 Aug 1909. He married Genevieve Helen Setick on 26 Oct 1932. He died on 8 Jan 1990 at age 80.
  455.   v.   Harlan A Lyon[1269] was born on 13 Mar 1911. He married Bessie M (--?--). He died on 8 Sep 1976 at age 65.[1270]

Bessie M (--?--) was born circa 1913.[1271]

[1256]United States 1900 Census, Fenton, Broome County, NY.
[1257]Lowry, *Morgan Lyon Biography*, page 73.
[1258]Ibid.
[1259]Ibid.
[1260]Lowry, *Morgan Lyon Biography*.
[1261]United States 1910 Census, La Porte, La Porte County, IN.
[1262]Ibid.
[1263]United States 1900 Census, Summit, Mason County, MI.
[1264]RootsWeb WorldConnect Project, Don LeClair database.
[1265]Find A Grave.
[1266]United States 1880 Census, Caledonia, Kent County, MI.
[1267]RootsWeb WorldConnect Project, Don LeClair database.
[1268]Find A Grave.
[1269]United States 1920 Census, Summit, Mason County, MI.
[1270]Michigan Death Records.
[1271]United States 1940 Census, Traverse City, Grand Traverse County, MI.

Emma Louise Tank was born on 18 Jan 1877 at Berlin, Germany. She married William Lefleur circa 1895.[1272]

There were no known children of L B Lyon and Emma Louise Tank.

298. Charles William Lyon (*Richard, William, Thomas, Thomas, John*) was born circa 1868 at Bowne, Kent County, MI. He married Bertha Mae McDonald on 25 Dec 1893 at New London, Waupaca County, WI.

Bertha Mae McDonald was born on 6 Nov 1870 at Maple Creek, Portage County, WI. She married Frank H Smith. She died on 18 May 1953 at Milwaukee, Milwaukee County, WI, at age 82.[1273]

Known children of Charles William Lyon and Bertha Mae McDonald were as follows:

+ 456.   i.   Carlton Ray Lyon was born on 30 Nov 1896 at New London, Waupaca County, WI. He married Lucy Lavina Hoyt on 9 Jan 1923 at Waukegan, Lake County, IL. He died on 6 Sep 1985 at Des Moines, King County, WA, at age 88.
   457.   ii.   Irene Lyon was born circa 1900 at Canada. She married Robert J Robinson circa 1920.[1274]

Robert J Robinson was born circa 1897 at WI.[1275]

304. Ulysses Clair Lyon (*Richard, William, Thomas, Thomas, John*) was born on 1 Apr 1893 at Kabetogama County, MN. He married Flora Hesser on 18 Mar 1917 at Glencoe, Payne County, OK. He died on 14 Sep 1968 at Sacramento, Sacramento County, CA, at age 75.[1276] He was buried at Sunset Memorial Park, Sacramento, Sacramento County, CA.[1277]

Flora Hesser was born on 2 Nov 1899. She died on 7 Jul 1998 at Sacramento County, CA, at age 98. She was buried at Sunset Memorial Park, Sacramento, Sacramento County, CA.[1278]

Known children of Ulysses Clair Lyon and Flora Hesser were as follows:

   458.   i.   Richard Carl Lyon was born on 5 Dec 1917 at Boise, Ada County, ID. He died on 30 Dec 1981 at Sacramento, Sacramento County, CA, at age 64. He was buried at East Lawn Sierra Hills Memorial Park, Sacramento, Sacramento County, CA.[1279]
   459.   ii.   George Roland Lyon was born circa 1921 at Ada County, ID. He married Frances Bertha Hanegan on 24 Oct 1942. He died on 5 Jun 1981 at Sacramento, Sacramento County, ID.[1280]
   460.   iii.   Ralph Lyon was born on 8 Jun 1927 at White Cross, Ada County, ID. He died on 14 Apr 1974 at Sacramento, Sacramento County, CA, at age 46.[1281]
   461.   iv.   Jack Lyon was born on 8 Jun 1927 at White Cross, Ada County, ID.[1282]
   462.   v.   Robert H Lyon[1283] was born circa 1929 at ID.
+ 463.   vi.   Arnold E Lyon was born circa 1931.

317. Dr May Eugenia Lyon (*Daniel, Daniel, Daniel, Thomas, John*)[1284] was born on 9 May 1861 at Tipton, Cedar County, IA. She married Dr Alonzo Achinson Cotton, son of Luzerne Cotton and Mary A Dwigans, on 17 Sep 1886 at Newton, Jasper County, IA. She died on 6 Oct 1936 at Detroit, Wayne County, MI, at age 75.[1285]

[1272] RootsWeb WorldConnect Project, Anna database.
[1273] Ancestry Family Trees, Bruce Lyon's U C Lyon Family Tree.
[1274] United States 1920 Census, Waupaca, Waupaca County, WI.
[1275] Ibid.
[1276] Ancestry Family Trees, Bruce Lyon's U C Lyon Family Tree.
[1277] Find A Grave.
[1278] Ibid.
[1279] Ancestry Family Trees, Bruce Lyon's U C Lyon Family Tree.
[1280] Ibid.
[1281] Ibid.
[1282] United States 1940 Census, West Chehalem, Yamhill County, OR.
[1283] Ancestry Family Trees, Bruce Lyon's U C Lyon Family Tree.

Dr Alonzo Achinson Cotton was born on 28 Nov 1861 at Cedar County, IA. He died in 1941 at Detroit, Wayne County, MI.[1286]

Known children of Dr May Eugenia Lyon and Dr Alonzo Achinson Cotton were as follows:

464. i. Earle Lyon Cotton[1287] was born on 24 Jun 1887 at IA. He married Marie Gerst.[1288] He died on 9 Jul 1975 at Woodbury County, IA, at age 88.[1289] He was buried at Calvary Cemetery, Sioux City, Woodbury County, IA.[1290]

Marie Gerst was born on 24 Jan 1890 at Holland, Sioux County, IA.[1291] She died in 1978.[1292] She was buried at Calvary Cemetery, Holland, Sioux County, IA.[1293]

465. ii. Carl L S Cotton was born on 5 Dec 1888 at IA. He married Maude Helen Callanan circa 1911.[1294]

Maude Helen Callanan was born in Mar 1888 at SD.[1295]

466. iii. Schuyler Opp Cotton[1296] was born on 19 Oct 1890 at Sioux City, Woodbury County, IA. He died on 21 Mar 1971 at Detroit, Wayne County, MI, at age 80. He was buried at White Chapel Memorial Park, Troy, Oakland County, MI.[1297]

467. iv. Daniel Lyon Cotton[1298] was born on 31 Oct 1894 at SD. He married Mildred R McDonald, daughter of A McDonald. He died in 1976 at Beresford, Union County, SD. He was buried at Emmanuel Lutheran Cemetery, Beresford, Union County, SD.[1299]

He was also known as Daniel Lengern Lyon.

Mildred R McDonald was born in Apr 1895 at SD.[1300] She died in 1987. She was buried at Emmanuel Lutheran Cemetery, Beresford, Union County, SD.[1301]

468. v. Alonzo A Cotton was born on 17 Sep 1896 at Vermillion, Clay County, SD.[1302] He married Hazel McDonald, daughter of A McDonald, on 29 Nov 1917 at Cook County, IL.[1303] He died on 22 May 1968 at Vermillion, Clay County, SD, at age 71.[1304]

Hazel McDonald was born in Oct 1896 at Clay County, SD. She died on 24 Jun 1973 at Vermillion, Clay County, SD, at age 76.[1305]

469. vi. Cornelia M Cotton was born on 9 Jul 1900 at Vermillion, Clay County, SD.[1306] She died on 24 Mar 1983 at Pasco County, FL, at age 82.

[1284]United States 1860 Census, Blue Grass, Scott County, IA.
[1285]RootsWeb WorldConnect Project, Victor Hillard database.
[1286]Ibid.
[1287]World War I Draft Records.
[1288]Birth Records, Iowa.
[1289]Tombstone.
[1290]Find A Grave.
[1291]Birth Records, Iowa.
[1292]Tombstone.
[1293]Find A Grave.
[1294]RootsWeb WorldConnect Project, Victor Hillard database.
[1295]Ibid.
[1296]United States 1900 Census, Vermilion, Clay County, IA.
[1297]Find A Grave.
[1298]United States 1900 Census, Vermilion, Clay County, IA.
[1299]Find A Grave.
[1300]United States 1900 Census, Spirit Mound, Clay County, SD.
[1301]Find A Grave.
[1302]World War I Draft Records.
[1303]Illinois Marriages Record Index, Cook County.
[1304]RootsWeb WorldConnect Project, Victor Hillard database.
[1305]Ibid.
[1306]Ibid.

318. Gertrude Augusta Lyon (*Daniel, Daniel, Daniel, Thomas, John*) was born on 11 Oct 1866 at Blue Grass, Scott County, IA. She married Dr Edward Nathan Smart. She died on 16 Jun 1940 at Norfolk, Madison County, NE, at age 73.[1307]

Dr Edward Nathan Smart was born on 9 Jan 1856 at Cleveland, Cuyahoga County, OH. He died on 17 Apr 1927 at Madison County, NE, at age 71.[1308]

Known children of Gertrude Augusta Lyon and Dr Edward Nathan Smart were:

470. i. Edward Lyon Smart was born on 6 May 1890 at Humphrey, Platte County, NE. He married Stella Elizabeth Bohn on 8 Apr 1920 at Council Bluffs, Pottawattamie County, IA. He died on 4 Nov 1971 at Los Angeles, Los Angeles County, CA, at age 81.[1309]

Stella Elizabeth Bohn was born on 3 Dec 1890 at Henrietta, Clay County, TX. She died on 22 Oct 1952 at Los Angeles, Los Angeles County, CA, at age 61.[1310]

323. Eugene Lyon (*Randolph, Truxton, Daniel, Thomas, John*) was born in Mar 1852 at PA. He married Lettie (--?--) circa 1880.[1311]

He was farmer.

Lettie (--?--) was born in Nov 1848 at PA.[1312]

Known children of Eugene Lyon and Lettie (--?--) both born at PA were as follows:

471. i. Blair Lyon was born in Jun 1881.[1313]

472. ii. Addie Lyon was born in Nov 1885.[1314]

324. Watson Lyon (*Randolph, Truxton, Daniel, Thomas, John*)[1315] was born in 1855 at Bradford County, PA. He married Sarah (--?--) say 1875. He married Alma L (--?--) circa 1888. He died in 1908 at Bradford County, PA.[1316] He was buried at Franklin Center Christian Cemetery, Franklindale, Bradford County, PA.[1317]

He was farmer. Living with Watson in 1900 was Lloyd Lyon born May 1888 and said to be a nephew.[1318]

Sarah (--?--) was born in 1848 at NJ. She died in 1882 at Bradford County, NY.[1319] She was buried at Franklin Center Christian Cemetery, Franklindale, Bradford County, NY.[1320]

Known children of Watson Lyon and Sarah (--?--) were as follows:

473. i. Jennie M Lyon was born circa 1877 at PA.[1321]

474. ii. Jessie J Lyon was born in Jan 1882 at Bradford County, PA.[1322]

Alma L (--?--) was born in 1864 at PA. She died in 1926 at Bradford County, PA.[1323] She was buried at Franklin Center Christian Cemetery, Franklindale, Bradford County, PA.[1324]

[1307]Ibid.
[1308]Ibid.
[1309]Ibid.
[1310]Ibid.
[1311]United States 1900 Census, Franklin, Bradford County, PA.
[1312]Ibid.
[1313]Ibid.
[1314]Ibid.
[1315]United States 1860 Census, Franklin, Bradford County, PA.
[1316]Tombstone.
[1317]Find A Grave.
[1318]United States 1900 Census, Moreton, Bradford County, PA.
[1319]Tombstone.
[1320]Find A Grave.
[1321]United States 1880 Census, Franklin, Bradford County, PA.
[1322]United States 1900 Census, Moreton, Bradford County, PA.
[1323]Tombstone.
[1324]Find A Grave.

There were no known children of Watson Lyon and Alma L (--?--).

326. Locke L Lyon (*William, Truxton, Daniel, Thomas, John*) was born on 9 Oct 1845 at Bradford County, PA.[1325] He married Sarah A Bowman.[1326] He died on 6 Oct 1907 at Denver, Denver County, CO, at age 61.[1327] He was buried at Fairmont Cemetery, Denver, Denver County, CO.[1328]

Sarah A Bowman[1329] was born circa 1852 at PA.
Known children of Locke L Lyon and Sarah A Bowman were as follows:
+ 475. i. Frank Randolph Lyon was born on 22 Sep 1871 at Lamoka, Bradford County, PA. He married Mary L (--?--) in 1906.
  476. ii. Alice Lyon was born circa 1875 at PA.[1330] She married (--?--) Jore.[1331]

327. Frank Fisher Lyon (*William, Truxton, Daniel, Thomas, John*) was born circa 1847 at Bradford County, PA.[1332] He married Mary DeVoe circa 1879.[1333] He died in 1916.[1334] He was buried at Monroeton Cemetery, Monroeton, Bradford County, PA.[1335]
He was civil engineer working with coal mining.

Mary DeVoe was born in 1860 at NY. She died in 1951.[1336]
Known children of Frank Fisher Lyon and Mary DeVoe were:
  477. i. Edith Lyon was born in Jul 1881 at PA.[1337] She married George J Krebs.[1338]

George J Krebs was born in Oct 1872 at PA.[1339]

328. Cordelia E Lyon (*William, Truxton, Daniel, Thomas, John*) was born on 27 Oct 1848 at Bradford County, PA.[1340] She married Levi Stevens (--?--) say 1870 at PA. She died on 25 May 1939 at Arapahoe County, CO, at age 90. She was buried at Fairmount Cemetery, Denver, Denver County, CO.[1341]

Levi Stevens (--?--) was born on 5 Feb 1843 at Verango, Verango County, PA. He died on 16 Jul 1896 at Callaway, Custer County, CO, at age 53. He was buried at Kingsbury Cemetery, Callaway, Custer County, CO.[1342] He was farmer.
Known children of Cordelia E Lyon and Levi Stevens (--?--) were as follows:
  478. i. Charles Stevens was born circa 1871 at PA.[1343] He died circa 1881.[1344]
  479. ii. William Laurence Stevens[1345] was born on 29 Nov 1874 at New Albany, Bradford County, PA. He married Syntha Ann Douglas. He died on 21 Jun 1954 at Rosemead, Los Angeles

[1325]RootsWeb WorldConnect Project, Victor Hillard database.
[1326]United States 1880 Census, Monroe, Bradford County, PA.
[1327]RootsWeb WorldConnect Project, Victor Hillard database.
[1328]Find A Grave.
[1329]RootsWeb WorldConnect Project, Victor Hillard database.
[1330]United States 1880 Census, Monroe, Bradford County, PA.
[1331]Find A Grave.
[1332]United States 1850 Census, Franklin, Bradford County, PA.
[1333]Find A Grave.
[1334]Tombstone.
[1335]Find A Grave.
[1336]Ibid.
[1337]United States 1900 Census, Somerset, Somerset County, PA.
[1338]RootsWeb WorldConnect Project, Victor Hillard database.
[1339]Ibid.
[1340]United States 1850 Census, Franklin, Bradford County, PA.
[1341]Find A Grave.
[1342]Ibid.
[1343]United States 1880 Census, Albany, Bradford County, PA.
[1344]RootsWeb WorldConnect Project, Victor Hillard database.

County, CA, at age 79. He was buried at Mountain View Cemetery, Alta-Dena, Los Angeles County, CA.[1346]

Syntha Ann Douglas was born in 1875. She died on 17 Oct 1955. She was buried at Mountain View Cemetery, Alta-Dena, Los Angeles County, CA.[1347]

480. iii. Ethel Stevens[1348] was born in Oct 1878 at PA. She married Perl Dewit.[1349] She died on 2 Jan 1906 at age 27.[1350]

481. iv. Edith H Stevens was born in Feb 1882 at PA.[1351] She married Marshall E Stout circa 1906.[1352]

Marshall E Stout was born in 1887 at NE.[1353]

330. Charles Fred Lyon (*William, Truxton, Daniel, Thomas, John*)[1354] was born in Feb 1852 at Bradford County, PA. He married Melessia M (--?--) circa 1876.[1355] He died in 1926.[1356] He was buried at Monroeton Cemetery, Monroeton, Bradford County, PA.[1357]

Melessia M (--?--) was born in Apr 1850 at PA.[1358] She died in 1920. She was buried at Monroeton Cemetery, Monroeton, Bradford County, PA.[1359]

Known children of Charles Fred Lyon and Melessia M (--?--) were as follows:

482. i. Lloyd Lyon was born in 1880 at Bradford County, PA. He died in 1883 at Bradford County, PA. He was buried at Monroeton Cemetery, Monroeton, Bradford County, PA.[1360]

483. ii. Harry H Lyon was born in Nov 1880.[1361] He married Gertrude E (--?--) circa 1919.[1362] He was civil engineer.

Gertrude E (--?--) was born circa 1891 at PA.[1363]

484. iii. Ralph Rodney Lyon was born on 31 Aug 1883 at Barclay, Bradford County, PA.[1364] He married Ruth (--?--). He died in 1942.[1365] He was buried at Monroeton Cemetery, Monroeton, Bradford County, PA.[1366]

Ruth (--?--) was born circa 1887 at PA.[1367] She was buried at Monroeton Cemetery, Franklindale, Bradford County, PA.[1368]

[1345]United States 1880 Census, Albany, Bradford County, PA.
[1346]Find A Grave.
[1347]Ibid.
[1348]United States 1880 Census, Albany, Bradford County, PA.
[1349]Find A Grave.
[1350]RootsWeb WorldConnect Project, Victor Hillard database.
[1351]United States 1900 Census, Delight, Custer County, NE.
[1352]United States 1910 Census, Arapahoe County, CO.
[1353]Ibid.
[1354]United States 1860 Census, Franklin, Bradford County, PA.
[1355]United States 1900 Census, Albany, Bradford County, PA.
[1356]Tombstone.
[1357]Find A Grave.
[1358]United States 1900 Census, Albany, Bradford County, PA.
[1359]Find A Grave.
[1360]Ibid.
[1361]United States 1900 Census, Albany, Bradford County, PA.
[1362]RootsWeb WorldConnect Project, Victor Hillard database.
[1363]Ibid.
[1364]United States 1900 Census, Albany, Bradford County, PA.
[1365]Tombstone.
[1366]Find A Grave.
[1367]United States 1940 Census, Monroe, Bradford County, PA.
[1368]Find A Grave.

331. Bell L Lyon (*William, Truxton, Daniel, Thomas, John*)[1369] was born in 1854 at Bradford County, PA. She married William Cole in 1877. She died in 1927.[1370] She was buried at Monroeton Cemetery, Monroeton, Bradford County, PA.[1371]

In the 1900 census Bell said she had had four children of which two were living. She was also known as Laura Isabell Lyon.

William Cole was born in Sep 1852 at PA. He died in 1923. He was buried at Monroeton Cemetery, Monroeton, Bradford County, PA.[1372]

Known children of Bell L Lyon and William Cole were:

485.   i.   Lizzie Cole was born in Sep 1878 at TN.[1373]

332. W Walter Lyon (*William, Truxton, Daniel, Thomas, John*)[1374] was born in Jan 1856 at Bradford County, PA. He married Teresa Horton circa 1883. He died in 1940.[1375] He was buried at Monroeton Cemetery, Monroeton, Bradford County, PA.[1376]

Teresa Horton was born in Jan 1857. She died in 1930. She was buried at Monroeton Cemetery, Monroeton, Bradford County, PA.[1377]

Known children of W Walter Lyon and Teresa Horton were:

486.   i.   J Waldo Lyon was born in Dec 1884 at PA.[1378] He died in 1918.[1379] He was buried at Monroeton Cemetery, Monroeton, Bradford County, PA.[1380]

345. George Osro Lyon Jr (*George, James, Alexander, Thomas, John*) was born on 21 Dec 1857 at Franklinville, Cattaraugus County, NY. He married Ella Madison on 5 Nov 1885.[1381] He died in 1929.[1382] He was buried at Chandlers Valley, Chandlers Valley, Warren County, PA.[1383]

Ella Madison was born in Nov 1867 at PA. She died in 1940.[1384] She was buried at Chandlers Valley, Chandlers Valley, Warren County, PA.[1385]

Known children of George Osro Lyon Jr and Ella Madison were as follows:

487.   i.   Hiran Edgar Lyon was born on 3 Jun 1888 at Titusville, Crawford County, PA. He died in 1948.[1386] He was buried at Hessel Valley Lutheran Cemetery, Chandlers Valley, Warren County, PA.[1387]

488.   ii.   Maude L Lyon was born in Dec 1889 at PA.[1388]

[1369]United States 1860 Census, Franklin, Bradford County, PA.
[1370]Tombstone.
[1371]Find A Grave.
[1372]Ibid.
[1373]United States 1900 Census, Waynesville, Haywood County, NC.
[1374]United States 1860 Census, Franklin, Bradford County, PA.
[1375]Tombstone.
[1376]Find A Grave.
[1377]Ibid.
[1378]United States 1900 Census, Towanda, Bradford County, PA.
[1379]Tombstone.
[1380]Find A Grave.
[1381]Cooley, *Rathbone Family*, page 246.
[1382]Tombstone.
[1383]Find A Grave.
[1384]Tombstone.
[1385]Find A Grave.
[1386]Tombstone.
[1387]Find A Grave.
[1388]United States 1900 Census, Jamestown, Chautauqua County, NY.

+ 489. iii. William Alexander Lyon was born on 25 Oct 1895 at Mayville, Chautauqua County, NY. He married Minnie M Cooper. He died on 28 May 1951 at age 55. He was buried at Youngsville Cemetery, Youngsville, Warren County, PA.

490. iv. Iva Lyon was born circa 1903 at PA.[1389]

491. v. Oliva A Lyon was born circa 1906 at PA.[1390]

492. vi. Ivan Eugene Lyon was born on 12 May 1908 at PA. He died on 25 Nov 1984 at age 76.[1391] He was buried at Chandlers Valley, Chandlers Valley, Warren County, PA.[1392]

348. Ellen M Lyon (*James, James, Alexander, Thomas, John*) was born circa 1847 at IN.[1393] She married Daniel N Dressler on 22 Feb 1866 at Marshall County, IN. She died in 1899 at IN.[1394] She was buried at City Cemetery, South Bend, St Joseph County, IN.[1395]

Daniel N Dressler was born in Mar 1842 at OH. He married Mary (--?--) say 1920.[1396] He died in 1927 at IN.[1397] He was buried at City Cemetery, South Bend, St Joseph County, IN.[1398] He was woodworker.

Known children of Ellen M Lyon and Daniel N Dressler were as follows:

493. i. William J Dressler was born circa 1868 at IN.[1399]

494. ii. Edgar J Dressler was born in Dec 1872 at IN. He married Martha J (--?--) circa 1899.[1400] He married Alice L (--?--) say 1915.[1401] He died in 1949.[1402] He was buried at Chenango Valley Cemetery, Binghamton, Broome County, NY.[1403]

Martha J (--?--) was born in Nov 1870 at PA.[1404]

Alice L (--?--)[1405] was born in 1882 at PA. She died in 1921 at Binghamton, Broome County, NY.[1406] She was buried at Chenango Valley Cemetery, Binghamton, Broome County, NY.[1407]

495. iii. Archie N Dressler was born circa 1876 at IN.[1408]

She was also known as Daniel N Dressler.

496. iv. Clarence S Dressler was born in Mar 1885 at KS.[1409]

366. Erwin E Lyon (*Benjamin, Alvah, Alexander, Thomas, John*) was born on 10 Sep 1858 at OH. He married Kate Hersch circa 1886.[1410] He died on 20 Jan 1917 at age 58.[1411] He was buried at Mount Washington Cemetery, Mount Washington, Hamilton County, OH.[1412]

[1389]United States 1910 Census, Youngsville, Warren County, PA.

[1390]Ibid.

[1391]Tombstone.

[1392]Find A Grave.

[1393]United States 1860 Census, Union, Marshall County, IN.

[1394]Tombstone.

[1395]Find A Grave.

[1396]United States 1900 Census, South Bend, St Joseph County, IN.

[1397]Tombstone.

[1398]Find A Grave.

[1399]Kansas, Cowley County 1885 Census.

[1400]United States 1900 Census, South Bend, St Joseph County, IN.

[1401]United States 1920 Census, Binghamton, Broome County, NY.

[1402]Tombstone.

[1403]Find A Grave.

[1404]United States 1900 Census, South Bend, St Joseph County, IN.

[1405]United States 1920 Census, Binghamton, Broome County, NY.

[1406]Tombstone.

[1407]Find A Grave.

[1408]Kansas, Cowley County 1885 Census.

[1409]United States 1900 Census, South Bend, St Joseph County, IN.

[1410]United States 1910 Census, Cincinnati, Hamilton County, OH.

[1411]Tombstone.

[1412]Find A Grave.

He was also known as Eunis E Lyon.

Kate Hersch was born circa 1859 at OH.[1413] She died on 13 Jul 1938.[1414] She was buried at Mount Washington Cemetery, Mount Washington, Hamilton County, OH.[1415]

Known children of Erwin E Lyon and Kate Hersch were:

497.   i. Walter Elston Lyon was born on 12 Jan 1890 at OH.[1416] He died on 15 Apr 1927 at age 37. He was buried on 15 Apr 1927 at Mount Washington Cemetery, Mount Washington, Hamilton County, OH.[1417]

367. Wesley M Lyon (*Benjamin, Alvah, Alexander, Thomas, John*) was born on 8 Sep 1866 at OH. He married Annie S (--?--) circa 1887.[1418] He died on 6 Jul 1928 at age 61.[1419] He was buried at Mount Washington Cemetery, Mount Washington, Hamilton County, OH.[1420]

He was railroad engineer.

Annie S (--?--) was born in Mar 1871 at OH.[1421]

Known children of Wesley M Lyon and Annie S (--?--) were as follows:

+ 498.   i. Howard Benjamin Lyon was born in Dec 1887 at OH. He married Elizabeth (--?--). He died on 7 Feb 1957 at age 69. He was buried at Mount Washington Cemetery, Mount Washington, Hamilton County, OH.

499.   ii. Florence S Lyon was born in Sep 1889 at OH.[1422]

+ 500.   iii. Harry F Lyon was born in Oct 1890. He married Louise B (--?--). He died on 26 Feb 1972 at age 81. He was buried at Gates of Heaven Cemetery, Montgomery, Hamilton County, OH.

501.   iv. Russell B Lyon was born in May 1894 at OH.[1423]

502.   v. Maud V Lyon was born in Jun 1896 at OH.[1424]

503.   vi. George A Lyon was born in Feb 1898 at OH.[1425]

504.   vii. Kenneth S Lyon was born on 24 Apr 1900 at OH. He married Mary L (--?--). He died on 2 May 1969 at age 69.[1426] He was buried at Gates of Heaven Cemetery, Montgomery, Hamilton County, OH.[1427]

Mary L (--?--) was born on 18 Apr 1903. She died on 22 Nov 1987 at age 84.[1428] She was buried at Gates of Heaven Cemetery, Montgomery, Hamilton County, OH.[1429]

399. Frank Willard Lyon (*Frank, Ozro, Alexander, Thomas, John*)[1430] was born on 28 Mar 1862 at Lander, Warren County, PA. He married Mary Catherine Moore on 30 Sep 1883. He died on 22 Aug 1926 at San Juan, Hidalgo County, TX, at age 64. He was buried at Ivy Cemetery, Admire, Lyon County, KS.[1431]

[1413] RootsWeb WorldConnect Project, Debbi's database.
[1414] Tombstone.
[1415] Find A Grave.
[1416] World War I Draft Records.
[1417] Tombstone.
[1418] United States 1900 Census, Cincinnati, Hamilton County, OH.
[1419] Tombstone.
[1420] Find A Grave.
[1421] United States 1900 Census, Cincinnati, Hamilton County, OH.
[1422] Ibid.
[1423] Ibid.
[1424] Ibid.
[1425] Ibid.
[1426] Tombstone.
[1427] Find A Grave.
[1428] Tombstone.
[1429] Find A Grave.
[1430] United States 1870 Census, Waterloo, Lyon County, KS.
[1431] Find A Grave.

Mary Catherine Moore was born on 4 Jul 1860 at Baldwin City, Douglas County, KS. She died on 15 Jul 1915 at Topeka, Shawnee County, KS, at age 55; Family records give her death as 28 Jul 1916. She was buried at Ivy Cemetery, Admire, Lyon County, KS.[1432]

Known children of Frank Willard Lyon and Mary Catherine Moore were as follows:

+ 505.   i.   Glen Ivan Lyon was born on 6 Dec 1885 at KS. He married Bessie Irene (--?--) on 4 Mar 1906. He died in 1959 at KS. He was buried at Admire Cemetery, Admire, Lyon County, KS.

+ 506.   ii.   Louis Harrison Lyon was born on 4 Mar 1889 at Admire, Lyon County, KS. He married Grace Ethel Ball on 28 Mar 1912. He died on 19 Jul 1950 at MO at age 61. He was buried at Ivy Cemetery, Admire, Lyon County, KS.

+ 507.   iii.   Edwin Ernest Lyon was born on 31 Mar 1899 at KS. He married Martha Pearl Oglesby. He died on 21 Jun 1935 at age 36. He was buried at Ivy Cemetery, Admire, Lyon County, KS.

508.   iv.   Frank Willard Lyon was born on 22 Sep 1901 at KS.[1433]
In 1940 he was institutionalized at the Central Oklahoma State Hospital.[1434]

404. John Melvin Lyon (*Charles, Ozro, Alexander, Thomas, John*) was born on 5 Feb 1875 at PA. He married Kate B Cowles, daughter of Dr Horace Hill Cowles and Cora Fanny Mahan, on 28 May 1902. He died on 12 Feb 1943 at age 68.[1435] He was buried at Foster Cemetery, Lander, Warren County, PA.[1436]
He was bookkeeper at an oil works.

Kate B Cowles was born in 1880 at PA. She died in 1962.[1437] She was buried at Foster Cemetery, Lander, Warren County, PA.[1438]

Known children of John Melvin Lyon and Kate B Cowles were:

509.   i.   Vera Belle Lyon[1439] was born on 2 Feb 1907. She died on 10 Mar 1963 at age 56.[1440] She was buried at Foster Cemetery, Lander, Warren County, PA.[1441]

405. Robert Elwood Lyon (*Charles, Ozro, Alexander, Thomas, John*)[1442] was born on 2 Dec 1877 at PA. He married Lena Maude Graves on 18 Jul 1904. He married Lucy Angeline Patch on 26 Sep 1931. He died on 13 Mar 1964 at age 86.[1443] He was buried at Collins Center Cemetery, Collins Center, Erie County, NY.[1444]
He was teacher, grain dealer, clerk in general store.

Lena Maude Graves was born on 24 Oct 1885. She died on 21 Mar 1921 at age 35.[1445] She was buried at Collins Center Cemetery, Collins Center, Erie County, NY.[1446]

Known children of Robert Elwood Lyon and Lena Maude Graves were:

+ 510.   i.   Doris Marguarita Lyon was born on 10 Jul 1905 at NY. She married William J Rennagle on 25 Jun 1927. She married Harold Anderson circa 1938. She died on 30 Aug 1994 at age 89.

[1432]Ibid.
[1433]United States 1910 Census, Colton, San Bernardino County, CA.
[1434]United States 1940 Census.
[1435]Tombstone.
[1436]Find A Grave.
[1437]Tombstone.
[1438]Find A Grave.
[1439]United States 1910 Census, Warren, Warren County, PA.
[1440]RootsWeb WorldConnect Project, Mary Beard database.
[1441]Find A Grave.
[1442]United States 1880 Census, Lander, Warren County, PA.
[1443]Tombstone.
[1444]Find A Grave.
[1445]Tombstone.
[1446]Find A Grave.

Lucy Angeline Patch was born on 15 Jun 1898. She died on 3 Jul 1976 at age 78.[1447] She was buried at Collins Center Cemetery, Collins Center, Erie County, NY.[1448]

There were no known children of Robert Elwood Lyon and Lucy Angeline Patch.

406. Stuart Ozro Lyon (*Charles, Ozro, Alexander, Thomas, John*) was born on 5 Feb 1879 at Lander, Warren County, PA. He married Mary Madeline Titus on 13 Aug 1918.[1449] He died on 17 Apr 1958 at age 79.[1450]

Mary Madeline Titus was born on 13 Apr 1891 at PA. She died in Jul 1966 at age 75.[1451]

Known children of Stuart Ozro Lyon and Mary Madeline Titus were as follows:

511.   i.   Charles William Lyon was born on 25 Sep 1919 at PA. He died on 12 Oct 1999 at age 80.[1452] He was also known as William C Lyon.

512.   ii.   Mary Frances Lyon was born on 23 Nov 1923. She married Leland Gordon Collins. She died in 1956.[1453]

Leland Gordon Collins was born on 2 May 1922. He died in 1956.[1454]

410. Roy Willard Lyon (*Edward, Ozro, Alexander, Thomas, John*) was born on 6 Dec 1873 at PA.[1455] He married Luella B Pritchard on 7 Jan 1897. He married Dolly Farley on 10 Mar 1925. He married Maudel (--?--) say 1942. He died on 7 Feb 1957 at Volusia County, FL, at age 83.[1456] He was buried at Hollywood Cemetery, Orange City, Volusia County, FL.[1457]

Luella B Pritchard was born in Sep 1876 at NY.[1458] She married Lorenz (--?--).

Known children of Roy Willard Lyon and Luella B Pritchard were as follows:

+ 513.   i.   Ralph Ozro Lyon was born on 28 Jun 1898 at NY. He married Evelyn Maria Sellers on 5 Jun 1932. He and Evelyn Maria Sellers were divorced in 1952 at Duval County, FL.

514.   ii.   Roy Willard Lyon was born on 1 May 1900 at NY. He died on 1 Aug 1905 at age 5; Drowned at age 5 years and 3 months.[1459]

515.   iii.   Francis R Lyon was born on 23 Jun 1902 at OH.[1460]

+ 516.   iv.   Myron J Lyon was born on 16 Jul 1903 at PA. He married Genevieve Irene Pritchard on 6 Jul 1928.

+ 517.   v.   Frederick W Lyon was born on 6 Aug 1906 at PA. He married Allene G Crick on 24 Aug 1929.

Dolly Farley was born on 6 Aug 1881 at WV. She died on 21 Nov 1941 at Volusia County, FL, at age 60.[1461] She was buried at Hollywood Cemetery, Orange City, Volusia County, FL.[1462]

Known children of Roy Willard Lyon and Dolly Farley were as follows:

518.   i.   Edward D Lyon was born on 21 Apr 1926 at NY.[1463]

[1447]Letter, Ronald E Sherry.

[1448]Find A Grave.

[1449]Letter, Ronald E Sherry.

[1450]RootsWeb WorldConnect Project, Mary Beard database.

[1451]Ibid.

[1452]Ibid.

[1453]Ibid.

[1454]Ibid.

[1455]World War I Draft Records.

[1456]Tombstone.

[1457]Find A Grave.

[1458]United States 1900 Census, Carroll, Chautauqua County, NY.

[1459]"The Lyon's Tale."

[1460]United States 1910 Census, Apalachicola, Franklin County, FL.

[1461]Tombstone.

[1462]Find A Grave.

519.   ii.   Mary E Lyon was born on 3 Apr 1929. She died on 20 Apr 1930 at age 1.[1464]

Maudel (--?--) was born circa 1894 at TN.[1465]
There were no known children of Roy Willard Lyon and Maudel (--?--).

411.   Belle Gertrude Lyon (*Edward, Ozro, Alexander, Thomas, John*) was born on 14 Sep 1876 at PA. She married Adelbert Reed on 15 Jul 1896.[1466] She and Adelbert Reed were divorced before 1910.
In the 1910 census Belle said she had had 6 children and all were living. The only child found associated with her is Cora L Reed.[1467]

Adelbert Reed was born on 19 Jul 1875 at NY.[1468]
Known children of Belle Gertrude Lyon and Adelbert Reed were as follows:
520.   i.   Edna J Reed married William H Stevens.[1469]

William H Stevens was born on 7 May 1897.[1470]
521.   ii.   Coralyl Agnes Reed was born on 30 Jul 1893. She married Leonard Foote.[1471]
522.   iii.   Anna S Reed was born on 23 Oct 1895. She married Herbert Bartlett on 6 Aug 1926. She died on 10 Aug 1931 at age 35.[1472]
523.   iv.   Harold C Reed was born on 7 Jul 1897.[1473]
524.   v.   Cora L Reed was born on 16 Sep 1897 at NY.[1474] She married Clarence J Bierwerth on 29 Jun 1921.[1475]

Clarence J Bierwerth was born on 25 Apr 1887.[1476]
525.   vi.   Edward Reed was born on 30 Nov 1898 at NY.[1477]
526.   vii.   Sarahleah Reed was born circa 1906 at NY.[1478]
527.   viii.   Christie E Reed was born circa 1907 at NY.[1479]

416.   Margaret E Lyon (*George, Ozro, Alexander, Thomas, John*) was born on 30 Dec 1879 at PA. She married Wayne H Branch on 7 Sep 1904.[1480]

Wayne H Branch was born on 29 Nov 1880.[1481]
Known children of Margaret E Lyon and Wayne H Branch were as follows:
528.   i.   Margaret E Branch was born on 16 Mar 1906. She married Ross I Webb on 20 Aug 1926.[1482]

[1463]United States 1930 Census, Enterprise, Volusia County, FL.
[1464]Letter, Ronald E Sherry.
[1465]Florida State 1945 Census, Volusia County, NY.
[1466]Letter, Ronald E Sherry.
[1467]United States 1910 Census, Ellicott, Chautauqua County, NY.
[1468]United States 1900 Census, Randolph, Cattaraugus County, NY.
[1469]"The Lyon's Tale."
[1470]Ibid.
[1471]Ibid.
[1472]Ibid.
[1473]Ibid.
[1474]United States 1900 Census, Randolph, Cattaraugus County, NY.
[1475]Letter, Ronald E Sherry.
[1476]Ibid.
[1477]"The Lyon's Tale."
[1478]United States 1920 Census, Ellington Chautauqua County, NY.
[1479]Ibid., Ellington, Chautauqua County, NY.
[1480]Letter, Ronald E Sherry.
[1481]Ibid.
[1482]Ibid.

Ross I Webb was born in 1905.[1483]

529.   ii.   Edna L Branch was born on 13 Mar 1908.[1484]

418. Dennis E Lyon (*George, Ozro, Alexander, Thomas, John*) was born on 31 Aug 1889 at PA. He married Verna Hartson on 27 Aug 1910.[1485] He died in 1966 at NY.[1486] He was buried at Pine Hill Cemetery, Falconer, Chautauqua County, NY.[1487]

He was machinist.

Verna Hartson was born circa 1891 at NY.[1488]

Known children of Dennis E Lyon and Verna Hartson both born at NY were as follows:

530.   i.   Lucille P Lyon[1489] was born on 10 Aug 1917. She died on 28 Jul 2000 at age 82. She was buried at Pine Hill Cemetery, Falconer, Chautauqua County, NY.[1490]

531.   ii.   Doris E Lyon was born on 20 Apr 1927.[1491]

419. Bernice B Lyon (*George, Ozro, Alexander, Thomas, John*) was born on 13 Jul 1891 at PA. She married Harry A Arnold on 3 Dec 1910.[1492]

Known children of Bernice B Lyon and Harry A Arnold were as follows:

532.   i.   Gordon L Arnold was born on 1 Mar 1915.[1493]

533.   ii.   Gerald R Arnold was born on 14 Sep 1918.[1494]

421. Leonard W Lyon (*Alexander, Ozro, Alexander, Thomas, John*) was born on 27 May 1877 at PA.[1495] He married Margaret M Lessler on 18 Feb 1903.[1496] He died in 1939.[1497] He was buried at Pine Grove Cemetery, Russell, Warren County, PA.[1498]

He was carpenter.

Margaret M Lessler was born in 1880 at PA. She died after 1940. She was buried at Pine Grove Cemetery, Russell, Warren County, PA.[1499]

Known children of Leonard W Lyon and Margaret M Lessler were:

+ 534.   i.   Mildred L Lyon was born on 28 Jun 1909 at IL. She married Earl Wilson on 3 Jun 1921.

422. William Garfield Lyon (*Alexander, Ozro, Alexander, Thomas, John*) was born on 16 Aug 1880.[1500] He married Jennie L Toner, daughter of William S Toner and Leona (--?--), on 13 Feb 1907. He died on 13 Jun 1965 at age 84.[1501] He was buried at Pine Grove Cemetery, Russell, Warren County, PA.[1502]

[1483] Ibid.
[1484] Ibid.
[1485] Ibid.
[1486] Tombstone.
[1487] Find A Grave.
[1488] United States 1920 Census, Ellicott, Chautauqua County, NY.
[1489] Ibid.
[1490] Find A Grave.
[1491] Letter, Ronald E Sherry.
[1492] Ibid.
[1493] Ibid.
[1494] Ibid.
[1495] Ibid.
[1496] "The Lyon's Tale."
[1497] Tombstone.
[1498] Find A Grave.
[1499] Ibid.
[1500] World War I Draft Records.
[1501] "The Lyon's Tale", Aug-Dec 1995, page 82. Betty Louise Lyon data.
[1502] Find A Grave.

He was teamster.

Jennie L Toner was born on 18 Oct 1884 at PA. She died on 22 May 1971 at Warren, Warren County, PA, at age 86.[1503] She was buried at Pine Grove Cemetery, Russell, Warren County, PA.[1504]

Known children of William Garfield Lyon and Jennie L Toner all born at PA were as follows:

    535.   i.   Mabel Emeline Lyon was born on 17 Mar 1909. She married (--?--) Phillips.[1505]

+ 536.   ii.   William Alexander Lyon was born on 1 Mar 1914. He married Catherine Elizabeth Meyer. He died on 3 Jan 1961 at age 46.

    537.   iii. Elsie L Lyon was born on 3 Nov 1916.[1506]

423. Sherman Henry Lyon (*Alexander, Ozro, Alexander, Thomas, John*) was born on 19 Oct 1890 at PA. He married Mildred E Rowland on 18 Jan 1911.[1507] He died on 5 Mar 1920 at age 29.[1508] He was buried at Pine Grove Cemetery, Russell, Warren County, PA.[1509]

He was also known as Henry S Lyon.

Known children of Sherman Henry Lyon and Mildred E Rowland were as follows:

    538.   i.   Phillip A Lyon Lyon was born on 13 Nov 1911.[1510]

    539.   ii.   Donald E Lyon was born on 6 Jan 1913.[1511]

424. Bertha M Lyon (*Jerome, Ozro, Alexander, Thomas, John*) was born on 25 Oct 1879 at NY. She married Harmon S King on 8 Aug 1900. She died on 20 Oct 1933 at age 53.[1512]

Harmon S King was born on 22 Nov 1880. He died on 20 Oct 1933 at age 52.[1513]

Known children of Bertha M Lyon and Harmon S King were as follows:

    540.   i.   Leo F King was born on 8 Mar 1901. He married Nellie Mills on 3 Aug 1929.[1514]

    541.   ii.   Claude H King was born on 24 Jan 1903. He married Ireta Farnsworth on 13 Aug 1924.[1515]

    542.   iii. Dorothy M King was born on 7 May 1912.[1516]

426. Nora E Lyon (*Jerome, Ozro, Alexander, Thomas, John*) was born on 30 Aug 1883 at NY. She married Earl V Taylor on 21 Dec 1910.[1517]

Earl V Taylor was born on 29 Jan 1888.[1518]

Known children of Nora E Lyon and Earl V Taylor were:

    543.   i.   Marion L Taylor was born on 31 May 1921.[1519]

[1503]Social Security Death Index.
[1504]Find A Grave.
[1505]"The Lyon's Tale", May-Aug 1985, page 1. Information from Mabel Emeline Lyon.
[1506]Letter, Ronald E Sherry.
[1507]Ibid.
[1508]Tombstone.
[1509]Find A Grave.
[1510]Letter, Ronald E Sherry.
[1511]Ibid.
[1512]Ibid.
[1513]"The Lyon's Tale."
[1514]Ibid.
[1515]Letter, Ronald E Sherry.
[1516]Ibid.
[1517]Ibid.
[1518]Ibid.
[1519]Ibid.

428. Elmer E Lyon (*Jerome, Ozro, Alexander, Thomas, John*) was born on 17 Feb 1888 at NY. He married Mabel L Shaut in 1910. He and Mabel L Shaut were divorced circa 1922. He married Mildred I Lind on 26 May 1923.[1520] He died on 26 Jul 1943 at age 55.[1521] He was buried at Sunset Hill Cemetery, Lakewood, Chautauqua County, NY.[1522]

He was director of the YMCA in Ashtabula OH in 1920 and an assistant metallurgist in 1940.

Mabel L Shaut was born on 13 Aug 1903.[1523] She married Glen Wyse circa 1923.[1524]

Known children of Elmer E Lyon and Mabel L Shaut were:

    544.   i.   Marie Louise Lyon was born on 23 Aug 1915 at NY.[1525]

Mildred I Lind[1526] was born on 13 Aug 1903 at PA. She married (--?--) Power circa 1950. She died on 3 Apr 1974 at age 70. She was buried at Sunset Hill Cemetery, Lakewood, Chautauqua County, NY.[1527]

Known children of Elmer E Lyon and Mildred I Lind were:

    545.   i.   Wallace Lyon was born say 1930.[1528]

429. Willis Charles Lyon (*Jerome, Ozro, Alexander, Thomas, John*) was born on 30 Mar 1891 at NY.[1529] He married Marguerite Walker on 9 Oct 1915.[1530] He died on 24 Sep 1975 at Plant City, Hillsborough County, FL, at age 84.[1531]

Marguerite Walker was born on 1 Jun 1894 at NY.[1532] Marguerite Lyon was an inmate of the Gowanda State Homeopathic Hospital in the 1930 and 1940 census.[1533]

Known children of Willis Charles Lyon and Marguerite Walker were as follows:

+ 546.   i.   James J Lyon was born on 29 Dec 1921 at NY. He married Henreitta L Poos on 11 Nov 1946.
+ 547.   ii. Irene Lyon was born on 11 Sep 1926. She married Gordon Feather.
   548.   iii. Daniel Lyon was born on 17 Apr 1928 at NY.[1534]

             Donald Lyon in the 1940 census is the Daniel Lyon listed in the 1930 census with Elmer and Mildred as "trying to adopt". He is the son of Elmer's brother Willis.[1535] He was also known as Donald Lyon.

   549.   iv. Julia Lyon was born on 17 Apr 1928. She died on 17 Apr 1928.

             Died at birth.[1536]

430. Raymond Wallace Lyon (*Jerome, Ozro, Alexander, Thomas, John*) was born on 21 Mar 1897 at Gerry, Chautauqua County, NY.[1537] He married Nora M Crawford on 31 Mar 1918. He died on 8 Apr 1992 at age 95.

Nora M Crawford was born on 6 Apr 1901 at NY. She died on 19 Dec 1984 at age 83.[1538]

[1520]Ibid.
[1521]Tombstone.
[1522]Find A Grave.
[1523]Letter, Ronald E Sherry.
[1524]United States 1930 Census, Hornell, Steuben County, NY.
[1525]Letter, Ronald E Sherry.
[1526]Ibid.
[1527]Find A Grave.
[1528]Letter, Ronald E Sherry.
[1529]United States 1900 Census, Gerry, Chautauqua County, NY.
[1530]Letter, Ronald E Sherry.
[1531]Florida Death Index.
[1532]Letter, Ronald E Sherry.
[1533]United States 1930 Census, Collins, Erie County, NY.
[1534]Letter, Ronald E Sherry.
[1535]Ibid.
[1536]Ibid.
[1537]World War I Draft Records.

Known children of Raymond Wallace Lyon and Nora M Crawford were as follows:

+ 550.   i.   Lawrence Raymond Lyon was born on 13 Apr 1919 at NY. He married Majorie Anne Krull.

    551.   ii.   Eleanor M Lyon was born on 8 Jan 1922 at Jamestown, Chautauqua County, NY. She married George Boynton Dillion on 25 Oct 1941.[1539] She died on 2 Jun 2002 at North Port, Sarasota County, FL, at age 80.[1540]

George Boynton Dillion was born on 3 Dec 1919 at Buffalo, Erie County, NY. He died on 22 Jun 1982 at Venice, Sarasota County, FL, at age 62.[1541]

436. Helen May Lyon (*Septimus, Charles, Alexander, Thomas, John*) was born on 10 May 1865 at NY.[1542] She married Lyman H Trotter circa 1889.[1543] She married Albert Davis before 1925.[1544] She died on 27 Sep 1940 at age 75.[1545] She was buried at Marietta Cemetery, Marietta, Marshall County, IA; There is an indication that she was buried with her first husband in Grant City MO but that record doesn't have a death date indicating she probably wasn't buried there.[1546]

Lyman H Trotter was born in 1856 at WI. He died in 1921.[1547] He was buried at Grant City Cemetery, Grant City, Worth County, MO.[1548]

Known children of Helen May Lyon and Lyman H Trotter were:

    552.   i.   Harry Trotter was born circa 1889 at OH.[1549]

Albert Davis was born circa 1869 at IA.[1550]

There were no known children of Helen May Lyon and Albert Davis.

437. Charles Howard Lyon (*Septimus, Charles, Alexander, Thomas, John*) was born on 23 Oct 1866 at Jamestown, Chautauqua County, NY. He married Minnie Luetta Hartman on 28 Feb 1895 at Saint Charles, Madison County, IA. He died on 5 May 1951 at Coupeville, Island County, WA, at age 84. He was buried at Coupeville, Island County, WA.[1551]

He was painter.

Minnie Luetta Hartman was born on 28 Feb 1874 at Saint Charles, Madison County, IA. She died on 27 Feb 1954 at Seattle, King County, WA, at age 79. She was buried at Sunnyside Cemetery, Coupeville, Island County, WA.[1552]

Known children of Charles Howard Lyon and Minnie Luetta Hartman were as follows:

+ 553.   i.   John "Jack" Chapin Lyon was born on 5 May 1896 at Saint Charles, Madison County, IA. He married Lora Mable Southard on 20 Feb 1920 at Seattle, King County, WA. He died on 7 May 1960 at Portland, Multnomah County, OR, at age 64.

+ 554.   ii.   Ruth A Lyon was born circa 1898 at IA. She married (--?--) Robinson.

[1538]Letter, Ronald E Sherry.
[1539]Ibid.
[1540]Social Security Death Index.
[1541]Florida Death Index.
[1542]Letter, Ronald E Sherry.
[1543]United States 1900 Census, Smith, Worth County, MO.
[1544]Iowa 1925 State Census, Marshalltown, Marshall County, IA.
[1545]Tombstone.
[1546]Find A Grave.
[1547]Tombstone.
[1548]Find A Grave.
[1549]Ibid.
[1550]Iowa 1925 State Census, Marshalltown, Marshall County, IA.
[1551]"The Lyon's Tale", Volume 49, issue 4, Oct 1998, page 182.
[1552]Ibid.

+ 555. iii. Charles Howard Lyon was born on 23 Apr 1903 at Coupville, Island County, WA. He married Beryl C White. He died on 25 Apr 1995 at Ventura, Ventura County, CA, at age 92.

439. Florence T Lyon (*Septimus, Charles, Alexander, Thomas, John*) was born on 28 Nov 1877 at IA.[1553] She married Ray G Simmons. She died on 23 Apr 1921 at NY at age 43.[1554] She was buried at Busti Cemetery, Busti, Chautauqua County, NY.[1555]

Ray G Simmons was born in 1870 at NY. He died in 1949.[1556] He was buried at Busti Cemetery, Busti, Chautauqua County, NY.[1557]

Known children of Florence T Lyon and Ray G Simmons all born at NY were as follows:

556. i. Taylor M Simmons was born on 6 Oct 1899. She married N E Nachtrie on 23 Jun 1921.[1558]

557. ii. Lynn L Simmons was born on 23 Jun 1904. She married Harry H Beck on 21 May 1927.[1559]

558. iii. Doris E Simmons was born on 25 Aug 1906. She married C E Andrews on 28 Feb 1926.[1560]

C E Andrews was born on 17 Sep 1903.

440. Frederick G Lyon (*Septimus, Charles, Alexander, Thomas, John*) was born on 4 Apr 1880 at St Charles, Madison County, IA. He married Mabel Benjamin. He and Mabel Benjamin were divorced before 1915.[1561] He married Lulu Ball circa 1915. He died on 4 Mar 1943 at Chautauqua County, NY, at age 62.[1562]

In 1900 he was living with his aunt Sarah D Lyon in Jamestown, NY. He was machinist.

Mabel Benjamin was born circa 1884 at NY.[1563] She was also known as Lulu M Lyon.

Known children of Frederick G Lyon and Mabel Benjamin were:

559. i. Walter Vincent Benjamin was born circa 1908 at NY.[1564]

Lulu Ball was born circa 1883 at NY. She died on 25 Feb 1954 at Chautauqua County, NY.[1565]

Known children of Frederick G Lyon and Lulu Ball were:

560. i. Frederick G Lyon[1566] was born on 3 Aug 1921 at NY.

441. Rosa Lyon (*Septimus, Charles, Alexander, Thomas, John*) was born on 14 Sep 1883 at IA. She married Henry N Sandberg.[1567] She died in 1969.[1568] She was buried at Sunset Hill Cemetery, Lakewood, Chautauqua County, NY.[1569]

She was also known as Rosebelle Lyon.

Henry N Sandberg was born circa 1885 at Sweden.[1570] He died in Feb 1969.[1571] He was buried at Sunset Hill Cemetery, Lakewood, Chautauqua County, NY.[1572]

[1553]United States 1880 Census, Saint Charles, Madison County, IA.

[1554]Letter, Ronald E Sherry.

[1555]Find A Grave.

[1556]Tombstone.

[1557]Find A Grave.

[1558]Letter, Ronald E Sherry.

[1559]Ibid.

[1560]Ibid.

[1561]United States 1920 Census, Portland, Chautauqua County, NY.

[1562]Barris, *Genealogical Information Reported in Dunkirk NY Newspapers*, 4 Mar 1943.

[1563]United States 1930 Census, Portland, Chautauqua County, NY.

[1564]United States 1920 Census, Portland, Chautauqua County, NY.

[1565]Barris, *Genealogical Information Reported in Dunkirk NY Newspapers*, 28 Feb 1954.

[1566]Letter, Ronald E Sherry.

[1567]Ibid.

[1568]Tombstone.

[1569]Find A Grave.

[1570]United States 1920 Census, Jamestown, Chautauqua County, NY.

Known children of Rosa Lyon and Henry N Sandberg were:

561.   i.   Hazel Glendean Sandberg was born on 6 Aug 1911 at NY.[1573]

[1571]Tombstone.
[1572]Find A Grave.
[1573]Letter, Ronald E Sherry.

Generation Seven

451. Florence Lyon (*L, Nelson, William, Thomas, Thomas, John*) was born in Feb 1891 at MI. She married Lawrence Christensen.[1574]

Lawrence Christensen was born circa 1886 at OH.[1575] He was machinist with a railroad.
Known children of Florence Lyon and Lawrence Christensen all born at MI were as follows:
- 562. i. Norene Christensen was born circa 1915.[1576]
- 563. ii. Arvis Christensen was born say 1916.[1577]
- 564. iii. Janet Christensen was born circa 1919.[1578]
- 565. iv. Lionel Christensen was born circa 1920.[1579]
- 566. v. Lois Christensen was born circa 1922.[1580]
- 567. vi. Mayilyn Christensen was born circa 1924.[1581]
- 568. vii. Clair Christensen was born circa 1926.[1582]
- 569. viii. Beverly Christensen was born circa 1930.[1583]

452. Morris Nelson Lyon (*L, Nelson, William, Thomas, Thomas, John*) was born on 18 Feb 1898 at MI.[1584] He married Elida M Houk. He died on 25 Jun 1963 at MI at age 65.[1585] He was buried at Lake View Cemetery, Ludington, Mason County, MI.[1586]
He was clerk in grocery store in 1940.

Elida M Houk was born on 6 Apr 1900. She died on 5 Jun 1983 at age 83. She was buried at Lake View Cemetery, Ludington, Mason County, MI.[1587]
Known children of Morris Nelson Lyon and Elida M Houk both born at MI are as follows:
- 570. i. Muriel E Lyon is still living.
- 571. ii. Doris M Lyon is still living.

453. Horace D Lyon (*L, Nelson, William, Thomas, Thomas, John*) was born circa 1903 at MI.[1588] He married Helme Gustafson.[1589]

Helme Gustafson was born circa 1905 at MI.[1590] She died in 1991.[1591] She was buried at Lake View Cemetery, Ludington, Mason County, MI.[1592]
Known children of Horace D Lyon and Helme Gustafson are:

[1574]RootsWeb WorldConnect Project, Anna database.
[1575]Ibid.
[1576]United States 1920 Census, Grand Rapids, Kent County, MI.
[1577]Ibid.
[1578]Ibid.
[1579]Ibid.
[1580]United States 1940 Census, Grand Rapids, Kent County, MI.
[1581]United States 1930 Census, Grand Rapids, Kent County, MI.
[1582]Ibid.
[1583]Ibid.
[1584]United States 1880 Census, Caledonia, Kent County, MI.
[1585]Tombstone.
[1586]Find A Grave.
[1587]Ibid.
[1588]United States 1920 Census, Summit, Mason County, MI.
[1589]United States 1930 Census, Ludington, Mason County, MI.
[1590]Ibid.
[1591]Tombstone.
[1592]Find A Grave.

572.   i.   Mary M Lyon is still living.

454. Armand Ronald Lyon (*L, Nelson, William, Thomas, Thomas, John*) was born on 9 Aug 1909 at MI. He married Genevieve Helen Setick on 26 Oct 1932.[1593] He died on 8 Jan 1990 at Ludington, Mason County, MI, at age 80.[1594]

Genevieve Helen Setick was born on 14 Jan 1911 at Manistee, Manistee County, MI.[1595]
Known children of Armand Ronald Lyon and Genevieve Helen Setick were as follows:
573.   i.   Barbara Lyon is still living.
574.   ii.   Ronald Lee Lyon was born on 10 Jul 1939 at MI. He died on 28 Feb 1977 at Marquette, Mason County, MI, at age 37.[1596] He was buried at Lake View Cemetery, Ludington, Mason County, MI.
575.   iii.   Judith Ann Lyon was born on 17 Apr 1945. She died on 24 Dec 2004 at age 59.[1597]

456. Carlton Ray Lyon (*Charles, Richard, William, Thomas, Thomas, John*) was born on 30 Nov 1896 at New London, Waupaca County, WI. He married Lucy Lavina Hoyt on 9 Jan 1923 at Waukegan, Lake County, IL. He died on 6 Sep 1985 at Des Moines, King County, WA, at age 88.[1598]

Lucy Lavina Hoyt was born on 14 Oct 1905 at Gordon, Douglas County, WI. She died on 3 Aug 1982 at Seattle, King County, WA, at age 76.[1599]
Known children of Carlton Ray Lyon and Lucy Lavina Hoyt were as follows:
576.   i.   Edwin Lyon was born circa 1924 at WI.[1600]
577.   ii.   Dorothy Lyon was born circa 1926.[1601]
+ 578.   iii.   Marie LaVerne Lyon was born on 11 Apr 1929 at Milwaukee, Milwaukee County, WI. She married Gordon James McGinnis on 11 Apr 1947 at Seattle, King County, WA.
579.   iv.   Joan Lyon is still living.
580.   v.   Ronald Lyon is still living.

463. Arnold E Lyon (*Ulysses, Richard, William, Thomas, Thomas, John*) was born circa 1931.[1602]

Known children of Arnold E Lyon include:
581.   i.   Bruce A Lyon is still living.

475. Frank Randolph Lyon (*Locke, William, Truxton, Daniel, Thomas, John*) was born on 22 Sep 1871 at Lamoka, Bradford County, PA.[1603] He married Mary L (--?--) in 1906.

Mary L (--?--) was born on 15 Mar 1882.[1604]
Known children of Frank Randolph Lyon and Mary L (--?--) were as follows:
582.   i.   Sarah B Lyon was born circa 1908 at PA.[1605]

[1593]Ibid.
[1594]RootsWeb WorldConnect Project, Don LeClair database.
[1595]Ibid.
[1596]Michigan Death Records.
[1597]RootsWeb WorldConnect Project, Don LeClair database.
[1598]McGinnis Lynda Kay, *Lynda Kay McGinnis Ancestry*.
[1599]Ibid.
[1600]United States 1940 Census, Lake, King County, WA.
[1601]Ibid.
[1602]Ibid., West Chehalem, Yamhill County, OR.
[1603]Passport application, 17 Jan 1921.
[1604]Passport application.
[1605]United States 1920 Census, Fairmont, Marion County, WV.

583. ii. Frank Lyon was born circa 1911 at PA.[1606]
584. iii. Robert Lyon was born circa 1915 at WV.[1607]

489. William Alexander Lyon (*George, George, James, Alexander, Thomas, John*) was born on 25 Oct 1895 at Mayville, Chautauqua County, NY.[1608] He married Minnie M Cooper. He died on 28 May 1951 at age 55.[1609] He was buried at Youngsville Cemetery, Youngsville, Warren County, PA.[1610]

He was mechanic, carpenter.

Minnie M Cooper was born on 4 Jul 1902 at PA. She died on 30 Oct 1966 at age 64.[1611] She was buried at Youngsville Cemetery, Youngsville, Warren County, PA.[1612]

Known children of William Alexander Lyon and Minnie M Cooper all born at PA were as follows:

+ 585. i. Harland E Lyon was born on 24 Sep 1919. He married Alice Lorraine Pattyson, daughter of Wilber W Pattyson and Bettie M (--?--). He died on 8 Dec 1967 at age 48.
  586. ii. Geneva E Lyon was born circa 1921.[1613]
  587. iii. Lloyd Lyon was born on 26 Dec 1921. He died on 11 Feb 2003 at age 81.[1614] He was buried at Wesleyan Cemetery, Sugar Grove, Warren County, PA.[1615]
+ 588. iv. Charles E Lyon was born on 22 Apr 1923. He married Belva Lucille Holmes. He died on 14 Feb 1996 at age 72.
  589. v. Josephine V Lyon was born circa 1925.[1616]
  590. vi. William A Lyon was born circa 1926.[1617]
  591. vii. Gerald J Lyon was born on 24 Feb 1927. He married Gloria F (--?--). He died on 25 May 1992 at age 65.[1618] He was buried at Pine Grove Cemetery, Russell, Warren County, PA.[1619]

   Gloria F (--?--) was born on 14 Nov 1932. She died on 18 May 1978 at age 45.[1620] She was buried at Pine Grove Cemetery, Russell, Warren County, PA.[1621]

  592. viii. Merle Lyon was born on 8 Mar 1928. He died on 18 Jul 2007 at age 79.[1622] He was buried at Wesleyan Cemetery, Sugar Grove, Warren County, PA.[1623]
+ 593. ix. Cecil J Lyon was born on 11 Apr 1929. He married Edith M (--?--). He died on 8 May 1999 at age 70.
  594. x. Allen R Lyon was born on 21 Jan 1932.[1624]
  595. xi. Alice L Lyon was born circa 1935.[1625]
  596. xii. John Almond Lyon was born on 21 Apr 1936.[1626] He died in Jan 1986 at Warren County, PA, at age 49.[1627]

[1606]Ibid.
[1607]Ibid.
[1608]World War I Draft Records.
[1609]Pennsylvania Veterans Records.
[1610]Ibid.
[1611]Tombstone.
[1612]Find A Grave.
[1613]United States 1930 Census, Youngsville, Warren County, PA.
[1614]Tombstone.
[1615]Find A Grave.
[1616]United States 1930 Census, Youngsville, Warren County, PA.
[1617]Ibid.
[1618]Tombstone.
[1619]Find A Grave.
[1620]Tombstone.
[1621]Find A Grave.
[1622]Tombstone.
[1623]Find A Grave.
[1624]United States 1940 Census, Youngsville, Warren County, PA.
[1625]Ibid.
[1626]Social Security Death Index.
[1627]Ibid.

498. Howard Benjamin Lyon (*Wesley, Benjamin, Alvah, Alexander, Thomas, John*) was born in Dec 1887 at OH.[1628] He married Elizabeth (--?--).[1629] He died on 7 Feb 1957 at age 69. He was buried at Mount Washington Cemetery, Mount Washington, Hamilton County, OH.[1630]

Elizabeth (--?--) was born circa 1893 at TN.[1631]

Known children of Howard Benjamin Lyon and Elizabeth (--?--) were:

597.   i.   Wesley Lyon was born circa 1920 at OH.[1632]

He was baker.

500. Harry F Lyon (*Wesley, Benjamin, Alvah, Alexander, Thomas, John*) was born in Oct 1890; Tombstone gives birth as 31 Oct 1891.[1633] He married Louise B (--?--). He died on 26 Feb 1972 at age 81.[1634] He was buried at Gates of Heaven Cemetery, Montgomery, Hamilton County, OH.[1635]

Louise B (--?--) was born on 3 Aug 1893. She died on 5 Feb 1992 at age 98.[1636]

Known children of Harry F Lyon and Louise B (--?--) were:

598.   i.   Raymond J Lyon was born on 21 Aug 1932. He died on 10 Jun 1979 at age 46. He was buried at Gates of Heaven Cemetery, Montgomery, Hamilton County, OH.[1637]

505. Glen Ivan Lyon (*Frank, Frank, Ozro, Alexander, Thomas, John*) was born on 6 Dec 1885 at KS; 1900 census gives birth year as 1884.[1638] He married Bessie Irene (--?--) on 4 Mar 1906. He died in 1959 at KS.[1639] He was buried at Admire Cemetery, Admire, Lyon County, KS.[1640]

Bessie Irene (--?--) was born on 18 Sep 1885 at KS. She died in 1973 at KS.[1641] She was buried at Admire Cemetery, Admire, Lyon County, KS.[1642]

Known children of Glen Ivan Lyon and Bessie Irene (--?--) all born at KS were as follows:

599.   i.   Frank Albion Lyon was born on 28 Oct 1907. He married Mary Isadora Heironmus on 1 Jan 1930.[1643]

Mary Isadora Heironmus was born on 7 Nov 1909.[1644]

600.   ii.   Marion Lois Lyon was born on 6 Feb 1910.[1645] She died in 1991.[1646] She was buried at Admire Cemetery, Admire, Lyon County, KS.[1647]

In the 1920 census this child is listed as a male but in the 1930 and 1940 census as a female.

[1628]United States 1900 Census, Cincinnati, Hamilton County, OH.
[1629]United States 1940 Census, Cincinnati, Hamilton County, OH.
[1630]Tombstone.
[1631]United States 1940 Census, Cincinnati, Hamilton County, OH.
[1632]Ibid.
[1633]United States 1900 Census, Cincinnati, Hamilton County, OH.
[1634]Tombstone.
[1635]Find A Grave.
[1636]Tombstone.
[1637]Ibid.
[1638]United States 1900 Census, Ivy, Lyon County, KS.
[1639]Tombstone.
[1640]Find A Grave.
[1641]Tombstone.
[1642]Find A Grave.
[1643]"The Lyon's Tale."
[1644]Letter, Ronald E Sherry.
[1645]United States 1910 Census, Ive, Lyon County, KS.
[1646]Tombstone.
[1647]Find A Grave.

601. iii. Wayne Ivan Lyon was born on 11 Dec 1913; Family records give birth as 5 Dec 1918.[1648] He married Harriet Lucille Griswold on 28 May 1938. He died on 21 Sep 1990 at KS at age 76.[1649] He was buried at Rossville Township Cemetery, Rossville, Shawnee County, KS.[1650]

Harriet Lucille Griswold was born on 27 Jul 1913 at Rossville, Shawnee County, KS.[1651] She died on 3 Aug 2010 at Bremen, Haralson County, GA, at age 97.[1652] She was buried at Rossville Township Cemetery, Rossville, Shawnee County, KS.[1653]

602. iv. June Irene Lyon was born on 5 Dec 1918. She died in 1991.[1654] She was buried at Admire Cemetery, Admire, Lyon County, KS.[1655]

She was also known as Ione Lyon.

506. Louis Harrison Lyon (*Frank, Frank, Ozro, Alexander, Thomas, John*) was born on 4 Mar 1889 at Admire, Lyon County, KS.[1656] He married Grace Ethel Ball on 28 Mar 1912. He died on 19 Jul 1950 at MO at age 61.[1657] He was buried at Ivy Cemetery, Admire, Lyon County, KS.[1658]

Grace Ethel Ball was born on 5 Jul 1889. She died on 7 Mar 1920 at age 30.[1659] She was buried at Ivy Cemetery, Admire, Lyon County, KS.[1660]

Known children of Louis Harrison Lyon and Grace Ethel Ball all born at KS were as follows:

603. i. Eunice Winona Lyon was born on 15 Jul 1914. She married Hubert Ringo on 22 Apr 1932.[1661] She died in 1968 at Hillsborough County, FL.[1662] She was buried at Garden of Memories, Tampa, Hillsborough County, FL.[1663]

Hubert Ringo was born on 9 Apr 1905. He died on 29 Jan 1997 at Hillsborough County, FL, at age 91.[1664]

604. ii. Louis Leroy Lyon was born on 2 Jan 1916.[1665]

605. iii. Winefred Lucille Lyon was born on 6 Jun 1918.[1666]

606. iv. Wilma Ruth Lyon was born on 3 Feb 1920.[1667]

+ 607. v. Harold L Lyon was born circa 1925. He married Martha Pearl Oglesby.

507. Edwin Ernest Lyon (*Frank, Frank, Ozro, Alexander, Thomas, John*) was born on 31 Mar 1899 at KS. He married Martha Pearl Oglesby. He died on 21 Jun 1935 at age 36.[1668] He was buried at Ivy Cemetery, Admire, Lyon County, KS.[1669]

[1648]Obituary, College of Emporia, Emporia, KS, 1991 yearbook.

[1649]Tombstone.

[1650]Find A Grave.

[1651]Tombstone.

[1652]Ibid.

[1653]Find A Grave.

[1654]Tombstone.

[1655]Find A Grave.

[1656]United States 1900 Census, Ivy, Lyon County, KS.

[1657]Find A Grave.

[1658]Ibid.

[1659]"The Lyon's Tale."

[1660]Find A Grave.

[1661]Letter, Ronald E Sherry.

[1662]Tombstone.

[1663]Find A Grave.

[1664]Florida Death Index.

[1665]United States 1930 Census, Osage City, Osage County, KS.

[1666]Letter, Ronald E Sherry.

[1667]Ibid.

[1668]Find A Grave.

[1669]Ibid.

Martha Pearl Oglesby was born on 19 Apr 1903 at KS.
Known children of Edwin Ernest Lyon and Martha Pearl Oglesby all born at KS were as follows:

608.   i.   Edwin Warren Lyon was born on 18 Aug 1923.[1670]
609.   ii.   Iris Laverne Lyon was born on 20 Nov 1925.[1671]
610.   iii.   Wanda Pearl Lyon was born on 12 Mar 1930.[1672]

510. Doris Marguarita Lyon (*Robert, Charles, Ozro, Alexander, Thomas, John*) was born on 10 Jul 1905 at NY. She married William J Rennagle on 25 Jun 1927.[1673] She married Harold Anderson circa 1938. She died on 30 Aug 1994 at age 89.[1674]

William J Rennagle was born on 6 Jun 1903. He died on 20 Jun 1936 at age 33.[1675]
Known children of Doris Marguarita Lyon and William J Rennagle were:

611.   i.   William Rennagle was born on 26 May 1930. He died on 11 Jul 1994 at age 64.[1676]

Harold Anderson was born circa 1912 at NY.[1677]
There were no known children of Doris Marguarita Lyon and Harold Anderson.

513. Ralph Ozro Lyon (*Roy, Edward, Ozro, Alexander, Thomas, John*) was born on 28 Jun 1898 at NY.[1678] He married Evelyn Maria Sellers on 5 Jun 1932. He and Evelyn Maria Sellers were divorced in 1952 at Duval County, FL.[1679]

Evelyn Maria Sellers was born on 5 Oct 1913 at FL. She died on 31 Aug 1978 at Duval County, FL, at age 64.[1680]
Known children of Ralph Ozro Lyon and Evelyn Maria Sellers all born at NY are as follows:

612.   i.   Gerald Eugene Lyon is still living.
613.   ii.   Marrice Lyon is still living.
614.   iii.   Rose Marie Lyon is still living.
615.   iv.   Lorraine Lyon is still living.

516. Myron J Lyon (*Roy, Edward, Ozro, Alexander, Thomas, John*) was born on 16 Jul 1903 at PA. He married Genevieve Irene Pritchard on 6 Jul 1928.[1681]

Genevieve Irene Pritchard was born on 25 Oct 1909 at NY. She died on 11 Sep 1989 at Santa Cruz County, CA, at age 79.[1682]
Known children of Myron J Lyon and Genevieve Irene Pritchard were as follows:

616.   i.   Myrna I Lyon was born on 16 Dec 1929 at OH.[1683]
617.   ii.   Betty Lou Lyon was born on 17 Mar 1930 at NY.[1684]

[1670]Letter, Ronald E Sherry.
[1671]"The Lyon's Tale."
[1672]Letter, Ronald E Sherry.
[1673]Ibid.
[1674]RootsWeb WorldConnect Project, Mary Beard database.
[1675]Ibid.
[1676]Florida Death Index.
[1677]United States 1940 Census, Eden, Erie County, NY.
[1678]United States 1900 Census, Carroll, Chautauqua County, NY.
[1679]RootsWeb WorldConnect Project, Pamela Miller database.
[1680]Florida Death Index.
[1681]Ibid., Jamestown, Chautauqua County, NY.
[1682]California Death Index.
[1683]Letter, Ronald E Sherry.
[1684]Ibid.

517. Frederick W Lyon (*Roy, Edward, Ozro, Alexander, Thomas, John*) was born on 6 Aug 1906 at PA. He married Allene G Crick on 24 Aug 1929.[1685]

He was restaurant owner.

Allene G Crick was born on 11 Feb 1910 at NY.
Known children of Frederick W Lyon and Allene G Crick were:
    618.   i.   Donald G Lyon was born on 16 Sep 1930 at NY.[1686]

534. Mildred L Lyon (*Leonard, Alexander, Ozro, Alexander, Thomas, John*) was born on 28 Jun 1909 at IL. She married Earl Wilson on 3 Jun 1921.[1687]

Known children of Mildred L Lyon and Earl Wilson were:
    619.   i.   Leonard E Wilson was born on 2 Dec 1922 at PA.[1688]

536. William Alexander Lyon (*William, Alexander, Ozro, Alexander, Thomas, John*) was born on 1 Mar 1914 at PA. He married Catherine Elizabeth Meyer. He died on 3 Jan 1961 at age 46. He was buried at Saint Joseph's Cemetery, Warren, Warren County, PA.[1689]

Catherine Elizabeth Meyer was born on 12 Jun 1914. She died on 7 Jun 2005 at age 90. She was buried at Saint Joseph's Cemetery, Warren, Warren County, PA.[1690]
Known children of William Alexander Lyon and Catherine Elizabeth Meyer are:
    620.   i.   Betty Louise Lyon is still living.

Douglas Allen Irving is still living.

546. James J Lyon (*Willis, Jerome, Ozro, Alexander, Thomas, John*) was born on 29 Dec 1921 at NY. He married Henreitta L Poos on 11 Nov 1946.[1691]

Henreitta L Poos was born on 7 Nov 1923.[1692]
Known children of James J Lyon and Henreitta L Poos are as follows:
    621.   i.   Cynthia M Lyon is still living.
    622.   ii.   Diane L Lyon is still living.

547. Irene Lyon (*Willis, Jerome, Ozro, Alexander, Thomas, John*) was born on 11 Sep 1926. She married Gordon Feather.[1693]

Gordon Feather was born on 13 Nov 1924.[1694]
Known children of Irene Lyon and Gordon Feather are as follows:
    623.   i.   Bruce Feather is still living.
    624.   ii.   Susan Feather is still living.
    625.   iii.   Anne Feather is still living.

[1685]Ibid.
[1686]Ibid.
[1687]Ibid.
[1688]Ibid.
[1689]Find A Grave.
[1690]Ibid.
[1691]"The Lyon's Tale."
[1692]Letter, Ronald E Sherry.
[1693]Ibid.
[1694]Ibid.

550. Lawrence Raymond Lyon (*Raymond, Jerome, Ozro, Alexander, Thomas, John*) was born on 13 Apr 1919 at NY. He married Majorie Anne Krull.[1695]

He was electrician.

Majorie Anne Krull was born on 2 Aug 1924 at Buffalo, Erie County, NY.[1696] She was also known as Marjorie A.

Known children of Lawrence Raymond Lyon and Majorie Anne Krull all born at Buffalo, Erie County, NY, are as follows:

+ 626.   i.   Gary Lawrence Lyon is still living.
+ 627.   ii.   Patricia Anne Lyon is still living.
+ 628.   iii.   James Kevin Lyon is still living.
+ 629.   iv.   John Dennis Lyon is still living.
+ 630.   v.   Jeffery Robert Lyon is still living.

553. John "Jack" Chapin Lyon (*Charles, Septimus, Charles, Alexander, Thomas, John*) was born on 5 May 1896 at Saint Charles, Madison County, IA. He married Lora Mable Southard on 20 Feb 1920 at Seattle, King County, WA. He died on 7 May 1960 at Portland, Multnomah County, OR, at age 64.[1697]

Lora Mable Southard was born on 18 May 1896 at Teoka, Whitman County, WA. She died on 16 Nov 1953 at Seattle, King County, WA, at age 57.[1698]

Known children of John "Jack" Chapin Lyon and Lora Mable Southard were:

+ 631.   i.   John "Mike" Chapin Lyon Jr was born on 28 Aug 1921 at Seattle, King County, WA. He married Marjorie Cecil Finan on 4 Nov 1944 at New Orleans, New Orleans Parish, LA.

554. Ruth A Lyon (*Charles, Septimus, Charles, Alexander, Thomas, John*) was born circa 1898 at IA. She married (--?--) Robinson.[1699]

(--?--) Robinson died before 1930.[1700]

Known children of Ruth A Lyon and (--?--) Robinson were:

632.   i.   William H Robinson was born circa 1920 at WA.[1701]

555. Charles Howard Lyon (*Charles, Septimus, Charles, Alexander, Thomas, John*) was born on 23 Apr 1903 at Coupville, Island County, WA. He married Beryl C White. He died on 25 Apr 1995 at Ventura, Ventura County, CA, at age 92.[1702]

He was lineman.

Beryl C White was born circa 1903 at CO.[1703] She died in Jan 1974 at Seattle, King County, WA.[1704]

Known children of Charles Howard Lyon and Beryl C White were:

633.   i.   Charles R Lyon[1705] was born circa 1926 at WA.[1706]

[1695]Ibid.

[1696]Ibid.

[1697]"The Lyon's Tale", Volume 49, issue 4, Oct 1998, page 182.

[1698]Ibid., Volume 49 issue 4 Oct 1998, page 182.

[1699]United States 1930 Census, Lake, King County, WA.

[1700]Ibid.

[1701]Ibid.

[1702]Death Records, California.

[1703]United States 1940 Census, Lake City, King County, WA.

[1704]Social Security Death Index.

[1705]United States 1940 Census, Lake City, King County, WA.

[1706]Ibid.

Generation Eight

578. Marie LaVerne Lyon (*Carlton, Charles, Richard, William, Thomas, Thomas, John*) was born on 11 Apr 1929 at Milwaukee, Milwaukee County, WI. She married Gordon James McGinnis on 11 Apr 1947 at Seattle, King County, WA.[1707]

Gordon James McGinnis was born on 31 Mar 1924 at Chilliwack, BC, Canada.
Known children of Marie LaVerne Lyon and Gordon James McGinnis are:
      634.   i.   Lynda Kay McGinnis is still living.

585. Harland E Lyon (*William, George, George, James, Alexander, Thomas, John*) was born on 24 Sep 1919 at PA. He married Alice Lorraine Pattyson, daughter of Wilber W Pattyson and Bettie M (--?--). He died on 8 Dec 1967 at age 48.[1708] He was buried at Tabor Cemetery, Kane, McKean County, PA.[1709]
He was finisher in a furniture factory.

Alice Lorraine Pattyson was born circa 1922 at NY. She married John A Snyder say 1970. She died on 11 Nov 1985 at Jamestown, Chautauqua County, NY.[1710] She was buried at Lake View Cemetery, Jamestown, Chautauqua County, NY.[1711]
Known children of Harland E Lyon and Alice Lorraine Pattyson are as follows:
      635.   i.   Howard Lyon is still living.
      636.   ii.   Ronald Lyon is still living.
      637.   iii. Bonnie Lyon is still living.
      638.   iv. Kenneth Lyon is still living.

588. Charles E Lyon (*William, George, George, James, Alexander, Thomas, John*) was born on 22 Apr 1923 at PA. He married Belva Lucille Holmes.[1712] He died on 14 Feb 1996 at age 72.[1713] He was buried at Pine Grove, Russell, Warren County, PA.[1714]

Belva Lucille Holmes was born on 22 Sep 1926 at McKean County, PA. She died on 1 Feb 2008 at Warren, Warren County, PA, at age 81. She was buried at Pine Grove, Warren, Warren County, PA.[1715]
Known children of Charles E Lyon and Belva Lucille Holmes are as follows:
      639.   i.   Charles E Lyon is still living.

                Betty Jean (--?--) was born on 1 Jan 1947 at Florence, Lauderdale County, AL. She died on 31 Mar 2008 at Warren, Warren County, PA, at age 61.[1716]
      640.   ii.   Larry Lyon is still living.

                Debra (--?--) is still living.
      641.   iii. David Lyon is still living.
      642.   iv. Joan Lyon is still living.

[1707] McGinnis Lynda Kay, *Lynda Kay McGinnis Ancestry*.
[1708] Burial Records, Pennsylvania Veteran's Records.
[1709] Ibid., Pennsylvania Veterans Records.
[1710] Tombstone, Charlotte, Chautauqua County, NY.
[1711] Find A Grave.
[1712] Ibid.
[1713] Tombstone.
[1714] Find A Grave.
[1715] Ibid.
[1716] Ibid.

Byran Colvin is still living.

593. Cecil J Lyon (*William, George, George, James, Alexander, Thomas, John*) was born on 11 Apr 1929 at PA. He married Edith M (--?--).[1717] He died on 8 May 1999 at Irving, Warren County, PA, at age 70.[1718] He was buried at Chandlers Valley Cemetery, Chandlers Valley, Warren County, PA.[1719]

Edith M (--?--) was born on 10 May 1929. She died on 21 Mar 2001 at age 71. She was buried at Chandlers Valley Cemetery, Chandlers Valley, Warren County, PA.[1720]
Known children of Cecil J Lyon and Edith M (--?--) were:
643.   i.   Daniel Lee Lyon was born on 28 Feb 1956.[1721] He died on 9 Jun 1998 at age 42. He was buried at Chandlers Valley Cemetery, Chandlers Valley, Warren County, PA.[1722]

607. Harold L Lyon (*Louis, Frank, Frank, Ozro, Alexander, Thomas, John*) was born circa 1925 at KS. He married Martha Pearl Oglesby.[1723]

Martha Pearl Oglesby was born circa 1904 at KS. She was also known as Pearl M.[1724]
Known children of Harold L Lyon and Martha Pearl Oglesby were as follows:
644.   i.   Edwin W Lyon was born on 9 Aug 1923 at TX. He died on 25 Feb 1991 at OK at age 67.[1725] He was buried at Ramona Cemetery, Washington County, KS.[1726]
645.   ii.   Iris Lavern Lyon was born circa 1926 at KS.[1727]
646.   iii.   Wanda P Lyon was born in 1930 at KS.[1728]

626. Gary Lawrence Lyon (*Lawrence, Raymond, Jerome, Ozro, Alexander, Thomas, John*) is still living.

Ann Malone is still living.
Known children of Gary Lawrence Lyon and Ann Malone both born at Buffalo, Erie County, NY, are as follows:
647.   i.   Dina Adrienne Lyon is still living.
648.   ii.   Michael Patrick Lyon is still living.

627. Patricia Anne Lyon (*Lawrence, Raymond, Jerome, Ozro, Alexander, Thomas, John*)[1729] is still living.

Ronald Eugene Sherry is still living.
Known children of Patricia Anne Lyon and Ronald Eugene Sherry are as follows:
649.   i.   Jennifer Anne Sherry is still living.

Michael Robert Abusherry[1730] is still living.
650.   ii.   Patrick Ronald Sherry is still living.

[1717]Ibid.
[1718]Tombstone.
[1719]Find A Grave.
[1720]Ibid.
[1721]Ibid.
[1722]Ibid.
[1723]United States 1930 Census, Ivy, Lyon County, KS.
[1724]Ibid., Iy, Lyon County, KS.
[1725]Tombstone.
[1726]Find A Grave.
[1727]United States 1930 Census, Ivy, Lyon County, KS.
[1728]Ibid.
[1729]Ibid.
[1730]Ibid.

628. James Kevin Lyon (*Lawrence, Raymond, Jerome, Ozro, Alexander, Thomas, John*)[1731] is still living.

Margaret R Kowalen is still living.
Known children of James Kevin Lyon and Margaret R Kowalen are:
    651.   i.   Timothy James Lyon is still living.

629. John Dennis Lyon (*Lawrence, Raymond, Jerome, Ozro, Alexander, Thomas, John*) is still living.

Barbara Brooks is still living.
Known children of John Dennis Lyon and Barbara Brooks are as follows:
    652.   i.   Kristofer Todd Lyon is still living.

              Melaine Martinelli is still living.
    653.   ii.   Timothy Owen Lyon is still living.

630. Jeffery Robert Lyon (*Lawrence, Raymond, Jerome, Ozro, Alexander, Thomas, John*) is still living.

Danita M Harkins is still living.
Known children of Jeffery Robert Lyon and Danita M Harkins are as follows:
    654.   i.   Kelly Marie Lyon is still living.
    655.   ii.   Jeremiah Robert Lyon is still living.

Catheleen Willson is still living.
Known children of Jeffery Robert Lyon and Catheleen Willson are:
    656.   i.   Matthew Larwence Lyon is still living.

631. John "Mike" Chapin Lyon Jr (*John, Charles, Septimus, Charles, Alexander, Thomas, John*) was born on 28 Aug 1921 at Seattle, King County, WA. He married Marjorie Cecil Finan on 4 Nov 1944 at New Orleans, New Orleans Parish, LA.[1732]

Marjorie Cecil Finan was born on 22 Jan 1925 at Newark, Wayne County, NY.[1733]
Known children of John "Mike" Chapin Lyon Jr and Marjorie Cecil Finan both born at Seattle, King County, WA, are as follows:
    657.   i.   Pamela Alice Lyon is still living.
    658.   ii.   James Michael Lyon is still living.

[1731]Letter, Ronald E Sherry.
[1732]"The Lyon's Tale", Volume 49, 4 Oct 1998, page 182.
[1733]Ibid.

Descendants of John [II] Lyon

Generation One

1001. John [II] Lyon was born circa 1740. He married Martha Burlingame, daughter of Daniel Burlingame and Rose Briggs, on 27 Oct 1763 at Cranston, Providence County, RI; marriage performed by William Burton.[1734] He died on 28 Jan 1803 at Foster, Providence County, RI; Providence Gazette, Sat 5 Feb 1803 article:

"Accident On Friday evening of last week" [28 Jan 1803] "As a Mr Lyon, of Foster, was driving a loaded cart into town, sitting on the tongue, being chilled with cold, he fell in alighting, when one of the wheels passed over him, and put an instant period to his life. We learn that he has left a wife and seven children to lament his fate. Accidents of this kind having heretofore occurred, our country friends would do well in quitting the very dangerous practice of riding on the tongues of carts or waggons."[1735]

John Lyon served in Col Harris' Regiment in 1760. The campaign of 1760 was to the Lake Champlain area and served under Lord Amherst and marched toward Montreal. The French surrendered on 8 Sep 1760 and the troops immediately returned home in 1760 at RI.[1736] John Lyon was made a freeman in Cranston, RI in 1763. John Lyon purchased land in Cranston RI and in Aug 1763 in Aug 1763. John Lyon of Cranston, Yeoman, sold the land he had purchased in 1763 back to the original owner who was William Carpenter of Cranston on 2 Jun 1764 at Cranston, Providence County, RI.[1737] John Lyon of Cranston RI (Yoeman) and Martha Lyon his wife, sold about one acre of land and a "frame" to Charles Higinbotham on 31 Jul 1764.[1738] A person by the name of John Lyon was a resident of White Creek, Charlotte County, NY [now Salem, Washington County, NY] when he signed a petition on 1 Dec. Thomas Lyon [I] who lived several miles east of this John Lyon also signed this petition.[1739] The Fitch Gazetteer says that _____ Lyon [John Lyon] carpenter, resided north of Black Creek and 15-20 rods opposite Reuben Cheney at Fitches Point Salem, NY [lot 98]. That he went "down country" into MA or CT during the retreat before Burgoyne's army [1777], returned after the danger was over. He "had sons Daniel, Alexander & Thomas."

This document was written 50 years after the event and seems to confuse the unidentified John Lyon who resided on this lot 98 with Thomas Lyon [I] who resided on lot 121 several miles to the east. The lack of knowing the given name of the principal casts doubt on the given names of the children and all that can be assumed is that this John Lyon did go "down country". Further, there is no evidence that this John Lyon returned to Charlotte County after the war. This John Lyon is possibly John Lyon [II] but that assertion cannot be proven.[1740]

John [II] sold the land on which he lived in Coventry RI in 1778. Martha and Reuben Lyon were appointed to administer the personal estate of John Lyon, late of Foster. An inventory of his estate was for a total of $783.75. It included farm items and 13 carpenter planes. Principal payments from the estate were to Cyrus Lyon for a $258.75 note and Dr Cyril Carpenter for $21.33 on 12 Feb 1803.[1741]

[1734] James N Arnold, *Vital Records of Rhode Island 1636-1850*. (Providence RI: Narragansett Press, 1892), Cranston Marriages Records Volume 1, page 253.

[1735] Vital Records, Foster, Providence County, RI, Wills, Book 1, page 331.

[1736] Howard M. Chapin, *Rhode Island in the Colonial Wars, A List of Rhode Island Soldiers & Sailors in the Old French & Indian War*. (Providence, RI: Rhode Island Historical Society, 1918).

[1737] Cranston, Providence County, RI, Land Records, Volume 1, page 437.

[1738] Arnold, *Vital Records of Rhode Island 1636-1850.*, Cranston Vital Records Volume 1, page 439.

[1739] E B O'Callaghan, *The Documentary History of the State of New York* (Albany, NY: Charles Van Benthuysen, 1851), Volume 4, page 888.

[1740] Kenneth A Perry, *The Fitch Gazetteer an Annotated Index to the Manuscript History of Washington County NY* (MD: Heritage Books, 1999), page 240.

[1741] Rhode Island Wills., Foster Will Book 1, pages 331, 332, 469 and 498.

Martha Burlingame[1742] was born on 11 Jun 1744 at Cranston, Kent County, RI.[1743] Martha received furniture and housewares from her fathers will suggesting she lived near Coventry RI when he died in 1794.

Known children of John [II] Lyon and Martha Burlingame were as follows:

+ 1002. i. Rhoda Lyon was born on 15 Oct 1764 at RI. She married Obediah Herrington, son of Obediah Herrington, on 6 Feb 1791 at Foster, Providence County, RI.

+ 1003. ii. John [III] Lyon was born circa 1765 at RI. He married Phebe Theodosia Carpenter, daughter of Dr Cyril Carpenter and Freelove Smith. He died on 14 Mar 1814 at Foster, Providence County, RI.

+ 1004. iii. Benjamin Lyon was born on 7 Jul 1767 at RI. He married Hannah Talbot, daughter of Benjamin Talbot and Margaret Richmond, circa 1793. He married Deborah (--?--) circa 1810. He died on 20 Nov 1854 at Sherburne, Chenango County, NY, at age 87.

+ 1005. iv. Mary (Polly) Lyon was born in 1768 at RI. She married Jeffery Amherst Fry, son of Col Thomas Fry, on 1 Mar 1789 at Foster, Providence County, RI.

+ 1006. v. Cyrus Lyon was born on 7 Dec 1773 at RI. He married Elizabeth Talbot, daughter of Benjamin Talbot and Margaret Richmond, on 1 May 1796 at RI. He married Sarah Grow on 30 Jul 1820 at Chenango County, NY. He died on 29 Sep 1840 at Sherburne, Chenango County, NY, at age 66. He was buried at Blackman Cemetery, Oxford, Chenango County, NY.

+ 1007. vi. Captain Reuben Lyon was born circa 31 Mar 1777 at Scituate, Providence County, RI. He married Susan Phillips circa 1800. He died on 23 Jul 1852 at Foster, Providence County, RI. He was buried at Lyon Lot Cemetery, Foster, Providence County, RI.

+ 1008. vii. Anna Lyon was born on 18 Oct 1786 at Foster, Providence County, RI. She married Benjamin Wickes, son of Joseph Wickes Esq, on 19 Jun 1803 at Coventry, Kent County, RI. She married Judge (--?--) Thompson at Chenango County, NY. She died in Jul 1860 at Norwich, Chenango County, NY, at age 73.

[1742] Arnold, *Vital Records of Rhode Island 1636-1850.*, Cranston Marriages Records Volume 1, page 253.
[1743] "The Lyon's Tale", Jan 2004, page 53.

Generation Two

1002. Rhoda Lyon (*John*) was born on 15 Oct 1764 at RI. She married Obediah Herrington, son of Obediah Herrington, on 6 Feb 1791 at Foster, Providence County, RI.[1744]

She was also known as Martha Lyon.

Known children of Rhoda Lyon and Obediah Herrington were as follows:

1009.   i.   Mary Herrington was born in 1797 at Foster, Providence County, RI. She married Cyrus Rice in 1818 at Oswego County. She died on 25 Aug 1880 at Warsaw, Wyoming County, NY.[1745] She was buried at Warsaw Cemetery, Warsaw, Wyoming County, NY.[1746]

        Cyrus Rice was born on 24 Mar 1792 at Canaan, Columbia County, NY. He died on 10 Jun 1832 at Warsaw, Wyoming County, NY, at age 40. He was buried at Warsaw Cemetery, Warsaw, Wyoming County, NY.[1747]

1010.   ii.   Charles Giles Herrington was born on 14 May 1812 at Oswego, Oswego County, NY. He married Charlotte Plant. He died on 12 Aug 1901 at Lawton, Van Buren County, MI, at age 89.[1748]

        Charlotte Plant was born on 17 Nov 1814 at Stafford, Genesso County, NY. She died on 17 Nov 1883 at Lawton, Van Buren County, NY, at age 69.[1749]

1003. John [III] Lyon (*John*) was born circa 1765 at RI. He married Phebe Theodosia Carpenter, daughter of Dr Cyril Carpenter and Freelove Smith.[1750] He died on 14 Mar 1814 at Foster, Providence County, RI.[1751]

He left a will on 29 Apr 1814 at Foster, Providence County, RI; John died intestate. Cyril Carpenter Lyon of Foster was appointed to administer his estate. The inventory of John Lyon's estate was valued at $4,795.1 on 22 Jun 1814.[1752]

Phebe Theodosia Carpenter was born circa 1765.[1753]

Known children of John [III] Lyon and Phebe Theodosia Carpenter were as follows:

1011.   i.   Cyril Carpenter Lyon was born on 21 Jun 1790 at RI. He died on 12 Oct 1859 at RI at age 69; Cause of death given as cerebral disease.[1754] He was buried at Cemetery 093, Foster, Providence County, RI.[1755]

        Cyril is buried in the Carpenter burial ground along with Dr Cyril Carpenter 1735-1816.

        Cyril probated the estate of John Lyon III in 1814.

        It is assumed that John III had married the daughter of Cyril Carpenter and that Cyril Carpenter Lyon was the oldest surviving son when his father died.

[1744] Arnold, *Vital Records of Rhode Island 1636-1850.*, Foster Vital Records Volume 1, page 22.

[1745] RootsWeb WorldConnect Project, Marv Miller database.

[1746] Ibid., Ryley Meagher database.

[1747] Ibid.

[1748] Ibid., Marv Miller database.

[1749] Ibid.

[1750] A B & G W A Lyon, *Lyon Memorial Massachusetts Families* (Detroit. MI: William Graham Printing, 1905), page 299.

[1751] Vital Records, Foster, Providence County, RI, Wills Volume 2, page 684.

[1752] Rhode Island Wills, Foster Will Book 3, page 14.

[1753] Amos B Carpenter, *History of the Rehoboth Carpenter Family.* (Amherst, MA: Carpenter & Morehouse, 1898), page 187.

[1754] Arnold, *Vital Records of Rhode Island 1636-1850.*, Foster Deaths, Volume 1851-1918, page 2.

[1755] Foster Rhode Island Cemetery records.

Cyril's estate along with Cynthia A Lyons estate were both probated 7 Nov 1859 in Foster, Providence County, RI. He was accountant in Providence, RI.

1012.   ii.   Christopher Smith Lyon was born circa 1793 at Foster, Providence County, RI. The last time Christopher S Lyon is known to be alive was on 28 Apr 1826.[1756]

1013.   iii.   Cynthia Ann Lyon was born in 1795 at RI.[1757]

In the 1850 Census Cynthia Ann Lyon was living with her brother Cyril Carpenter Lyon. When Cyril died his executor, Harris A Vanghn was appointed Cynthia's guardian. She received 1/2 Cyril's estate and was boarded for several years with various people. In the 1870 and 1880 Foster RI census Cynthia was living in the town poorhouse.[1758]

1004. Benjamin Lyon (*John*) was born on 7 Jul 1767 at RI. He married Hannah Talbot, daughter of Benjamin Talbot and Margaret Richmond, circa 1793. He married Deborah (--?--) circa 1810. He died on 20 Nov 1854 at Sherburne, Chenango County, NY, at age 87.[1759]

He was tailor in 1794. Benjamin sold his land in Foster RI to his brother Reuben on 25 Nov 1803. Biographical Sketches of Leading citizens of Chenango County NY, says he arrived in Sherburne, Chenango County, NY in 1804. He left a will on 13 Mar 1844; proven 15 Jan 1855. Mentions wife Deborah, sons Benjamin T, Alden, John and Reuben, daughter Eliza Jackson. Son Benjamin T Lyon executor.[1760]

Hannah Talbot was born circa 1771. She died on 16 May 1808 at Sherburne, Chenango County, NY.[1761]
Known children of Benjamin Lyon and Hannah Talbot were as follows:

+ 1014.   i.   Alden Lyon was born on 14 Feb 1794 at Foster, Providence County, RI. He married Thankful (--?--).

1015.   ii.   Eliza Lyon was born on 23 Mar 1795 at Foster, Providence County, RI. She married Richard Jackson.[1762]

She resided in 1855 at Ithaca, Tompkins County, NY.

+ 1016.   iii.   Benjamin Talbot Lyon was born on 26 Nov 1796 at Foster, Providence County, RI. He married Mary Comstock circa 1824. He married Mary Umphrey Rogers, daughter of Alva Rogers and Desire Eaton, circa 1830. He died on 30 May 1865 at Chenango County, NY, at age 68.

+ 1017.   iv.   John Lyon was born on 13 Nov 1798 at RI. He married Sena Spencer on 13 Dec 1823 at NY. He died on 9 Mar 1875 at Hawkeye, Fayette County, IA, at age 76. He was buried at Eden Cemetery, Saint Lucas, Fayette County, IA.

+ 1018.   v.   Reuben Lyon was born on 21 Feb 1802 at RI. He married Sarah Venable say 1830. He married Caroline Fish Chamberlain say 1835. He died on 8 Apr 1874 at Angelica, Allegany County, NY, at age 72.

1019.   vi.   Cyrus Lyon was born on 9 Mar 1804 at Sherburne, Chenango County, NY. He died on 20 Aug 1827 at age 23.[1763]

1020.   vii.   Richmond Lyon was born on 29 Mar 1806 at Sherburne, Chenango County, NY. He died on 10 Mar 1807.[1764]

Deborah (--?--) was born in 1779 at VT. She died on 10 Nov 1859.[1765]

[1756]Rhode Island Land Records, Foster, Volume 8, page 157.
[1757]United States 1850 Census, Foster, Providence County, RI.
[1758]Rhode Island Wills, Foster Will Book 9, page 298.
[1759]Lyon, *Lyon Memorial Massachusetts Families*, page 300.
[1760]*Will*, Chenango County NY, Volume G, page 130.
[1761]Lyon, *Lyon Memorial Massachusetts Families*, page 300.
[1762]Ibid.
[1763]Ibid.
[1764]Ibid.
[1765]Ibid.

There were no known children of Benjamin Lyon and Deborah (--?--).

1005. Mary (Polly) Lyon (*John*) was born in 1768 at RI.[1766] She married Jeffery Amherst Fry, son of Col Thomas Fry, on 1 Mar 1789 at Foster, Providence County, RI.[1767]

Jeffery Amherst Fry was born in 1764 at East Greenwich, Kent County, RI. He died on 20 Jun 1807 at Foster, Providence County, RI.[1768]

Known children of Mary (Polly) Lyon and Jeffery Amherst Fry were as follows:

1021.   i.   Richard Fry was born on 5 Aug 1789.[1769]

1022.   ii.   George Fry was born in 1792.[1770]

1023.   iii.   Lucy Fry was born in 1794.[1771]

1024.   iv.   Elizabeth Fry was born in 1796.[1772]

1025.   v.   Amherst Fry was born in 1798 at Foster, Providence County, RI. He married Mary Burlingame in 1824. He died in 1845 at Peoria, Peoria County, IL.[1773]

1026.   vi.   Phebe Fry was born in 1800.[1774]

1027.   vii.   Olney Fry was born on 2 Feb 1802 at Foster, Providence County, RI. He married Celinda Bennett in 1821 at Providence, Providence County, RI. He married Dorcus Ross in 1868. He married Elizabeth Perry after 1869. He died in 1894 at Albany, Lynn County, OR.[1775]

        Celinda Bennett was born in 1802 at Providence, Providence County, RI. She died in 1859 at Albany.[1776]

1028.   viii.   Olive Fry was born in 1804.[1777]

1029.   ix.   Harriet Fry was born in 1806.[1778]

1006. Cyrus Lyon (*John*) was born on 7 Dec 1773 at RI. He married Elizabeth Talbot, daughter of Benjamin Talbot and Margaret Richmond, on 1 May 1796 at RI. He married Sarah Grow on 30 Jul 1820 at Chenango County, NY. He died on 29 Sep 1840 at Sherburne, Chenango County, NY, at age 66.[1779] He was buried at Blackman Cemetery, Oxford, Chenango County, NY.

Cyrus was called a gentleman in 1797. Cyrus Lyon, yeoman of Foster RI sold his land to his father. His wife Elizabeth signed with a mark in 1803. He left a will on 13 Feb 1840; Proven 14 Dec 1840 at Oxford. Mentions wife Sarah, sons Alfred of Sherburne, Alexander, Daniel, Richmond. Grandson Cyrus son of Alexander. Granddaughters Hannah, Mariah Lyon and Sarah Talbot (under 18) Betsey Talbot and Mary Talbot. Daniel and Alexander Lyon were not residing in NY State.[1780]

Elizabeth Talbot was born on 12 May 1773 at Foster, Providence County, RI. She died on 15 Feb 1820 at Chenango County, NY, at age 46.[1781] She was buried at North Norwich Cemetery, North Norwich, Chenango County, NY.[1782] She was also known as Betsey Lyon.[1783]

[1766]Thomas A, PhD Gorton, *Samuel Gorton of Rhode Island and his Descendants* (Baltimore, MD: Gateway Press, 1985).

[1767]Arnold, *Vital Records of Rhode Island 1636-1850.*, Foster Vital Records Volume 1, page 21.

[1768]Gorton, *Samuel Gorton of Rhode*, page 637.

[1769]Ibid.

[1770]Ibid.

[1771]Ibid.

[1772]Ibid.

[1773]Ibid.

[1774]Ibid.

[1775]Ibid.

[1776]Ibid.

[1777]Ibid.

[1778]Ibid.

[1779]Lyon, *Lyon Memorial Massachusetts Families*, page 299.

[1780]Probate Records, Chenango County, NY, Wills, Liber E folio 13.

[1781]Lyon, *Lyon Memorial Massachusetts Families*, page 300.

Known children of Cyrus Lyon and Elizabeth Talbot were as follows:

+ 1030. i. Alexander Lyon was born on 3 May 1797 at RI. He married Alice Millard on 12 Jul 1818 at Darrington, NY. He married Nancy A (--?--) before 1850. He married P Sarah (--?--) say 1862. He died circa 1890 at Hooperville, Weber County, UT.

+ 1031. ii. Elizabeth Lyon was born on 20 Jan 1799 at RI. She married James Talbot on 5 Jan 1819.

  1032. iii. Patty Lyon[1784] was born on 4 Jan 1802 at RI.[1785] She died on 26 Sep 1803 at RI at age 1.[1786]

+ 1033. iv. Daniel Lyon was born on 11 Oct 1807 at Sherburne, Chenango County, NY. He married Harriet Carpenter, daughter of Joseph Carpenter, circa 1825 at Chenango County, NY. He died in 1866 at Chenango County, NY.

+ 1034. v. Alfred Lyon was born on 20 Apr 1809 at Sherburne, Chenango County, NY. He married Polly Benedict on 23 Apr 1832 at Chenango County, NY. He died on 21 May 1874 at New London, Waupaca County, WI, at age 65.

  1035. vi. Richmond Lyon was born on 29 Oct 1811 at Sherburne, Chenango County, NY.[1787]

Sarah Grow[1788] was born on 14 Jul 1777.[1789] She died on 26 Aug 1863 at WI at age 86.[1790]
There were no known children of Cyrus Lyon and Sarah Grow.

1007. Captain Reuben Lyon (*John*) was born circa 31 Mar 1777 at Scituate, Providence County, RI; Death record gives birth as 30 Mar 1778. He married Susan Phillips circa 1800.[1791] He married Nabby Tabor on 7 Oct 1846 at Johnston, Providence County, RI.[1792] He died on 23 Jul 1852 at Foster, Providence County, RI; Cause of death given as dropsy in the chest.[1793] He was buried at Lyon Lot Cemetery, Foster, Providence County, RI.[1794]

He was farmer. He left a will on 21 Feb 1850; proven 4 Sep 1852. Mentions wife Nabby. Son Shelton P Lyon who was bequeathed the Real Estate. Eight children (unnamed) of his son Gardner who was deceased. Daughter Louisa Bates wife of William Bates. Grandson Reuben Wilcox. Grandson Emery Dorsetus Lyon son of his son John. Granddaughter Ann Eliza Lyon, daughter of son John.[1795]

Susan Phillips was born in 1779. She died on 6 Jun 1842 at Foster, Providence County, RI. She was buried at Lyon Lot Cemetery, Foster, Providence County, RI.[1796] She was also known as Susannah.[1797]

Known children of Captain Reuben Lyon and Susan Phillips all born at Foster, Providence County, RI, were as follows:

  1036. i. Richard S Lyon was born on 21 May 1802. He married Amy Fish say 1825.[1798] He married Hannah (--?--) say 1835.[1799] He died on 21 Dec 1866 at Foster, Providence County, RI, at age 64; Foster Cemetery records give death date as 1885. He was buried at Lyon Lot Cemetery, Foster, Providence County, RI.[1800]

[1782]Find A Grave www.findagrave.com.
[1783]Tombstone.
[1784]Lyon, *Lyon Memorial Massachusetts Families*, page 300.
[1785]Ibid.
[1786]Ibid.
[1787]Ibid.
[1788]Ibid.
[1789]Ibid.
[1790]Ibid.
[1791]Arnold, *Vital Records of Rhode Island 1636-1850.*, Foster Marriages, Volume 1, page 86.
[1792]Ibid., Johnston Vital Records Volume 1, page 187.
[1793]Ibid., Foster Deaths, Volume 1851-1918, page 1.
[1794]Vital Records, Foster, Providence County, RI, Cemetery Index.
[1795]Rhode Island Wills, Foster Will Book 8, page 443.
[1796]Vital Records, Foster, Providence County, RI, Lyon Lot Cemetery.
[1797]Rhode Island Land Records, Foster, Volume 6, page 343.
[1798]Vital Records, Foster, Providence County, RI, Lyon Lot Cemetery.
[1799]Rhode Island Wills, Foster Will Book 10.
[1800]Vital Records, Foster, Providence County, RI, Lyon Lot Cemetery.

He was farmer. In 1846 Richard S Lyon was living in the Shaker Village in Enfield, CT.[1801] He left a will on 23 Oct 1866; mentions wife Hannah, brother Sheldon P Lyon and nephew Emery D Lyon. The inventory of Richard S Lyon's estate was valued at $3,092.[1802]

Amy Fish was born in 1801. She died on 10 May 1830 at Foster, Providence County, RI. She was buried at Lyon Lot Cemetery, Foster, Providence County, RI.[1803]

Hannah (--?--) died after 1866.[1804]

+ 1037. ii. Gardner Lyon was born on 11 Apr 1804. He married Anna Phillips, daughter of Asaph Phillips and Esther Whipple, on 17 Mar 1823 at Foster, Providence County, RI. He married Patience (--?--) circa 1846. He died on 20 Jun 1849 at age 45.

+ 1038. iii. Hannah B Lyon was born on 5 Apr 1806. She married (--?--) Wilcox circa 1825. She died on 24 Dec 1828 at age 22.

  1039. iv. Martha Lyon was born in 1808. She died on 14 Feb 1811 at Foster, Providence County, RI. She was buried at Lyon Lot Cemetery, Foster, Providence County, RI.[1805]

+ 1040. v. John P Lyon was born on 21 Jul 1809. He married Mary Bennett, daughter of Nathaniel Bennett, on 8 Nov 1829 at Foster, Providence County, RI. He died on 4 Jul 1836 at age 26.

  1041. vi. Reuben Lyon Jr[1806] was born on 22 May 1811.[1807] He died in Feb 1828 at Foster, Providence County, RI, at age 16.[1808]

  1042. vii. Alden Lyon was born in 1814. He died on 29 Mar 1825 at RI. He was buried at Lyon Lot Cemetery, Foster, Providence, RI.[1809]

  1043. viii. Israel Lyon was born in 1814. He died on 13 Sep 1818. He was buried at Lyon Lot Cemetery, Foster, Providence, RI.[1810]

  1044. ix. Louisa Lyon was born on 21 Oct 1816. She married (--?--) Butes.[1811] She died on 30 Dec 1886 at age 70.[1812]

+ 1045. x. Sheldon P Lyon was born on 21 Jun 1822. He married Mary E Hill, daughter of Jonathan Hill and Mary (--?--), on 10 Nov 1844 at Coventry, Kent County, RI. He died on 9 Dec 1875 at age 53.

Nabby Tabor[1813] was born say 1825 at Foster, Providence County, RI.

There were no known children of Captain Reuben Lyon and Nabby Tabor.

1008. Anna Lyon (*John*) was born on 18 Oct 1786 at Foster, Providence County, RI. She married Benjamin Wickes, son of Joseph Wickes Esq, on 19 Jun 1803 at Coventry, Kent County, RI; Marriage performed by John Hammand, Elder.[1814] She married Judge (--?--) Thompson at Chenango County, NY.[1815] She died in Jul 1860 at Norwich, Chenango County, NY, at age 73.[1816]

Benjamin Wickes was born in 1784.[1817]

[1801]United States 1850 Census, Enfield, Hartford County, CT.
[1802]Rhode Island Wills, Foster Will Book 10 page 247.
[1803]Vital Records, Foster, Providence County, RI, Lyon Lot Cemetery.
[1804]Rhode Island Wills, Foster Will Book 10.
[1805]Vital Records, Foster, Providence County, RI, Lyon Lot Cemetery.
[1806]Ibid., Cemetery records, Lyon Lot Cemetery.
[1807]Ibid.
[1808]Ibid.
[1809]Vital Records, Foster, Providence County, RI.
[1810]Ibid.
[1811]Rhode Island Wills, Foster Will Book 9, page 495.
[1812]Ancestry Family Trees, Wilcox and Allied Families.
[1813]Arnold, *Vital Records of Rhode Island 1636-1850.*, Johnston Vital Records Volume 1, page 187.
[1814]Vital Records, Coventry, Kent County, RI, Births, Marriages & Deaths, Volume 1, page 187.
[1815]Lyon, *Lyon Memorial Massachusetts Families*, page 301.
[1816]Ibid.
[1817]Ibid.

Known children of Anna Lyon and Benjamin Wickes were as follows:

1046.　i.　Waity Wickes died on 14 Jan 1806.[1818]

1047.　ii.　William Wickes.[1819]

1048.　iii.　Marvin Wickes was born on 27 Jul 1809 at Norwich, Chenango County, NY.[1820] He married Erisa (--?--).[1821] He married Elvira Hitchcock.[1822] He died on 16 Sep 1870 at Norwich, Chenango County, NY, at age 61.[1823]

　　　　He was chair maker.

　　　　Erisa (--?--) was born circa 1811 at NY.[1824]

　　　　Elvira Hitchcock was born on 1 Aug 1812. She died on 22 May 1874 at Brockport, Monroe County, NY, at age 61.[1825]

There were no known children of Anna Lyon and Judge (--?--) Thompson.

[1818]Ibid.

[1819]Ibid.

[1820]Ibid.

[1821]United States 1850 Census, Norwich, Chenango County, NY.

[1822]Lyon, *Lyon Memorial Massachusetts Families*, page 304.

[1823]Ibid., page 301.

[1824]United States 1850 Census, Norwich, Chenango County, NY.

[1825]Lyon, *Lyon Memorial Massachusetts Families*, page 304.

Generation Three

1014. Alden Lyon (*Benjamin, John*) was born on 14 Feb 1794 at Foster, Providence County, RI; Tombstone give birth as 1796.[1826] He married Thankful (--?--).[1827]

He resided in 1855 at Alden, Erie County, NY.[1828]

Thankful (--?--) was born circa 1794 at NY. She died in 1857 at Allegany County, NY.[1829] She was buried at Until the Day of Dawn Cemetery, Angelica, Allegany County, NY.[1830]

Known children of Alden Lyon and Thankful (--?--) were as follows:

    1049.   i.   Eliza Lyon.[1831]

+ 1050. ii.   Willard C Lyon was born in 1822 at Ithaca, Tompkins County, NY. He married Elane Ann Hooker, daughter of Margaret (--?--). He died on 17 Jan 1898 at Allegany County, NY. He was buried at Until the Day of Dawn Cemetery, Angelica, Allegany County, NY.

    1051. iii. Adelia H Lyon was born circa 1827 at NY.[1832] She married Charles Chilson (--?--) before 1860. She married William Thompson between 1870 and 1880.[1833]

                Charles Chilson (--?--) died before 1880.

                William Thompson was born circa 1828 at NY.[1834] He died before 1900.

    1052. iv. Amelia Lyon was born circa 1829 at NY.[1835]

    1053. v.   Deborah Lyon was born circa 1833 at NY.[1836]

+ 1054. vi. Helen Lyon was born on 1 Mar 1835 at Allegany County, NY. She married Nathan Emerson circa 1854. She died on 18 Mar 1906 at Harrisville, Alcona County, MI, at age 71.

    1055. vii. George Lyon was born circa 1841 at NY.

                Killed in the Civil War.[1837]

1016. Benjamin Talbot Lyon (*Benjamin, John*) was born on 26 Nov 1796 at Foster, Providence County, RI. He married Mary Comstock circa 1824. He married Mary Umphrey Rogers, daughter of Alva Rogers and Desire Eaton, circa 1830. He died on 30 May 1865 at Chenango County, NY, at age 68.

He was both a farmer and he had a shoe shop. He left a will on 31 May 1864 at Chenango County, NY; proven 1 Jun 1865. The will mentions his wife Mary U Lyon. Sons Lucion, William W, and Edward P Lyon and four unnamed children that are minors. Daughters Hannah L Comstock, Mary L McComber Delia E Squires, Cornelia Dixon, Roxana Lyon, Cynthia Rixford, Ellen W Lyon and Catherine Lyon. Also grandchild Alfred M Brooks son of daughter Amy Brooks deceased.[1838]

Mary Comstock was born circa 1807 at CT. She died on 1 Feb 1865 at Sherburne, Chenango County, NY. The cause of death was consumption.[1839]

Known children of Benjamin Talbot Lyon and Mary Comstock were as follows:

[1826]Arnold, *Vital Records of Rhode Island 1636-1850.*, Foster Vital Records Volume 1, page 66.

[1827]Lyon, *Lyon Memorial Massachusetts Families*, page 301.

[1828]*Surrogate Court of Chenango County, NY*, Will of Benjamin Lyon.

[1829]Tombstone.

[1830]Find A Grave.

[1831]Lyon, *Lyon Memorial Massachusetts Families*, page 301.

[1832]United States 1880 Census, Alfred, Allegheny, NY.

[1833]Lyon, *Lyon Memorial Massachusetts Families*, page 301.

[1834]United States 1880 Census, Alfred, Allegheny, NY.

[1835]United States 1850 Census, Alfred, Allegheny, NY.

[1836]Ibid.

[1837]Lyon, *Lyon Memorial Massachusetts Families*, page 301.

[1838]Family History Library, Film 0860305, Unpublished Wills, Chenango County, NY.

[1839]Ibid.

+ 1056. i.   Hannah Lyon was born on 21 Sep 1823 at Chenango County, NY. She married Calvin Comstock, son of Amon Comstock and Irena (--?--), on 12 Mar 1845 at Sherburne, Chenango County, NY. She died on 15 Feb 1872 at Sherburne, Chenango County, NY, at age 48. She was buried at Westernville cemetery, Westernville, Oneida County, NY.

  1057. ii.   Lucian A Lyon was born on 26 Apr 1825 at NY. He married Emily Kiingsbury, daughter of Isreal Kiingsbury and Mary (--?--).[1840] He died on 9 Oct 1873 at Boonville, Oneida County, NY, at age 48. He was buried at Boonville Cemetery, Boonville, Oneida County, NY.[1841]

            Emily Kiingsbury was born circa Aug 1833 at Oneida County, NY. She died on 5 Feb 1894. She was buried at Boonville Cemetery, Boonville, Oneida County, NY.[1842]

  1058. iii. Arnon Lyon was born on 17 Sep 1826 at Sherburne, Chenango County, NY. He married Evaline Sexton on 26 Aug 1850 at Sherburne, Chenango County, NY. He died on 25 Sep 1851 at Earlville, Madison County, NY, at age 25.[1843]

            Evaline Sexton[1844] was born circa 1823 at NY.

+ 1059. iv. Mary Comstock Lyon was born on 20 Feb 1828 at Chenango County, NY. She married Joel McComber on 8 Oct 1856 at Sherburne, Chenango County, NY. She died on 5 May 1897 at Brooklyn, Kings County, NY, at age 69.

Mary Umphrey Rogers was born circa 1808. She died in 1866.[1845]

Known children of Benjamin Talbot Lyon and Mary Umphrey Rogers were as follows:

+ 1060. i.   Amie Mahala Lyon was born on 17 Apr 1832 at Chenango County, NY. She married William Brooks on 12 Jun 1861 at Sherburne, Chenango County, NY. She died on 13 May 1864 at Sherburne, Chenango County, NY, at age 32. She was buried at Sherburne West Hill Cemetery, Sherburne, Chenango County, NY.

+ 1061. ii.   Delia Eliza Lyon was born on 20 Dec 1833 at Chenango County, NY. She married James P Squires on 10 Oct 1860. She died on 1 Sep 1866 at Sherburne, Chenango County, NY, at age 32.

  1062. iii. Charles Rollin Lyon was born on 12 Jul 1836 at Sherburne, Chenango County, NY. He died on 13 Feb 1838 at Sherburne, Chenango County, NY, at age 1.[1846]

+ 1063. iv. Cornelia Lyon was born on 6 Jun 1838 at Sherburne, Chenango County, NY. She married Alanzo K Dixon on 9 Oct 1861 at Chenango County, NY. She died on 6 Dec 1899 at Brooklyn, Kings County, NY, at age 61.

+ 1064. v.   Roxie Anna Lyon was born on 17 Sep 1840 at Sherburne, Chenango County, NY. She married Kenyon Terry on 16 Oct 1872 at Smyrna, Chenango County, NY.

  1065. vi. Cynthia Lovonia Lyon was born circa 1843 at NY. She married Sidney D Rexford on 2 Mar 1864 at Sherburne, Chenango County, NY. She married Prof Charles E Boss on 20 Jul 1881.[1847]

            Sidney D Rexford died at Smyrna, Chenango County, NY.[1848]

+ 1066. vii. Ellen Lyon was born on 19 Aug 1844 at NY. She married James P Squires circa 1867.

  1067. viii. Catherine Lois Lyon was born on 11 Feb 1847 at Sherburne, Chenango County, NY.

[1840]Lyon, *Lyon Memorial Massachusetts Families*, page 302.
[1841]Find A Grave.
[1842]Ibid.
[1843]Lyon, *Lyon Memorial Massachusetts Families*, page 302.
[1844]Ibid.
[1845]*Book of Biographies, Biographical Sketches of Leading Citizens of Chenango County NY.* (Buffalo, NY: Biographical Publishing Co, 1898).
[1846]Lyon, *Lyon Memorial Massachusetts Families*, page 302.
[1847]Ibid., page 306.
[1848]Ibid.

She was also known as Kate Lyon. Kate was living with her sister Mary C McComber in New York City in 1880.[1849]

+ 1068. ix. William Wicks Lyon was born on 30 Dec 1849 at Sherburne, Chenango County, NY. He married Cora A Karr, daughter of Huse Karr and Ruth (--?--), on 16 Aug 1876 at Smyrna, Chenango County, NY.

+ 1069. x. Edward Percy Lyon was born on 9 Apr 1855 at Sherburne, Chenango County, NY. He married Mary E Shepardson on 20 Sep 1887 at Smyrna, Chenango County, NY. He died on 28 Nov 1928 at Brooklyn, Kings County, NY, at age 73.

1017. John Lyon (*Benjamin, John*) was born on 13 Nov 1798 at RI. He married Sena Spencer on 13 Dec 1823 at NY. He died on 9 Mar 1875 at Hawkeye, Fayette County, IA, at age 76.[1850] He was buried at Eden Cemetery, Saint Lucas, Fayette County, IA.[1851]

He resided in 1855 at Smyrna, Chenango County, NY.

Sena Spencer was born on 29 Apr 1805 at Butternuts, Otsego County, NY.[1852] She died on 29 Oct 1892 at Hawkeye, Fayette County, IA, at age 87.[1853] She was buried at Eden Cemetery, Saint Lucas, Fayette County, IA.[1854]

Known children of John Lyon and Sena Spencer all born at Smyrna, Chenango County, NY, were as follows:

1070. i. Eliza Lyon was born on 11 Feb 1825. She died on 18 Feb 1831 at Smyrna, Chenango County, NY, at age 6.[1855]

1071. ii. (--?--) Lyon was born on 3 Sep 1826. He/she died on 10 Oct 1826 at Smyrna, Chenango County, NY.[1856]

1072. iii. Cyrus Lyon was born on 9 Sep 1827. He died on 3 Mar 1831 at Smyrna, Chenango County, NY, at age 3.[1857]

+ 1073. iv. Hiram Spencer Lyon was born on 15 Sep 1831. He married Cornelia B Packard on 14 Oct 1861.

+ 1074. v. John Whitman Lyon was born on 17 May 1833. He married Hannah U Thompson on 11 Feb 1877. He died in 1917.

+ 1075. vi. Sarah Deborah Lyon was born on 5 Jun 1836. She married Sidney Ferris on 24 Sep 1857 at Smyrna, Chenango County, NY. She died on 25 Mar 1905 at age 68.

+ 1076. vii. Benjamin Theodore Lyon was born on 26 Nov 1846. He married Emma R (--?--) on 11 Nov 1868 at Plymouth, Chenango County, NY. He died on 26 Apr 1910 at age 63.

1018. Reuben Lyon (*Benjamin, John*) was born on 21 Feb 1802 at RI. He married Sarah Venable say 1830. He married Caroline Fish Chamberlain say 1835. He died on 8 Apr 1874 at Angelica, Allegany County, NY, at age 72.[1858]

He was marble dealer in 1850. He resided in 1855 at Homer, Cortland County, NY.

Known children of Reuben Lyon and Sarah Venable were:

[1849]United States 1880 Census, Ney York City, New York County, NY.
[1850]Lyon, *Lyon Memorial Massachusetts Families*, page 300.
[1851]Find A Grave.
[1852]Lyon, *Lyon Memorial Massachusetts Families*, page 302.
[1853]Ibid.
[1854]Find A Grave.
[1855]Lyon, *Lyon Memorial Massachusetts Families*, page 302.
[1856]Ibid.
[1857]Ibid.
[1858]Ibid., page 300.

+ 1077.   i. Samuel Venable Lyon was born circa 1825 at Norwich, Chenango County, NY. He married Julia Frances Duryea.

Caroline Fish Chamberlain was born in 1809 at NY.[1859] She died on 16 Oct 1871 at Elmira, Chemung County, NY.[1860]

Known children of Reuben Lyon and Caroline Fish Chamberlain were as follows:

1078.   i. Cyrus Lyon[1861] was born say 1836.
+ 1079.   ii. John E Lyon was born circa 1837 at Norwich, Chenango County, NY.
1080.   iii. Julia Frances Lyon was born on 8 Aug 1839 at Norwich, Chenango County, NY. She married Amos Yale. She died on 25 Dec 1883 at Paris, France, at age 44.[1862]

Amos Yale died circa 1875 at Syracuse, Onondaga County, NY.[1863]

1081.   iv. Margaret G Lyon was born circa 1840 at Norwich, Chenango County, NY.[1864] She married George Rowe.
1082.   v. Caroline Eliza Lyon was born circa 1845 at Norwich, Chenango County, NY. She married Milo Addison Bell at Elmira, Chemung County, NY.[1865]
1083.   vi. Amelia S Lyon was born in 1847 at Norwich, Chenango County, NY. She married (--?--) Dunkleburger after 1900 at Nevada, Story County, IA.[1866]
Lived in Nevada, IA.
1084. vii. Fay Franklin Lyon was born in 1850 at Norwich, Chenango County, NY. He married Mary L Sonart.[1867] He died circa 1930.
He was furniture finisher.
1085. viii. Agnes Lyon was born circa 1853 at Homer, Cortland County, NY. She married Thomas H Crummey.[1868]
Lived in Los Angeles, CA 1905.[1869]
+ 1086.   ix. Hattie Bell Lyon was born on 29 Jun 1856 at Ithaca, Tompkins County, NY. She married Iram Brewer.

1030. Alexander Lyon (*Cyrus, John*) was born on 3 May 1797 at RI. He married Alice Millard on 12 Jul 1818 at Darrington, NY.[1870] He married Nancy A (--?--) before 1850.[1871] He married P Sarah (--?--) say 1862.[1872] He died circa 1890 at Hooperville, Weber County, UT; Alexander Lyon of Hooperville was dropped from the pension rolls for failure to collect his pension.[1873]

Known children of Alexander Lyon and Alice Millard were as follows:

+ 1087.   i. Cyrus Lyon was born circa 1819 at NY. He married Sarah Ann Cozine, daughter of William Cozine, on 23 Mar 1854 at Carroll County, MO. He died on 13 Jul 1864. He was buried at Old Pleasant Park Cemetery, Carroll County, MO.

[1859]Ibid., page 303.
[1860]Ibid.
[1861]Ibid.
[1862]Ibid.
[1863]Ibid.
[1864]United States 1850 Census, Norwich, Chenango County, NY.
[1865]Lyon, *Lyon Memorial Massachusetts Families*, page 303.
[1866]Ibid.
[1867]Ibid.
[1868]Ibid.
[1869]Ibid.
[1870]Ibid., page 300.
[1871]United States 1850 Census, Carroll County, MO.
[1872]United States 1880 Census, Hooper, Weber County, UT.
[1873]1812 War Index, New York State, Pension payment record for Alexander Lyon, New York State Archives, Albany, NY.

+ 1088. ii. Elizabeth Lyon was born on 10 Jan 1821. She married George W Laughlin circa 1840. She died on 9 May 1909 at Dover, Cuyahoga County, OH, at age 88.
+ 1089. iii. Lucius Millard Lyon was born on 6 Sep 1825 at DeRuyter, Madison County, NY. He married Lucinda Lucetta Kittridge, daughter of William Kittridge, on 5 Sep 1850 at MI. He died on 23 Sep 1891 at Fairhaven, Whatcom County, WA, at age 66. He was buried at Mount Pleasant Cemetery, Seattle, King County, WA.

Nancy A (--?--) was born circa 1791 at CT.[1874]
There were no known children of Alexander Lyon and Nancy A (--?--).

P Sarah (--?--) was born circa 1830 at MA.[1875]
Known children of Alexander Lyon and P Sarah (--?--) both born at UT were as follows:
1090. i. Theodore Lyon was born circa 1864.[1876]
1091. ii. J Adelaide Lyon was born circa 1866.[1877]

1031. Elizabeth Lyon (*Cyrus, John*) was born on 20 Jan 1799 at RI.[1878] She married James Talbot on 5 Jan 1819.[1879]

James Talbot was born on 31 Dec 1794 at Edmeston, Otsego County, NY. He died on 15 Aug 1866 at Edmeston, Otsego County, NY, at age 71. He was buried at Taylor Hill Cemetery, Edmeston, Otsego County, NY.[1880]
Known children of Elizabeth Lyon and James Talbot were as follows:
1092. i. Betsey Talbot was born before 1822. She died after 1840.[1881]
1093. ii. Mary Talbot was born before 1822. She died after 1840.[1882]
1094. iii. Sarah Talbot was born between 1822 and 1840. She died after 1840.[1883]

1033. Daniel Lyon (*Cyrus, John*) was born on 11 Oct 1807 at Sherburne, Chenango County, NY.[1884] He married Harriet Carpenter, daughter of Joseph Carpenter, circa 1825 at Chenango County, NY. He died in 1866 at Chenango County, NY.[1885]

Harriet Carpenter was born circa 1806 at NY; The Hamilton County History says she was born in PA.[1886] She died in 1870 at Chenango County, NY.[1887] 1850 census gives birth as NY.[1888]
Known children of Daniel Lyon and Harriet Carpenter were as follows:
+ 1095. i. Polly Lyon was born in Oct 1827 at Chenango County, NY. She married Hiram Gustin say 1852. She died in 1907 at Madison County, NY. She was buried at Earlville Cemetery, Earlville, Madison County, NY.
1096. ii. Sarah Lyon was born circa 1829 at Chenango County, NY.[1889]

[1874]United States 1850 Census, Carroll County, MO.
[1875]Ibid.
[1876]United States 1880 Census, Hooper, Weber County, UT.
[1877]Ibid.
[1878]Lyon, *Lyon Memorial Massachusetts Families*, page 300.
[1879]Ibid.
[1880]RootsWeb WorldConnect Project, Kim Branagan Database.
[1881]Probate Records, Chenango County, Wills, Liber E folio 1.
[1882]Ibid.
[1883]Ibid.
[1884]Lyon, *Lyon Memorial Massachusetts Families*, page 300.
[1885]C F Royce, *Biographical and Historical Memoirs of Adams, Clay, Hall and Hamilton Counties, Nebraska.* (Chicago, IL: Goodspeed Publishing Company, 1890).
[1886]United States 1850 Census, Lincklaen, Chenango County, NY.
[1887]Royce, *Biographical and Historical Memoirs of Adams, Clay, Hall and Hamilton Counties, Nebraska.*
[1888]United States 1850 Census, Lincklaen, Chenango County, NY.

+ 1097. iii. Cyrus Ralph Lyon was born circa 1831 at NY. He married Lucy (--?--) say 1858.
+ 1098. iv. Jason James Lyon was born on 22 May 1833 at Lincklaen, Chenango County, NY. He married Rosella Lucinda Gould, daughter of William Gould and Hannah Austin, on 24 Sep 1856 at Springfield, Sangamon County, IL. He died on 15 Apr 1914 at Trumbull, Clay County, NE, at age 80. He was buried at Greenwood Cemetery, Hastings, Adams County, NE.
+ 1099. v. Myron D Lyon was born circa 1836 at NY. He married Olive (--?--).
  1100. vi. Sarah Lyon was born circa 1838 at NY.[1890]
       She was also known as Sarah Henrietta Lyon.
  1101. vii. William Lyon was born circa 1840 at NY.[1891]
  1102. viii. Ezra Lyon was born circa 1843 at Chenango County, NY.[1892]
  1103. ix. Ira Lyon was born circa 1845 at NY.[1893]

1034. Alfred Lyon (*Cyrus, John*) was born on 20 Apr 1809 at Sherburne, Chenango County, NY. He married Polly Benedict on 23 Apr 1832 at Chenango County, NY.[1894] He died on 21 May 1874 at New London, Waupaca County, WI, at age 65.[1895]

Polly Benedict was born on 22 Mar 1810 at Chenango County, NY. She died on 1 Aug 1867 at New London, Waupaca County, WI, at age 57.[1896]

Known children of Alfred Lyon and Polly Benedict were as follows:

+ 1104. i. Charles C Lyon was born on 16 Jan 1833 at Sherburne, Chenango County, NY. He married Charlotte Antoinette Owen circa 1855. He married Clara M Daugherty, daughter of Alonzo Daugherty and Thankful (--?--), on 13 Jun 1877. He died on 12 Nov 1903 at New London, Waupaca County, WI, at age 70.
  1105. ii. Sidney Lyon[1897] was born on 24 Oct 1835 at Sherburne, Chenango County, NY.[1898] He married Martha Green on 25 Sep 1867.[1899] He died on 14 Feb 1898 at New London, Waupaca County, Wi, at age 62.[1900]
  1106. iii. Milo Lyon[1901] was born on 1 Jun 1837 at Sherburne, Chenango County, NY.[1902] He died on 14 Jul 1837 at Sherburne, Chenango County, NY.[1903]
  1107. iv. Esther Melinda Lyon was born on 28 Nov 1838 at Sherburne, Chenango County, NY. She died on 3 Dec 1858 at New London, Waupaca County, WI, at age 20.[1904]
+ 1108. v. Milo Alfred Lyon was born on 14 Apr 1841 at Sherburne, Chenango County, NY. He married Helen A Robinson, daughter of John Robinson and Sophia (--?--), on 19 Jun 1864 at New London, Waupaca County, WI. He died in 1941 at Monrovia, Los Angeles County, CA.
+ 1109. vi. Sarah S Lyon was born on 18 Dec 1847 at Sherburne, Chenango County, NY. She married Samuel W Bennett on 20 Oct 1862. She married Stephen H Snyder on 11 Jan 1902. She

[1889] Royce, *Biographical and Historical Memoirs of Adams, Clay, Hall and Hamilton Counties, Nebraska.*
[1890] United States 1850 Census, Lincklaen, Chenango County, NY.
[1891] Ibid.
[1892] Royce, *Biographical and Historical Memoirs of Adams, Clay, Hall and Hamilton Counties, Nebraska.*
[1893] United States 1850 Census, Lincklaen, Chenango County, NY.
[1894] Lyon, *Lyon Memorial Massachusetts Families*, page 303.
[1895] Ibid., page 300.
[1896] Lyons, *William Lyon of Roxbury, MA and Some of his Descendants*, p 133.
[1897] Lyon, *Lyon Memorial Massachusetts Families*, page 303.
[1898] Ibid.
[1899] Ibid.
[1900] Ibid.
[1901] Ibid., page 304.
[1902] Ibid.
[1903] Ibid.
[1904] Ibid.

died on 19 Feb 1930 at Green Bay, Brown County, WI, at age 82. She was buried at Fort Howard Memorial Park, Green Bay, Brown County, WI.

1110.   vii.   Franklin Lyon was born circa 1851 at NY. He died in Nov 1869 at Waupaca, WI.[1905]

1037. Gardner Lyon (*Reuben, John*) was born on 11 Apr 1804 at Foster, Providence County, RI. He married Anna Phillips, daughter of Asaph Phillips and Esther Whipple, on 17 Mar 1823 at Foster, Providence County, RI.[1906] He married Patience (--?--) circa 1846.[1907] He died on 20 Jun 1849 at Foster, Providence County, RI, at age 45. He was buried at Lyon Lot Cemetery, Foster, Providence County, RI.[1908]

The inventory of Gardner Lyon's estate was valued at $160.39 on 27 Aug 1849.[1909]

Anna Phillips was born on 6 Feb 1804 at Foster, Providence County, RI.[1910] She died in 1845 at Foster, Providence County, RI. She was buried at Lyon Lot Cemetery, Foster, Providence County, RI.[1911]

Known children of Gardner Lyon and Anna Phillips were as follows:

1111.   i.   Annis Lyon was born on 19 May 1825 at Foster, Providence County, RI.[1912] She married George N Corbin.

George N Corbin was born circa 1822 at RI.[1913]

1112.   ii.   Albert Lyon was born on 1 Oct 1827 at Foster, Providence County, RI.[1914]

1113.   iii.   Alder Lyon was born say 1829 at Foster, Providence County, RI.[1915]

1114.   iv.   Jason Lyon was born in 1831 at Foster, Providence County, RI. He died on 4 Apr 1854 at Foster, Providence County, RI; Cause of death given as dropsy of the heart.[1916] He was buried at Lyon Lot Cemetery, Foster, Providence County, RI.[1917]

1115.   v.   Hannah Lyon was born in 1835 at Foster, Providence County, RI. She died on 17 Apr 1853.[1918]

In 1860 Hannah was living with her older sister Annis Corbin in Smithfield, Providence County, RI.

1116.   vi.   Esther Lyon[1919] was born circa 1837 at Foster, Providence County, RI.[1920]

In 1860 Esther was living with her older sister Annis Corbin in Smithfield, Providence County, RI. In 1860 she was living with her uncle Sheldon P Lyon in Foster RI.[1921]

1117.   vii.   Susan Lyon[1922] was born in 1837 at Foster, Providence County, RI.[1923] She died on 16 Feb 1853.[1924] She was buried at Lyon Lot Cemetery, Foster, Providence County, RI.[1925]

In 1860 Susan was living with her older sister Annis Corbin in Smithfield, Providence County, RI.[1926]

[1905]U S Census Mortality Schedule, year ending 1 Jun 1870.
[1906]Arnold, *Vital Records of Rhode Island 1636-1850.*, Foster Vital Records Volume 1, page 86.
[1907]Rhode Island Wills, Foster Will Book 8, page 308.
[1908]Vital Records, Foster, Providence County, RI, Cemetery records, Lyon Lot Cemetery.
[1909]Rhode Island Wills, Foster Will Book 8, page 319.
[1910]Arnold, *Vital Records of Rhode Island 1636-1850.*, Foster Births and Deaths, Volume 1, page 58.
[1911]Vital Records, Foster, Providence County, RI, Cemetery records, Lyon Lot Cemetery.
[1912]Arnold, *Vital Records of Rhode Island 1636-1850.*, Foster Vital Records.
[1913]United States 1850 Census, Smithfield, Providence County, RI.
[1914]Lyons, *William Lyon of Roxbury, MA and Some of his Descendants*, P 134.
[1915]Rhode Island Wills, Foster Will Book 9, page 495.
[1916]Arnold, *Vital Records of Rhode Island 1636-1850.*, Foster Deaths, Volume 1851-1918, page 1.
[1917]Vital Records, Foster, Providence County, RI, Cemetery records, Lyon Lot Cemetery.
[1918]Ibid., Lyon Lot Cemetery.
[1919]United States 1850 Census, Smithfield, Providence County, RI.
[1920]Ibid.
[1921]Ibid.
[1922]Vital Records, Foster, Providence County, RI, Cemetery records, Lyon Lot Cemetery.
[1923]Ibid.
[1924]Ibid.
[1925]Ibid.
[1926]United States 1850 Census, Smithfield, Providence County, RI.

1118. viii. Samantha Lyon[1927] was born circa 1842 at RI.[1928]

In the 1850 census Samantha was living with Daniel Howard who had children or grandchildren but no wife. Along with Samantha Lyon age 8, were Patience Lyon age 43, and Albert Lyon age 22. Patience was Gardner Lyon's second wife and Albert is his son.

Patience (--?--) was born circa 1807 at RI. After Gardner's death Patience Lyon, "widow of Gardner Lyon" was appointed guardian of his minor children Susan, Esther and Samantha. In the 1850 census Patience was living with Daniel Howard who had children or grandchildren but no wife. Along with Patience were Samantha Lyon age 8 and Albert Lyon age 22.[1929]

There were no known children of Gardner Lyon and Patience (--?--).

1038. Hannah B Lyon (*Reuben, John*) was born on 5 Apr 1806 at Foster, Providence County, RI. She married (--?--) Wilcox circa 1825. She died on 24 Dec 1828 at Foster, Providence County, RI, at age 22. She was buried at Lyon Lot Cemetery, Foster, Providence County, RI.[1930]

Known children of Hannah B Lyon and (--?--) Wilcox were:

1119. i. Reuben Lyon Wilcox was born in 1828. He married Caroline (--?--). He died on 12 May 1889. He was buried at Lyon Lot Cemetery, Foster, Providence County, RI.[1931]

1040. John P Lyon (*Reuben, John*) was born on 21 Jul 1809 at Foster, Providence County, RI. He married Mary Bennett, daughter of Nathaniel Bennett, on 8 Nov 1829 at Foster, Providence County, RI. He died on 4 Jul 1836 at Foster, Providence County, RI, at age 26.[1932] He was buried at Lyon Lot Cemetery, Foster, Providence, RI.[1933]

Mary Bennett was born in 1809 at Foster, Providence County, RI. She died on 30 Jun 1840.[1934] She was buried at Lyon Lot Cemetery, Foster, Providence, RI.[1935] She was also known as Polly Bennett.

Known children of John P Lyon and Mary Bennett were as follows:

1120. i. Susan Lyon was buried at Lyon Lot Cemetery, Foster, Providence, RI.[1936]

1121. ii. Ann Eliza Lyon married (--?--) Walper.[1937]

+ 1122. iii. Emory Darastur Lyon was born circa 1830 at Foster, Providence County, RI. He married Julia M Hill. He died on 8 Jul 1914 at Foster, Providence County, RI. He was buried at Lyon Lot Cemetery, Foster, Providence County, RI.

1045. Sheldon P Lyon (*Reuben, John*) was born on 21 Jun 1822 at Foster, Providence County, RI. He married Mary E Hill, daughter of Jonathan Hill and Mary (--?--), on 10 Nov 1844 at Coventry, Kent County, RI. He died on 9 Dec 1875 at Foster, Providence County, RI, at age 53; Cause of death given as dropsy in the chest.[1938] He was buried at Lyon Lot Cemetery, Foster, Providence County, RI.

He was farmer.

[1927] Ibid., Foster, Providence County, RI.

[1928] Ibid.

[1929] Ibid.

[1930] Vital Records, Foster, Providence County, RI, Cemetery records, Lyon Lot Cemetery.

[1931] Ibid.

[1932] Ancestry Family Trees, Wilcox and Allied Families.

[1933] Vital Records, Foster, Providence County, RI, Cemetery records, Lyon Cemetery, #103.

[1934] Ancestry Family Trees, Wilcox and Allied Families.

[1935] Vital Records, Foster, Providence County, RI, Cemetery records, Lyon Lot Cemetery.

[1936] Vital Records, Foster, Providence County, RI.

[1937] Rhode Island Wills, Foster Will Book 9, page 495.

[1938] Arnold, *Vital Records of Rhode Island 1636-1850.*, Foster Deaths, Volume 1851-1918, page 17.

Mary E Hill was born in 1825 at Foster, Providence County, RI. She died on 14 Sep 1889 at Foster, Providence County, RI; Cause of death given as apoplexy.[1939] She was buried at Lyon Lot Cemetery, Foster, Providence County, RI. She left a will on 31 Oct 1888; mentions son John W Lyon.[1940]

Known children of Sheldon P Lyon and Mary E Hill all born at Foster, Providence County, RI, were as follows:

1123.　i.　John Witter Lyon was born on 23 Sep 1849. He married Emogene Preston circa 1876. He died on 22 Feb 1917 at Scituate, Providence County, RI, at age 67.[1941] He was buried at North Scituate Cemetery, Scituate, Providence County, RI.[1942]

　　　　He was grocer. He was also known as John Walter Lyon.

　　　　Emogene Preston[1943] was born on 5 Oct 1850 at Foster, Providence County, RI.[1944] She married George Augustus Stone on 8 Apr 1923.[1945] She died on 4 Jan 1935 at Providence, Providence County, RI, at age 84.[1946]

+ 1124.　ii.　George Phillips Lyon was born on 3 Oct 1853. He married Adella M Johnson, daughter of William H Johnson and Susan A (--?--), circa 1875. He married Genevieve P Wilbur, daughter of Peleg Wilbur and Sarah Blanchard, circa 1881. He married Ella F Jencks, daughter of Nathan D Jencks and Cornelia F Dexter, circa 1900. He died on 1 Mar 1918 at age 64.

+ 1125.　iii.　Emily C Lyon was born on 4 Feb 1854. She married George K Tyler circa 1872. She died on 16 Apr 1909 at age 55.

[1939]Vital Records, Foster, Providence County, RI, Cemetery records, Lyon Lot Cemetery.
[1940]Rhode Island Wills, Foster Will Book 12 page 110.
[1941]Tombstone.
[1942]Find A Grave.
[1943]Tombstone.
[1944]Ibid.
[1945]Find A Grave.
[1946]Tombstone.

Generation Four

1050. Willard C Lyon (*Alden, Benjamin, John*) was born in 1822 at Ithaca, Tompkins County, NY. He married Elane Ann Hooker, daughter of Margaret (--?--). He died on 17 Jan 1898 at Allegany County, NY.[1947] He was buried at Until the Day of Dawn Cemetery, Angelica, Allegany County, NY.[1948]

Elane Ann Hooker was born in Nov 1829. She married Eilan Hooker.[1949] She died on 28 Jan 1915 at Dunkirk, Chautauqua County, NY, at age 85.[1950]

Known children of Willard C Lyon and Elane Ann Hooker all born at Alleghany County, NY, were as follows:

- 1126. i. Calvin W Lyon was born circa 1850. He died on 17 May 1891 at Huntington, IN; 18 May 1891.[1951]
- 1127. ii. Harriet A Lyon was born circa 1852. She married Willard H Hooker circa 1885.[1952]
- + 1128. iii. Frank J Lyon was born circa 1855. He married Ella (--?--).
- + 1129. iv. Della A Lyon was born circa 1857. She married Hiram Mattison.
- + 1130. v. Martin Grover Lyon was born on 26 Jul 1862. He married Lillan Julia Pugh on 27 Dec 1892 at Dunkirk, Chautauqua County, NY. He died on 28 Jun 1934 at age 71.
- 1131. vi. Harry Benjamin Lyon DD L was born on 15 Mar 1873. He married Marjorie Alling on 25 Apr 1899 at Buffalo, Erie County, NY. He married Jane C Connolly on 6 Apr 1917.[1953] He died on 6 May 1974 at age 101.[1954] He was buried at Forest Hills Cemetery, Fredonia, Chautaugua County, NY.[1955]

  He was dentist and postmaster.

  Marjorie Alling was born on 25 Dec 1873 at Dunkery, Chatuauqua County, NY. She died on 10 Jul 1902 at age 28.[1956] She was buried at Forest Hills Cemetery, Fredonia, Chautaugua County, NY.[1957]

  Jane C Connolly was born in 1874 at Canada. She died on 17 Dec 1962 at Chautauqua County, NY.[1958] She was buried at Forest Hills Cemetery, Fredonia, Chautaugua County, NY.[1959]

1054. Helen Lyon (*Alden, Benjamin, John*) was born on 1 Mar 1835 at Allegany County, NY. She married Nathan Emerson circa 1854.[1960] She died on 18 Mar 1906 at Harrisville, Alcona County, MI, at age 71.[1961]

Nathan Emerson was born in 1828 at Allegany County, NY. He died on 10 Dec 1905 at Harrisville, Alcona County, MI.[1962] He was buried at Springport Cemetery, Harrisville, Alcona, MI.[1963]

[1947]Lois M Barris, *Genealogical Information Reported in Dunkirk NY Newspapers*.
[1948]Find A Grave.
[1949]Ibid.
[1950]Ibid.
[1951]Barris, *Genealogical Information Reported in Dunkirk NY Newspapers*.
[1952]United States 1900 Census, Foster, McKean County, PA.
[1953]John P Downs, *History of Chautauqua County, NY and its People* (Boston: American Historical Society, 1921).
[1954]Tombstone.
[1955]Find A Grave.
[1956]Tombstone.
[1957]Find A Grave.
[1958]Barris, *Genealogical Information Reported in Dunkirk NY Newspapers*, 17 Dec 1962.
[1959]Find A Grave.
[1960]Michigan Death Records.
[1961]Ibid.
[1962]Ibid.
[1963]Find A Grave.

Known children of Helen Lyon and Nathan Emerson were as follows:

1132. i. Ella Emerson was born circa 1855 at Allegany County, NY.[1964]
1133. ii. Orella Emerson was born circa 1857 at Allegany County, NY.[1965]
            She was also known as Aurelia Emerson.
1134. iii. Alice Emerson was born circa 1859 at Allegany County, NY.[1966]
1135. iv. Hattie Emerson was born circa 1861 at Allegany County, NY.[1967]
1136. v. Willard Emerson was born on 31 Aug 1866 at Allegany County, NY.[1968] He died on 16 Mar 1913 at Traverse City, Grand Traverse County, MI, at age 46.[1969] He was buried at Springport Cemetery, Traverse City, Grand Traverse County, MI.
1137. vi. James F Emerson was born circa 1868.[1970]
1138. vii. George Emerson was born circa 1872 at Allegany County, NY.[1971]
1139. viii. Gertrude Emerson was born circa 1874 at Allegany County, NY.[1972]
1140. ix. Edward Emerson was born circa 1876 at Alcona, MI.[1973]

1056. Hannah Lyon (*Benjamin, Benjamin, John*) was born on 21 Sep 1823 at Chenango County, NY. She married Calvin Comstock, son of Amon Comstock and Irena (--?--), on 12 Mar 1845 at Sherburne, Chenango County, NY. She died on 15 Feb 1872 at Sherburne, Chenango County, NY, at age 48. She was buried at Westernville cemetery, Westernville, Oneida County, NY.[1974]

Calvin Comstock was born on 24 Feb 1822 at NY. He married Rachel (--?--) after 1872. He died on 21 Apr 1888 at Western, Oneida County, NY, at age 66.[1975] He was buried at Westernville cemetery, Western, Oneida County, NY.[1976]

Known children of Hannah Lyon and Calvin Comstock were as follows:

1141. i. Dr Arron Comstock was born circa 1846 at Oneida County, NY.[1977] He died on 10 Dec 1879.[1978]
1142. ii. Dr Frederick Comstock was born on 14 May 1849. He married Alice Brand, daughter of Nathan Brand and Clarinda (--?--). He died on 11 Jan 1904 at age 54.[1979] He was buried at Armory Hill Cemetery, Ilion, Herkimer County, NY.[1980]

            Alice Brand was born in 1852 at NY. She died in 1924.[1981] She was buried at Armory Hill Cemetery, Ilion, Herkimer County, NY.[1982]

1059. Mary Comstock Lyon (*Benjamin, Benjamin, John*) was born on 20 Feb 1828 at Chenango County, NY. She married Joel McComber on 8 Oct 1856 at Sherburne, Chenango County, NY. She died on 5 May 1897 at Brooklyn, Kings County, NY, at age 69.[1983]

[1964]United States 1860 Census, Scio, Allegany County, NY.
[1965]Ibid.
[1966]Ibid.
[1967]United States 1870 Census, Scio, Allegany County, NY.
[1968]Ibid.
[1969]Find A Grave.
[1970]United States 1870 Census, Scio, Allegany County, NY.
[1971]United States 1880 Census, Harrisville, Alcona County, MI.
[1972]Ibid.
[1973]Ibid.
[1974]Find A Grave.
[1975]Tombstone.
[1976]Find A Grave.
[1977]United States 1850 Census, Western, Oneida County, NY.
[1978]Lyon, *Lyon Memorial Massachusetts Families*, page 304.
[1979]Ibid.
[1980]Find A Grave.
[1981]Tombstone.
[1982]Find A Grave.

Joel McComber was born circa 1827 at NY. He died on 4 Feb 1897 at Brooklyn, Kings County, NY.[1984] He was manufacturer of boots, shoes and lasts.

Known children of Mary Comstock Lyon and Joel McComber were:

1143.   i.   Corrie D McComber was born on 17 Jun 1847 at NY.[1985]

        She was writer.

1060. Amie Mahala Lyon (*Benjamin, Benjamin, John*) was born on 17 Apr 1832 at Chenango County, NY. She married William Brooks on 12 Jun 1861 at Sherburne, Chenango County, NY. She died on 13 May 1864 at Sherburne, Chenango County, NY, at age 32.[1986] She was buried at Sherburne West Hill Cemetery, Sherburne, Chenango County, NY.[1987]

William Brooks was born in 1833 at Chenango County, NY. He died in Oct 1893 at Norwich, Chenango County, NY.[1988] He was buried at Sherburne West Hill Cemetery, Sherburne, Chenango County, NY.[1989]

Known children of Amie Mahala Lyon and William Brooks both born at Norwich, Chenango County, NY, were as follows:

1144.   i.   Merton Brooks was born on 20 Apr 1863. He died in 1865 at Norwich, Chenango County, NY.[1990] He was buried at Sherburne West Hill Cemetery, Sherburne, Chenango County, NY.[1991]

        He was also known as Alford.

1145.   ii.   (--?--) Brooks was born on 20 Apr 1864. She died on 30 Apr 1864 at Norwich, Chenango County, NY. She was buried in 1865 at Sherburne West Hill Cemetery, Sherburne, Chenango County, NY.[1992]

1061. Delia Eliza Lyon (*Benjamin, Benjamin, John*) was born on 20 Dec 1833 at Chenango County, NY. She married James P Squires on 10 Oct 1860. She died on 1 Sep 1866 at Sherburne, Chenango County, NY, at age 32.[1993]

James P Squires married Ellen Lyon, daughter of Benjamin Talbot Lyon and Mary Umphrey Rogers, circa 1867.

Known children of Delia Eliza Lyon and James P Squires all born at Sherburne, Chenango County, NY, were as follows:

1146.   i.   Fred Deville Squires was born on 20 Aug 1861. He married Mary Wright on 7 May 1885.[1994]

        Mary Wright.

1147.   ii.   Archie Lyon Squires was born on 11 Nov 1862. He married Julitta Davis on 7 Dec 1886.[1995]

        He was also known as Arther L Squiers.

        Julitta Davis was born circa 1867 at NY.[1996]

[1983]Lyon, *Lyon Memorial Massachusetts Families*, page 302.

[1984]Ibid., page 305.

[1985]Ibid.

[1986]Ibid., page 302.

[1987]Find A Grave.

[1988]Lyon, *Lyon Memorial Massachusetts Families*, page 305.

[1989]Find A Grave.

[1990]Lyon, *Lyon Memorial Massachusetts Families*, page 305.

[1991]Find A Grave.

[1992]Ibid.

[1993]Lyon, *Lyon Memorial Massachusetts Families*, page 302.

[1994]Ibid., page 310.

[1995]United States 1900 Census, Sherburne, Chenango County, NY.

[1996]Ibid.

1148. iii. Lydia Ann Squires was born on 13 Sep 1864. She died on 13 May 1865 at Sherburne, Chenango County, NY.[1997]

1149. iv. Edward Pierce Squires was born on 1 Sep 1866. He died in Apr 1868 at Sherburne, Chenango County, NY, at age 1.[1998]

1063. Cornelia Lyon (*Benjamin, Benjamin, John*) was born on 6 Jun 1838 at Sherburne, Chenango County, NY. She married Alanzo K Dixon on 9 Oct 1861 at Chenango County, NY. She died on 6 Dec 1899 at Brooklyn, Kings County, NY, at age 61.[1999]
Attended the 1883 Lyon reunion as a descendant of Betsey T Lyon.[2000]

Known children of Cornelia Lyon and Alanzo K Dixon both born at Smyrna, Chenango County, NY, were as follows:

1150. i. Dr Herbert Sidney Dixon was born on 18 Jan 1866. He married Ethel Merritt.[2001]
Attended the 1883 Lyon reunion as a descendant of Betsey T Lyon.

1151. ii. Mary Lyon Dixon was born on 19 May 1870. She married Clarence Riggs on 30 Jun 1898.[2002]
Attended the 1883 Lyon reunion as a descendant of Betsey T Lyon.

1064. Roxie Anna Lyon (*Benjamin, Benjamin, John*) was born on 17 Sep 1840 at Sherburne, Chenango County, NY. She married Kenyon Terry on 16 Oct 1872 at Smyrna, Chenango County, NY.
Attended the 1883 Lyon reunion as a descendant of Betsey T Lyon.[2003]

Kenyon Terry died on 28 Jun 1900 at Norwich, Chenango County, NY.[2004]
Known children of Roxie Anna Lyon and Kenyon Terry were as follows:

1152. i. Elvira N Terry.[2005]

1153. ii. Laura Ethel Terry was born at Norwich, Chenango County, NY. She died on 15 Mar 1885 at Chenango County, NY.[2006]
Attended the 1883 Lyon reunion as a descendant of Betsey T Lyon.

1066. Ellen Lyon (*Benjamin, Benjamin, John*) was born on 19 Aug 1844 at NY.[2007] She married James P Squires circa 1867.
Attended the 1883 Lyon reunion as a descendant of Betsey T Lyon.

James P Squires married Delia Eliza Lyon, daughter of Benjamin Talbot Lyon and Mary Umphrey Rogers, on 10 Oct 1860.
Known children of Ellen Lyon and James P Squires both born at Sherburne, Chenango County, NY, were as follows:

1154. i. Arnon Squires was born on 6 Oct 1869. He married Caroline Wylie on 28 May 1895. He married Gertrude Cooper on 24 Sep 1902.[2008]

Caroline Wylie died on 24 Apr 1901.[2009]

[1997] Lyon, *Lyon Memorial Massachusetts Families*, page 305.
[1998] Ibid.
[1999] Ibid., page 302.
[2000] *Lyon Reunion of 1883.*
[2001] Lyon, *Lyon Memorial Massachusetts Families*, page 310.
[2002] Ibid.
[2003] *1883 Lyon Reunion.*
[2004] Lyon, *Lyon Memorial Massachusetts Families*, page 306.
[2005] *Surrogate Court Records, Chenango County, NY*, Liber J, page 353.
[2006] Lyon, *Lyon Memorial Massachusetts Families*, page 306.
[2007] Ibid., page 302.
[2008] Ibid., page 311.

Gertrude Cooper.
1155.   ii.   Delia Eliza Squires was born on 9 Aug 1871. She died on 9 Sep 1871 at Sherburne, Chenango County, NY.[2010]

1068. William Wicks Lyon (*Benjamin, Benjamin, John*) was born on 30 Dec 1849 at Sherburne, Chenango County, NY. He married Cora A Karr, daughter of Huse Karr and Ruth (--?--), on 16 Aug 1876 at Smyrna, Chenango County, NY.

At age 23 William W Lyon started clerking in the A K Dixon hardware store. Later he and C L Ferris bought out Dixon and under the name of Lyon and Ferris opened a store with a full line of stoves; hardware, whips, paints, oils & agricultural implements on School St.
He was liberal in religious views, a stanch Republican, trustee of the village corporation and grandmaster of the IOOF lodge of Smyrna. He was hardware store.

Cora A Karr was born in 1856.[2011] She died on 28 Jun 1901 at Chenango County, NY. She was buried at Sherburne West Hill cemetery, Sherburne, Chenango County, NY.[2012]
Known children of William Wicks Lyon and Cora A Karr were:
+ 1156.   i.   Edward Benjamin Lyon was born on 4 Apr 1879 at Smyrna, Chenango County, NY. He married Blanch Boynton.

1069. Edward Percy Lyon (*Benjamin, Benjamin, John*) was born on 9 Apr 1855 at Sherburne, Chenango County, NY. He married Mary E Shepardson on 20 Sep 1887 at Smyrna, Chenango County, NY. He died on 28 Nov 1928 at Brooklyn, Kings County, NY, at age 73.[2013]
Edward P Lyon was living with his sister Mary C McComber in New York City.

Mary E Shepardson died on 5 Mar 1929 at Brooklyn, Kings County, NY. She was lawyer in New York City.[2014]
Known children of Edward Percy Lyon and Mary E Shepardson were as follows:
1157.   i.   Edna Shepardson Lyon was born on 12 Jul 1888 at New York Ciity, New York County, NY.[2015]
1158.   ii.   Percy Shepardson Lyon was born on 31 Dec 1890 at Brooklyn, Kings County, NY. He married Elizabeth Fragas Jones on 17 Jan 1925 at Dover, Kent County, DE.[2016] He died in Jan 1970 at Philadelphia, Philadelphia County, PA, at age 79.[2017]
He was mechanical engineer.
Elizabeth Fragas Jones was born circa 1897 at Dover, Kent County, DE.[2018]
1159.   iii.   Harold Shepardson Lyon was born on 26 May 1894 at Brooklyn, Kings County, NY. He married Ruth K (--?--).[2019] He died in Sep 1967 at New York Ciity, New York County, NY, at age 73.[2020]
+ 1160.   iv.   Dorothy Shepardson Lyon was born on 22 Feb 1897 at Brooklyn, Kings County, NY. She married Arthur L Nelson on 20 Sep 1920 at Brooklyn, Kings County, NY. She and Arthur L Nelson were divorced on 20 Jan 1940. She died on 16 Sep 1946 at Waban, Middlesex County, MA, at age 49.

[2009]Ibid.
[2010]Ibid., page 305.
[2011]Tombstone.
[2012]Find A Grave.
[2013]"The Lyon's Tale", May 1991, page 29.
[2014]Lyon, *Lyon Memorial Massachusetts Families*, page 307.
[2015]Ibid.
[2016]Marriage Record, Delaware.
[2017]Social Security Death Index.
[2018]Marriage Record, Delaware.
[2019]World War II Draft Records.
[2020]Social Security Death Index.

1073. Hiram Spencer Lyon (*John, Benjamin, John*) was born on 15 Sep 1831 at Smyrna, Chenango County, NY. He married Cornelia B Packard on 14 Oct 1861.[2021]

He was carpenter and fruit grower.[2022]

Cornelia B Packard was born on 18 Jul 1841.[2023]
Known children of Hiram Spencer Lyon and Cornelia B Packard all born at WI were as follows:
1161.   i.   Alice Millerd Lyon was born on 19 Jul 1863.[2024]
+ 1162. ii. Cyrus Willard Lyon was born on 16 Mar 1878. He married Celia (--?--) circa 1898.
1163.   iii. Mary Lovinia Lyon was born on 26 Jul 1880.[2025]
1164.   iv. Sena Rosina Lyon was born on 10 Dec 1883.[2026]
            She was worked at a chair factory.

1074. John Whitman Lyon (*John, Benjamin, John*) was born on 17 May 1833 at Smyrna, Chenango County, NY. He married Hannah U Thompson on 11 Feb 1877. He died in 1917 at Fayette County, IA.[2027] He was buried at Eden Cemetery, Saint Lucas, Fayette County, IA.[2028]

Hannah U Thompson was born in Apr 1848 at WI. She died on 26 Jan 1914 at Fayette County, IA, at age 65. She was buried at Eden Cemetery, Saint Lucas, Fayette County, IA.[2029]
Known children of John Whitman Lyon and Hannah U Thompson were:
+ 1165.   i.   Alice L Lyon was born on 26 Jan 1878 at IA. She married Abraham Lincoln Ridley on 10 Jan 1899.

1075. Sarah Deborah Lyon (*John, Benjamin, John*)[2030] was born on 5 Jun 1836 at Smyrna, Chenango County, NY.[2031] She married Sidney Ferris on 24 Sep 1857 at Smyrna, Chenango County, NY.[2032] She died on 25 Mar 1905 at age 68.[2033]

Sidney Ferris[2034] was born circa 1826 at NY.[2035]
Known children of Sarah Deborah Lyon and Sidney Ferris were as follows:
1166.   i.   Norman E Ferris[2036] was born on 26 Jul 1860 at Plymouth, Chenango County, NY.[2037] He married Jennie P Burrel on 15 Dec 1885.[2038] He died in Sep 1898 at Sumner, Bremer County, IA, at age 38.[2039]
1167.   ii. Cora M Ferris[2040] was born on 27 Jul 1862 at IL.[2041,2042] She married Frank Becker on 15 Mar 1881.

[2021]Lyon, *Lyon Memorial Massachusetts Families*, page 307.
[2022]Ibid.
[2023]Ibid.
[2024]Ibid.
[2025]Ibid.
[2026]Ibid.
[2027]Tombstone.
[2028]Find A Grave.
[2029]Ibid.
[2030]Lyon, *Lyon Memorial Massachusetts Families*, page 303.
[2031]Ibid.
[2032]Ibid., page 307.
[2033]Ibid., page 303.
[2034]Ibid., page 307.
[2035]United States 1880 Census, Windsor, Fayette County, IA.
[2036]Lyon, *Lyon Memorial Massachusetts Families*, page 308.
[2037]Ibid.
[2038]Ibid., page 311.
[2039]Ibid., page 308.
[2040]Ibid.

Frank Becker was born in Jul 1854 at WI.[2043]

1168.   iii.   Hattie A Ferris[2044] was born on 15 Nov 1869 at Sumner, Republic County, IA.[2045] She died on 3 Jan 1879 at Sumner, Republic County, IA, at age 9.[2046]

1076. Benjamin Theodore Lyon (*John, Benjamin, John*) was born on 26 Nov 1846 at Smyrna, Chenango County, NY. He married Emma R (--?--) on 11 Nov 1868 at Plymouth, Chenango County, NY.[2047] He died on 26 Apr 1910 at age 63.[2048] He was buried at White Rock Cemetery, Sumner, Republic County, KS.[2049]

Emma R (--?--) was born in May 1849 at NY. She died on 27 Feb 1919 at Republic County, KS, at age 69.[2050] She was buried at White Rock Cemetery, Sumner, Republic County, KS.[2051]

Known children of Benjamin Theodore Lyon and Emma R (--?--) both born at Sumner, Republic County, IA, were as follows:

1169.   i.   Carrie Minnie Lyon was born on 3 Apr 1870. She died on 17 Mar 1879 at Sumner, Republic County, IA, at age 8.[2052] She was buried at White Rock Cemetery, Sumner, Republic County, KS.[2053]

1170.   ii.   Clara May Lyon was born on 8 Nov 1880. She died on 2 Dec 1902 at KS at age 22.[2054] She was buried at White Rock Cemetery, Sumner, Republic County, KS.[2055]

1077. Samuel Venable Lyon (*Reuben, Benjamin, John*) was born circa 1825 at Norwich, Chenango County, NY. He married Julia Frances Duryea.[2056]
He was marble worker.

Julia Frances Duryea was born in Dec 1825 at NY.[2057]
Known children of Samuel Venable Lyon and Julia Frances Duryea all born at NY were as follows:

1171.   i.   Henry D Lyon was born circa 1849.[2058]
           He was marble worker.

+ 1172.   ii.   William V Lyon was born in May 1852. He married Sarah E (--?--) circa 1874.

1173.   iii.   Charles Lyon was born circa 1861.[2059]

1174.   iv.   Flora Lyon was born in Mar 1865.[2060]

1079. John E Lyon (*Reuben, Benjamin, John*) was born circa 1837 at Norwich, Chenango County, NY.[2061] He married Emma Burbank.[2062]

[2041]Ibid.

[2042]United States 1880 Census, Windsor, Fayette County, IA.

[2043]United States 1900 Census, Taylor, Harrison County, IA.

[2044]Lyon, *Lyon Memorial Massachusetts Families*, page 308.

[2045]Ibid.

[2046]Ibid.

[2047]Ibid.

[2048]Tombstone.

[2049]Find A Grave.

[2050]Tombstone.

[2051]Ibid.

[2052]Lyon, *Lyon Memorial Massachusetts Families*, page 308.

[2053]Find A Grave.

[2054]Lyon, *Lyon Memorial Massachusetts Families*, page 308.

[2055]Find A Grave.

[2056]United States 1870 Census, Norwich, Chenango County, NY.

[2057]United States 1900 Census, Norwich, Chenango County, NY.

[2058]United States 1870 Census, Norwich, Chenango County, NY.

[2059]Ibid.

[2060]United States 1900 Census, Norwich, Chenango County, NY.

[2061]United States 1850 Census, Norwich, Chenango County, NY.

[2062]Lyon, *Lyon Memorial Massachusetts Families*, page 303.

He was also known as Emory Lyon.

Known children of John E Lyon and Emma Burbank were:
1175.   i.   Nellie Burbank Lyon.[2063]

1086. Hattie Bell Lyon (*Reuben, Benjamin, John*) was born on 29 Jun 1856 at Ithaca, Tompkins County, NY. She married Iram Brewer.[2064]

Known children of Hattie Bell Lyon and Iram Brewer were:
1176.   i.   Frederick Brewer was born in Aug 1882 at IA.[2065]

1087. Cyrus Lyon (*Alexander, Cyrus, John*) was born circa 1819 at NY; Tombstone gives birth as 13 May 1813 but the census imply c 1819. Additional information says he was born in Madison County, NY which is north of Chenango County NY and adjacent to it. He married Sarah Ann Cozine, daughter of William Cozine, on 23 Mar 1854 at Carroll County, MO.[2066] He died on 13 Jul 1864; "Killed by Bloody Bill Anderson's Guerillas."[2067] He was buried at Old Pleasant Park Cemetery, Carroll County, MO.[2068]
    He was farmer.

Sarah Ann Cozine was born circa 1833 at KT.[2069] She married Falton Blevans on 18 Jan 1866 at Carroll County, MO.[2070] She married James Wheatley on 1 Jan 1878 at Carroll County, MO.[2071]
    Known children of Cyrus Lyon and Sarah Ann Cozine all born at MO were as follows:
1177.   i.   George A Lyon was born circa 1855. He married Maura McCumber on 15 Oct 1877 at Carroll County, MO.[2072]
1178.   ii.   Sarah Alice Lyon was born circa 1858. She married James L McCumber on 15 Oct 1877 at Carroll County, MO.[2073]
                James L McCumber died before 1880.[2074]
+ 1179.   iii. "General" Patterson Lyon was born in Jul 1861. He married Hattie L Hanlon. He died on 17 Jun 1951 at age 89.

1088. Elizabeth Lyon (*Alexander, Cyrus, John*) was born on 10 Jan 1821. She married George W Laughlin circa 1840. She died on 9 May 1909 at Dover, Cuyahoga County, OH, at age 88.[2075]

George W Laughlin was born on 3 Aug 1815 at PA. He died on 29 May 1872 at OH at age 56.[2076]
Known children of Elizabeth Lyon and George W Laughlin all born at OH were as follows:
1180.   i.   Eliza Laughlin was born circa 1843.[2077]
1181.   ii.   Laura Laughlin was born circa 1844.[2078]
1182.   iii. Mary Ann Laughlin was born circa 1847.[2079]

[2063] Ibid.
[2064] Ibid.
[2065] United States 1900 Census, Philadelphia, Philadelphia County, PA.
[2066] Missouri Marriage Records, Carroll County.
[2067] Tombstone.
[2068] Find A Grave.
[2069] United States 1880 Census, Rea, Carroll County, MO.
[2070] Missouri Marriage Records, Carroll County.
[2071] Marriage Record, Carroll County, MO.
[2072] Missouri Marriage Records, Carroll County.
[2073] Ibid.
[2074] United States 1880 Census, Rea, Carroll County, MO.
[2075] Death Records, Cuyahoga County.
[2076] Tombstone.
[2077] United States 1850 Census, Dover, Cuyahoga County, OH.
[2078] Ibid.

1183.   iv.   Frederick Laughlin was born in Feb 1851.[2080] He married Agusta (--?--).

Agusta (--?--) was born in Nov 1863 at OH.[2081]

1184.   v.   Alice Laughlin was born circa 1854.[2082]

1185.   vi.   George Laughlin was born circa 1857.[2083]

1186.   vii.   Rosa Laughlin was born circa 1859.[2084]

1187.   viii.   Cyrus W Laughlin was born in Oct 1864.[2085] He married Mamy A (--?--).

Mamy A (--?--) was born in Aug 1866 at OH.[2086]

1089. Lucius Millard Lyon (*Alexander, Cyrus, John*) was born on 6 Sep 1825 at DeRuyter, Madison County, NY.[2087] He married Lucinda Lucetta Kittridge, daughter of William Kittridge, on 5 Sep 1850 at MI. He died on 23 Sep 1891 at Fairhaven, Whatcom County, WA, at age 66. He was buried at Mount Pleasant Cemetery, Seattle, King County, WA.[2088]

He was gardener. Lucius Lyon died in Washington State but the death records indicate that he was a resident on Ease Scyricus, MI and list his father as being Alexander Lyon who was born in NY.[2089]

Lucinda Lucetta Kittridge[2090] was born on 16 Jul 1829 at Hartland, Windsor County, VT. She died on 21 Dec 1900 at WA at age 71.[2091] She was buried at Mount Pleasant Cemetery, Seattle, King County, WA.[2092]

Known children of Lucius Millard Lyon and Lucinda Lucetta Kittridge were as follows:

+ 1188.   i.   Alice Maria Lyon was born on 20 Sep 1851 at Lapeer County, MI. She married Francis Adelbert Warner. She died on 10 Mar 1947 at Jacksonville, Duval County, FL, at age 95.

1189.   ii.   Cyrus W Lyon was born on 25 Oct 1853 at Allison, Lapeer County, MI.[2093] He married Emma (--?--) circa 1884.

He was farmer.

Emma (--?--) was born in Jul 1863 at MI.[2094]

1190.   iii.   Lucius Millard Lyon was born in Sep 1856 at Allison, Lapeer County, MI.[2095]

+ 1191.   iv.   William Kittridge Lyon was born in Nov 1859 at MI. He married Lottie Loretta Stevens circa 1887. He died on 21 Oct 1942 at Bellingham, Whatcom County, WA, at age 82. He was buried at Bayview Cemetery, Bellingham, Whatcom County, WA.

+ 1192.   v.   Frank B Lyon was born in Dec 1861 at MI. He married Margaret Anne Still circa 1887.

1095. Polly Lyon (*Daniel, Cyrus, John*) was born in Oct 1827 at Chenango County, NY. She married Hiram Gustin say 1852. She died in 1907 at Madison County, NY.[2096] She was buried at Earlville Cemetery, Earlville, Madison County, NY.[2097]

[2079]Ibid.

[2080]United States 1900 Census, Dover, Cuyahoga County, OH.

[2081]Ibid.

[2082]United States 1860 Census, Dover, Cuyahoga County, OH.

[2083]Ibid.

[2084]Ibid.

[2085]United States 1900 Census, Dover, Cuyahoga County, OH.

[2086]Ibid.

[2087]"The Lyon's Tale", Oct 1999, Volume 50, issue 4, page 137.

[2088]Tim Merrill, *Descendants of Alexander Lyon* (2 Dec 1999), Descendants of Alexander Lyon, dated 2 Dec 1999.

[2089]Washington State Death Records.

[2090]Michigan Death Records, East Saginaw, Saginaw County, MI.

[2091]Tombstone.

[2092]Find A Grave.

[2093]RootsWeb WorldConnect Project, Tim Merrill database.

[2094]United States 1900 Census, Saginaw, Saginaw County, MI.

[2095]United States 1910 Census, Wrangell, AK.

[2096]Tombstone.

[2097]Find A Grave.

In the 1900 census Maria said she had had 3 children and all were living. She was also known as Maria Lyon.[2098]

Hiram Gustin was born in 1824 at NY. He died in 1908 at Madison County, NY. He was buried at Earlville Cemetery, Earlville, Madison County, NY.[2099]

Known children of Polly Lyon and Hiram Gustin all born at NY were as follows:

1193.   i.   Lucius A Gustin was born in 1854.[2100] He married Josephine T (--?--). He married Mary Knott in 1874. He died in 1921. He was buried at Christ Church Cemetery, Sherburne, Chenango County, NY.[2101]

   Josephine T (--?--) died on 21 Dec 1884 at Chenango County, NY. She was buried at Christ Church Cemetery, Sherburne, Chenango County, NY.[2102]

1194.   ii.   Alice Gustin was born in 1863.[2103]

1195.   iii. Theresa Gustin was born in 1866.[2104] She married Frank Merit Lyon, son of Merritt L Lyon and Mary Ette (--?--).[2105] She died in 1944.[2106]

   Frank Merit Lyon was born in 1866. He died in 1934.[2107]

1097. Cyrus Ralph Lyon (*Daniel, Cyrus, John*) was born circa 1831 at NY. He married Lucy (--?--) say 1858.

He was cooper.

Lucy (--?--) was born circa 1837 at NY.[2108]

Known children of Cyrus Ralph Lyon and Lucy (--?--) were:

1196.   i.   Arlon Lyon was born circa 1860.[2109]

1098. Jason James Lyon (*Daniel, Cyrus, John*) was born on 22 May 1833 at Lincklaen, Chenango County, NY. He married Rosella Lucinda Gould, daughter of William Gould and Hannah Austin, on 24 Sep 1856 at Springfield, Sangamon County, IL. He died on 15 Apr 1914 at Trumbull, Clay County, NE, at age 80.[2110] He was buried at Greenwood Cemetery, Hastings, Adams County, NE.[2111]

He was cattleman and sold windmills.

Rosella Lucinda Gould was born on 8 Mar 1839 at Greenfield, Greene County, IL. She died on 13 Sep 1920 at Trumbull, Clay County, NE, at age 81. She was buried at Greenwood Cemetery, Hastings, Adams County, NE.[2112]

Known children of Jason James Lyon and Rosella Lucinda Gould were as follows:

1197.   i.   Lawrence L Lyon.[2113]

[2098]Lyons, *William Lyon of Roxbury, MA and Some of his Descendants*, page 133.

[2099]Tombstone.

[2100]Find A Grave.

[2101]Ibid.

[2102]Ibid.

[2103]Ibid.

[2104]Ibid.

[2105]Ibid.

[2106]Ibid.

[2107]Ibid.

[2108]United States 1870 Census, Otselic, Chenango County, NY.

[2109]Ibid.

[2110]Tombstone.

[2111]Find A Grave.

[2112]Ibid.

[2113]Royce, *Biographical and Historical Memoirs of Adams, Clay, Hall and Hamilton Counties, Nebraska*.

1198. ii. Alice Lyon was born circa 1859 at IL. She married Archie Murdock. She died in 1885.[2114]

Archie Murdock was born circa 1850 at Scotland.[2115]

+ 1199. iii. Frank M Lyon was born in Apr 1860 at IL. He married Samantha M Collins, daughter of Isaac Collins and Ellen M (--?--), circa 1885.

+ 1200. iv. Alfred Sheriden Lyon was born circa 1866 at IL. He married Mabel D Wright.

+ 1201. v. William D Lyon was born circa 1868 at IL. He married Afka M Johnson. He died in 1954.

+ 1202. vi. Lovina Harriett Lyon was born in Apr 1869 at IL. She married John E Schertz. She died on 31 Jan 1933 at Nampa, Canyon County, ID, at age 63. She was buried at Kohlerlawn Cemetery, Nampa, Canyon County, ID.

+ 1203. vii. Charles Jason Lyon was born on 7 Feb 1871 at Loami, Sangamon County, IL. He married Emeline Deborah Maxson, daughter of Orson Maxson and Adelia (--?--), on 3 Jul 1896. He died on 5 Sep 1937 at Hastings, Adams County, NE, at age 66. He was buried at Greenwood Cemetery, Hastings, Adams County, NE.

1204. viii. Maggie I Lyon was born circa 1876 at NE.[2116]

1205. ix. Sarah E Lyon was born in Jan 1879 at NE.[2117]

+ 1206. x. Florence Lucretia Lyon was born in 1881 at NE. She married George J Maraott. She died in 1961. She was buried at Greenwood Cemetery, Hastings, Adams County, NE.

1099. Myron D Lyon (*Daniel, Cyrus, John*) was born circa 1836 at NY.[2118] He married Olive (--?--).[2119]

Olive (--?--) was born circa 1838 at NY.[2120]
Known children of Myron D Lyon and Olive (--?--) were:
1207. i. Vernelia H Lyon was born circa 1870 at NY.[2121]

1104. Charles C Lyon (*Alfred, Cyrus, John*) was born on 16 Jan 1833 at Sherburne, Chenango County, NY. He married Charlotte Antoinette Owen circa 1855. He married Clara M Daugherty, daughter of Alonzo Daugherty and Thankful (--?--), on 13 Jun 1877. He died on 12 Nov 1903 at New London, Waupaca County, WI, at age 70.[2122]

Charlotte Antoinette Owen was born circa 1831 at NJ. She died on 1 Jun 1873 at WI.[2123] She was buried at Maple Creek Cemetery #1, New London, Outagamie County, WI.[2124]

Known children of Charles C Lyon and Charlotte Antoinette Owen all born at New London, Waupaca County, WI, were as follows:

+ 1208. i. Charles L Lyon was born on 18 Nov 1856. He married Lillian Payton circa 1884.

1209. ii. Anna Melinda Lyon was born on 15 Jun 1860. She died on 19 May 1863 at New London, Waupaca County, WI, at age 2.[2125]

She was also known as Charlotte Lyon.

+ 1210. iii. Alfred Austin Lyon was born on 17 Mar 1864. He married Mary Rief circa 1892.

[2114] Ibid.
[2115] United States 1880 Census, Scoville, Hamilton County, NY.
[2116] Ibid., Scovllle, Hamilton County, NE.
[2117] Ibid.
[2118] United States 1850 Census, Lincklaen, Chenango County, NY.
[2119] United States 1880 Census, Scovllle, Hamilton County, NE.
[2120] Ibid.
[2121] Ibid.
[2122] Lyon, *Lyon Memorial Massachusetts Families*, page 308.
[2123] Ibid.
[2124] Find A Grave.
[2125] Lyon, *Lyon Memorial Massachusetts Families*, page 308.

1211. iv. Albert Lyon was born on 24 Dec 1868. He died on 4 Jun 1872 at age 3.[2126] He was buried at Maple Creek Cemetery #1, New London, Outagamie County, WI.[2127]

Clara M Daugherty was born circa 1843 at WI. She married (--?--) Webber.[2128]
There were no known children of Charles C Lyon and Clara M Daugherty.

1108. Milo Alfred Lyon (*Alfred, Cyrus, John*) was born on 14 Apr 1841 at Sherburne, Chenango County, NY. He married Helen A Robinson, daughter of John Robinson and Sophia (--?--), on 19 Jun 1864 at New London, Waupaca County, WI.[2129] He died in 1941 at Monrovia, Los Angeles County, CA.[2130]

Helen A Robinson was born circa 1845 at IL.[2131]
Known children of Milo Alfred Lyon and Helen A Robinson were as follows:
+ 1212. i. Ida Lyon was born on 27 Jan 1869 at WI. She married Bert A Lipke on 9 Jul 1889.
+ 1213. ii. John C Lyon was born on 1 Apr 1873 at New London, Waupaca County, WI. He married Mable R Trayser on 18 Oct 1899 at New London, Waupaca County, WI. He died in 1967 at New London, Waupaca County, WI.

1109. Sarah S Lyon (*Alfred, Cyrus, John*) was born on 18 Dec 1847 at Sherburne, Chenango County, NY. She married Samuel W Bennett on 20 Oct 1862. She married Stephen H Snyder on 11 Jan 1902.[2132] She died on 19 Feb 1930 at Green Bay, Brown County, WI, at age 82.[2133] She was buried at Fort Howard Memorial Park, Green Bay, Brown County, WI.[2134]

Samuel W Bennett was born on 3 Jul 1835 at Binghamton, Broome County, NY. He died on 29 Jul 1897 at Brown County, WI, at age 62.[2135] He was buried at Fort Howard Memorial Park, Green Bay, Brown County, WI.[2136]
Known children of Sarah S Lyon and Samuel W Bennett were as follows:
1214. i. Harlow J Bennett was born on 24 Aug 1864 at WI. He married Catherine (--?--).

Catherine (--?--) was born circa 1870 at OH.[2137]
1215. ii. Sidney A Bennett was born on 15 Apr 1866.[2138] He died on 3 Jan 1869 at age 2.[2139]
1216. iii. Helen M Bennett was born on 25 Mar 1868.[2140] She died on 14 Jul 1894 at age 26.[2141]
1217. iv. Alfred Lyon Bennett was born on 22 Mar 1870 at New London, Waupaca County, WI. He married Cora D Snyder on 5 Sep 1889. He died on 13 Oct 1940 at Marinette, Marinette County, WI, at age 70.[2142]

[2126]Tombstone.
[2127]Find A Grave.
[2128]United States 1880 Census, New London, Waupaca County, WI.
[2129]Lyon, *Lyon Memorial Massachusetts Families*, page 308.
[2130]Lyons, *William Lyon of Roxbury, MA and Some of his Descendants*, p 212.
[2131]United States 1870 Census, New London, Waupaca County, WI.
[2132]Lyon, *Lyon Memorial Massachusetts Families*, page 308.
[2133]Lyons, *William Lyon of Roxbury, MA and Some of his Descendants*, p 221.
[2134]Find A Grave.
[2135]Tombstone.
[2136]Find A Grave.
[2137]United States 1920 Census, Omaha, Douglas County, NE.
[2138]Lyon, *Lyon Memorial Massachusetts Families*, page 309.
[2139]Ibid.
[2140]Ibid.
[2141]Lyons, *William Lyon of Roxbury, MA and Some of his Descendants*, p 212.
[2142]Ibid., p 295.

Cora D Snyder was born on 14 May 1870 at Wisconsin Rapids, Wood County, WI. She died on 16 Apr 1925 at Menominee, Menominee County, MI, at age 54.[2143]

1218.   v.   Leon L Bennett was born on 29 Jan 1873. He died on 27 Aug 1874 at age 1.[2144]

1219.   vi.   Martha M Bennett was born on 13 Dec 1875.[2145]

1220.   vii.   Ruth Ann Bennett was born on 14 Dec 1877.[2146] She was buried at Fort Howard Memorial Park, Green Bay, Brown County, WI.[2147]

1221.   viii.   John C Bennett was born on 9 May 1880.[2148]

1222.   ix.   George L Bennett was born on 9 Sep 1882. He died on 14 Jul 1883.[2149]

1223.   x.   Samuel W Bennett was born on 7 Feb 1884. He died on 10 Apr 1960 at Brown County, OH, at age 76.[2150] He was buried at Fort Howard Memorial Park, Green Bay, Brown County, OH.[2151]

1224.   xi.   Melinda E Bennett was born on 10 Sep 1886.[2152]

1225.   xii.   Jennie May Bennett was born on 19 May 1889. She died on 4 Feb 1956 at Brown County, WI, at age 66.[2153] She was buried at Fort Howard Memorial Park, Green Bay, Brown County, WI.[2154]

Stephen H Snyder was born on 10 Apr 1841 at NY. He died on 28 Oct 1841 at Brown County, WI.[2155] He was buried at Fort Howard Memorial Park, Green Bay, Brown County, WI.[2156]

There were no known children of Sarah S Lyon and Stephen H Snyder.

1122.   Emory Darastur Lyon (*John, Reuben, John*) was born circa 1830 at Foster, Providence County, RI. He married Julia M Hill. He died on 8 Jul 1914 at Foster, Providence County, RI; Cause of death was heart disease.[2157] He was buried at Lyon Lot Cemetery, Foster, Providence County, RI.[2158]

He was carpenter than farmer.

Julia M Hill was born on 2 Feb 1830 at Foster, Providence County, RI. She died on 6 Feb 1911 at Foster, Providence County, RI, at age 81; cause of death was Bright's Disease.[2159] She was buried at Lyon Lot Cemetery, Foster, Providence County, RI.[2160]

Known children of Emory Darastur Lyon and Julia M Hill were as follows:

+ 1226.   i.   Mary Etta Lyon was born circa 1854 at RI. She married Henry Lester Place. She died in 1919 at RI. She was buried at Pocasset Cemetery, Cranston, Providence County, RI.

1227.   ii.   Idella Maria Lyon was born on 1 Jul 1861 at Foster, Providence County, RI. She married Eugene F Bennett. She died in 1939.[2161] She was buried at Pocasset Cemetery, Cranston, Providence County, RI.[2162]

[2143] Ibid.

[2144] Ibid., page 212.

[2145] Lyon, *Lyon Memorial Massachusetts Families*, page 309.

[2146] Ibid.

[2147] Find A Grave.

[2148] Lyon, *Lyon Memorial Massachusetts Families*, page 309.

[2149] Ibid.

[2150] Tombstone.

[2151] Find A Grave.

[2152] Lyon, *Lyon Memorial Massachusetts Families*, page 309.

[2153] Tombstone.

[2154] Find A Grave.

[2155] Tombstone.

[2156] Find A Grave.

[2157] Vital Records, Foster, Providence County, RI, Lyon Lot Cemetery.

[2158] Ibid.

[2159] Ibid.

[2160] Ibid.

[2161] Tombstone.

[2162] Find A Grave.

Eugene F Bennett was born in 1856. He died in 1939.[2163] He was buried at Pocasset Cemetery, Cranston, Providence County, RI.[2164]

1124. George Phillips Lyon (*Sheldon, Reuben, John*) was born on 3 Oct 1853 at Foster, Providence County, RI. He married Adella M Johnson, daughter of William H Johnson and Susan A (--?--), circa 1875. He married Genevieve P Wilbur, daughter of Peleg Wilbur and Sarah Blanchard, circa 1881. He married Ella F Jencks, daughter of Nathan D Jencks and Cornelia F Dexter, circa 1900. He died on 1 Mar 1918 at age 64; Cause of death given as Angina Pectoris.[2165] He was buried at Lyon Lot Cemetery, Foster, Providence County, RI.[2166]

In the 1910 census George's wife was said to be Ella F Lyon and that he had been married three times.

Adella M Johnson was born on 15 Oct 1857. She died on 28 Jun 1880 at age 22; Adella's death was due to cancer.[2167]

There were no known children of George Phillips Lyon and Adella M Johnson.

Genevieve P Wilbur was born on 15 Feb 1868 at Coventry, Providence County, RI. She died on 24 Jun 1897 at age 29; cause of death was consumption.[2168]

Known children of George Phillips Lyon and Genevieve P Wilbur were:

    1228.   i.   Elsie M Lyon was born on 17 Mar 1896 at Foster, Providence County, RI. She died on 9 Mar 1906 at Foster, Providence County, RI, at age 9; cause of death was consumtpion.[2169] She was buried at Lyon Lot Cemetery, Foster, Providence, RI.[2170]

Ella F Jencks was born in 1855. She died in 1938.[2171] She was buried at Ballou Cemetery, Cumberland, Providence County, RI; Ella Lyon is listed as the third wife of George P Lyon on his families tombstone but her inscription on it wasn't completed and there is no individual stone for her in the Lyon Lot Cemetery. Instead, she was buried in the Ballow Cemetery in Cumberland.[2172]

There were no known children of George Phillips Lyon and Ella F Jencks.

1125. Emily C Lyon (*Sheldon, Reuben, John*) was born on 4 Feb 1854 at Foster, Providence County, RI. She married George K Tyler circa 1872. She died on 16 Apr 1909 at age 55.[2173] She was buried at Moosup Valley Cemetery, Foster, Providence County, RI.[2174]

George K Tyler was born on 26 Aug 1843 at RI. He died on 25 Aug 1913 at age 69.[2175] He was buried at Moosup Valley Cemetery, Foster, Providence County, RI.[2176]

Known children of Emily C Lyon and George K Tyler both born at RI were as follows:

    1229.   i.   Herbert E Tyler was born on 10 Nov 1872. He died on 2 Aug 1888 at age 15.[2177] He was buried at Moosup Valley Cemetery, Foster, Providence County, RI.[2178]

[2163]Tombstone.

[2164]Find A Grave.

[2165]Arnold, *Vital Records of Rhode Island 1636-1850.*, Foster Deaths, Volume 1912-1926, page 7.

[2166]Vital Records, Foster, Providence County, RI, Lyon Lot Cemetery.

[2167]Arnold, *Vital Records of Rhode Island 1636-1850.*, Foster Deaths, Volume 1851-1918, page 22.

[2168]Find A Grave.

[2169]Arnold, *Vital Records of Rhode Island 1636-1850.*, Foster Deaths, Volume 1851-1918, page 48.

[2170]Vital Records, Foster, Providence County, RI.

[2171]Tombstone.

[2172]Find A Grave.

[2173]Tombstone.

[2174]Find A Grave.

[2175]Tombstone.

[2176]Find A Grave.

[2177]Tombstone.

1230.   ii.   Leonora E Tyler was born in Jul 1876.[2179]

[2178]Find A Grave.
[2179]United States 1900 Census, Warwick, Kent County, RI.

Generation Five

1128. Frank J Lyon (*Willard, Alden, Benjamin, John*) was born circa 1855 at Alleghany County, NY. He married Ella (--?--).[2180]

Ella (--?--) was born in Jul 1861 at NY.[2181]

Known children of Frank J Lyon and Ella (--?--) were as follows:

+ 1231.   i.   Daniel H Lyon was born in May 1882 at NY. He married Jennie M (--?--).

1232.   ii.   Ethel M Lyon was born in Sep 1884 at NY.[2182]

1233.   iii.   Raymond F Lyon was born in Aug 1898 at NY.[2183]

1234.   iv.   Jennie M Lyon was born circa 1901.[2184]

1129. Della A Lyon (*Willard, Alden, Benjamin, John*) was born circa 1857 at Alleghany County, NY. She married Hiram Mattison.[2185]

She was also known as Adella Lyon.

Hiram Mattison was born circa 1854 at NY.[2186]

Known children of Della A Lyon and Hiram Mattison were:

1235.   i.   Lyonel Mattison was born circa 1890 at NY.[2187]

1130. Martin Grover Lyon (*Willard, Alden, Benjamin, John*) was born on 26 Jul 1862 at Alleghany County, NY. He married Lillan Julia Pugh on 27 Dec 1892 at Dunkirk, Chautauqua County, NY.[2188] He died on 28 Jun 1934 at age 71.[2189] He was buried at Forest Hills Cemetery, Fredonia, Chautaugua County, NY.[2190]

Lillan Julia Pugh was born on 25 Mar 1868 at NY. She died on 19 Jan 1951 at age 82.[2191] She was buried at Forest Hills Cemetery, Fredonia, Chautaugua County, NY.[2192]

Known children of Martin Grover Lyon and Lillan Julia Pugh were:

1236.   i.   Edith G Lyon was born in Oct 1893 at NY.[2193] She married Richard Wright VanScoter on 30 Jul 1919.[2194]

1156. Edward Benjamin Lyon (*William, Benjamin, Benjamin, John*) was born on 4 Apr 1879 at Smyrna, Chenango County, NY. He married Blanch Boynton.[2195]

He was automobile dealer.

Known children of Edward Benjamin Lyon and Blanch Boynton were:

[2180]Ibid., Angelica, Allegheny, NY.

[2181]Ibid.

[2182]Ibid.

[2183]Ibid.

[2184]United States 1910 Census, Angelica, Allegheny, NY.

[2185]United States 1930 Census, Dunkirk, Chautauqua, NY.

[2186]Ibid.

[2187]Ibid.

[2188]Barris, *Genealogical Information Reported in Dunkirk NY Newspapers*.

[2189]Tombstone, Angelica, Allegheny, NY.

[2190]Find A Grave.

[2191]Tombstone.

[2192]Find A Grave.

[2193]United States 1900 Census, Dunkirk, Chautauqua County, NY.

[2194]Barris, *Genealogical Information Reported in Dunkirk NY Newspapers*, 31 Jul 1919.

[2195]Lyon, *Lyon Memorial Massachusetts Families*, page 306.

+ 1237. i. Margaret L Lyon was born circa 1907 at Chenango County, NY. She married Chester McPherson.

1160. Dorothy Shepardson Lyon (*Edward, Benjamin, Benjamin, John*) was born on 22 Feb 1897 at Brooklyn, Kings County, NY. She married Arthur L Nelson on 20 Sep 1920 at Brooklyn, Kings County, NY. She and Arthur L Nelson were divorced on 20 Jan 1940. She died on 16 Sep 1946 at Waban, Middlesex County, MA, at age 49.[2196]

Arthur L Nelson was born on 15 Jun 1892 at Boston, Suffolk County, MA. He died on 2 Aug 1959 at San Antonio, TX, at age 67.[2197]

Known children of Dorothy Shepardson Lyon and Arthur L Nelson were as follows:
1238. i. Percy Lyon Nelson was born in 1922.[2198] He married Mary H Palmerton.
1239. ii. Margaret Lyon Nelson was born on 20 Mar 1925 at Jamaica Plains, MA. She married James Moore Hornbrook on 22 Feb 1951 at Waban, Middlesex County, MA.[2199]

1162. Cyrus Willard Lyon (*Hiram, John, Benjamin, John*) was born on 16 Mar 1878 at WI.[2200] He married Celia (--?--) circa 1898.

Celia (--?--) was born in Jul 1877 at WI.
Known children of Cyrus Willard Lyon and Celia (--?--) were:
1240. i. Lullian Lyon was born circa 1906 at WI.[2201]

1165. Alice L Lyon (*John, John, Benjamin, John*) was born on 26 Jan 1878 at IA. She married Abraham Lincoln Ridley on 10 Jan 1899.[2202]

Abraham Lincoln Ridley was born circa 1866 at WI.[2203]

Known children of Alice L Lyon and Abraham Lincoln Ridley both born at Fayette County, IA, were as follows:
1241. i. Alberta Ione Ridley was born on 18 Apr 1904.[2204]
1242. ii. Irene Ridley was born on 30 Aug 1911. She married Frazen (--?--). She died on 19 Feb 1993 at Los Angeles, Los Angeles County, CA, at age 81.[2205]

1172. William V Lyon (*Samuel, Reuben, Benjamin, John*) was born in May 1852 at NY.[2206] He married Sarah E (--?--) circa 1874.

Sarah E (--?--) was born in Feb 1858 at NY.[2207]

Known children of William V Lyon and Sarah E (--?--) were as follows:
+ 1243. i. Cora Bell Lyon was born circa 1875 at NY. She married Frederick Philley.
1244. ii. Lillian M Lyon was born in Jul 1877.[2208]

[2196] "The Lyon's Tale", May 1991, page 29.
[2197] Ibid.
[2198] Ibid., Dec 2003, page 274.
[2199] Ibid., May 1991, page 29.
[2200] Lyon, *Lyon Memorial Massachusetts Families*, page 307.
[2201] United States 1940 Census, Janesville, Rock County, WI.
[2202] Lyon, *Lyon Memorial Massachusetts Families*, page 307.
[2203] United States 1910 Census, Windsor, Fayette County, IA.
[2204] Lyon, *Lyon Memorial Massachusetts Families*, page 307.
[2205] California Death Index.
[2206] United States 1900 Census, Norwich, Chenango County, NY.
[2207] Ibid.
[2208] Ibid.

1245. iii. Samuel E Lyon was born in Mar 1879 at NY.[2209]

+ 1246. iv. Fannie H Lyon was born in Jan 1891. She married Raymond Mooney in 1909.

+ 1247. v. Lisle F Lyon was born circa 1902 at NY. He married Florence A Taylor.

1179. "General" Patterson Lyon (*Cyrus, Alexander, Cyrus, John*) was born in Jul 1861 at MO. He married Hattie L Hanlon.[2210] He died on 17 Jun 1951 at Lincoln County, OR, at age 89.[2211] He was buried at Fern Ridge Cemetery, Seal Rock, Lincoln County, OR.[2212]

He was also known as John P Lyon.[2213]

Hattie L Hanlon was born in Mar 1869 at IL. She died in 1933.[2214] She was buried at Fern Ridge Cemetery, Seal Rock, Lincoln County, IL.[2215]

Known children of "General" Patterson Lyon and Hattie L Hanlon all born at OR were as follows:

1248. i. Bessie Mable Lyon was born on 19 Aug 1891. She died on 14 Feb 1905 at age 13.[2216] She was buried at Fern Ridge Cemetery, Seal Rock, Lincoln County, OR.[2217]

+ 1249. ii. Jessie P Lyon was born in Mar 1894. She married John Barton circa 1913.

1250. iii. Katie B Lyon was born in May 1896.[2218]

1251. iv. George L Lyon was born in Feb 1900.[2219]

1252. v. Dolly S Lyon was born circa 1905.[2220]

1253. vi. Rosa M Lyon was born in 1910.[2221]

1188. Alice Maria Lyon (*Lucius, Alexander, Cyrus, John*) was born on 20 Sep 1851 at Lapeer County, MI. She married Francis Adelbert Warner. She died on 10 Mar 1947 at Jacksonville, Duval County, FL, at age 95.[2222]

Francis Adelbert Warner was born in 1849 at East Liverpool, Columbiana County, OH. He died on 12 Aug 1907 at Jacksonville, Duval County, FL.[2223]

Known children of Alice Maria Lyon and Francis Adelbert Warner were as follows:

1254. i. Alya Winford Warner was born on 24 Sep 1873 at Pontiac, Oakland County, MI. She married William R Porter on 17 Mar 1894 at Jacksonville, Duval County, FL. She married Lee Eugene Bigelow on 2 Sep 1903 at Jacksonville, Duval County, FL. She died on 3 Oct 1939 at Jacksonville, Duval County, FL, at age 66.[2224]

William R Porter was born circa 1869 at IN. He died in Feb 1900 at Nashville, TN.[2225]
Lee Eugene Bigelow[2226] was born on 2 Dec 1872 at FL.[2227] He died in 1940 at Jacksonville, Duval County, FL.[2228]

[2209]Ibid.

[2210]Ibid., Beaver, Lincoln County, OR.

[2211]Tombstone.

[2212]Find A Grave.

[2213]United States 1870 Census, Grand River, Carroll County, MO.

[2214]Tombstone.

[2215]Find A Grave.

[2216]Tombstone.

[2217]Find A Grave.

[2218]United States 1900 Census, Beaver, Lincoln County, OR.

[2219]Ibid.

[2220]United States 1910 Census, Yaquina, Lincoln County, OR.

[2221]Ibid.

[2222]"The Lyon's Tale", Volume 50, issue 4, page 137.

[2223]RootsWeb WorldConnect Project, Tim Merrill database.

[2224]Ibid.

[2225]Ibid.

[2226]Ibid.

[2227]Ibid.

1255.   ii.   Pearl Ada Warner was born circa 1879 at Saginaw, Saginaw County, MI.[2229]

1256.   iii. Elmer Leslie Warner was born on 28 Aug 1881 at Saginaw, Saginaw County, MI.[2230] He married Mary Conners. He died on 19 Aug 1963 at Jacksonville, Duval County, FL, at age 81.[2231]

        He was secretary of a wholesale turpentine company.

        Mary Conners was born circa 1889 at FL.[2232]

1257.   iv.   Louis Lionel Warner was born on 3 Jan 1884 at Saginaw, Saginaw County, MI. He married Effie White. He died in Apr 1965 at Daytona Beach, Volusia County, FL, at age 81.[2233]

        Effie White was born circa 1885 at NY.[2234]

1191. William Kittridge Lyon (*Lucius, Alexander, Cyrus, John*) was born in Nov 1859 at MI. He married Lottie Loretta Stevens circa 1887. He died on 21 Oct 1942 at Bellingham, Whatcom County, WA, at age 82.[2235] He was buried at Bayview Cemetery, Bellingham, Whatcom County, WA.[2236]

He was truck gardener.

Lottie Loretta Stevens was born in Nov 1869 at MI. She died on 28 Aug 1942 at Bayview Cemetery, Bellingham, Whatcom County, WA, at age 72.[2237]

    Known children of William Kittridge Lyon and Lottie Loretta Stevens all born at MI were as follows:

1258.   i.   Herbert Stevens Lyon was born on 12 Jul 1888. He died on 15 Jan 1908 at age 19.[2238] He was buried at Bayview Cemetery, Bellingham, Whatcom County, WA.[2239]

1259.   ii.   Luciuc M Lyon was born in Feb 1891. He died on 5 Jan 1908 at age 16.[2240] He was buried at Bayview Cemetery, Bellingham, Whatcom County, WA.[2241]

1260.   iii. Clarence M Lyon was born in Jul 1900. He died on 3 Oct 1908 at Whatcom County, WA, at age 8.[2242] He was buried at Bayview Cemetery, Bellingham, Whatcom County, WA.[2243]

1192. Frank B Lyon (*Lucius, Alexander, Cyrus, John*) was born in Dec 1861 at MI. He married Margaret Anne Still circa 1887.

He was carpenter in 1892 and a druggist in 1900. In 1920 Frank B Lyon was living with Fred S Kittrideg in Bellingham, Whatcon County, WA. He as employed as a ship carpenter and divorced.

Margaret Anne Still was born in Dec 1862 at Ontario, Canada. She died in 1934.[2244] She was buried at Evergreen Washelli Memorial Park, Seattle, King County, WA.[2245]

    Known children of Frank B Lyon and Margaret Anne Still were:

[2228]Ibid.

[2229]Ibid.

[2230]Ibid.

[2231]Florida Death Index.

[2232]United States 1940 Census, Jacksonville, Duval, FL.

[2233]RootsWeb WorldConnect Project, Tim Merrill database.

[2234]United States 1940 Census, Atlanta, Fulton County, GA.

[2235]Washington State Death Records.

[2236]Find A Grave.

[2237]Washington State Death Records.

[2238]Tombstone.

[2239]Find A Grave.

[2240]Tombstone.

[2241]Find A Grave.

[2242]Washington State Death Records.

[2243]Find A Grave.

[2244]Ibid.

[2245]Ibid.

+ 1261. i. Fred Rosco Lyon was born in Feb 1895 at WA. He married Vera D (--?--) say 1935. He died on 22 Jul 1944 at Seattle, King County, WA, at age 49. He was buried at Evergreen Washelli Memorial Park, Seattle, King County, WA.

1199. Frank M Lyon (*Jason, Daniel, Cyrus, John*) was born in Apr 1860 at IL. He married Samantha M Collins, daughter of Isaac Collins and Ellen M (--?--), circa 1885.[2246]

He was also known as Mary F Lyon. He was also known as Francis M Lyon.

Samantha M Collins was born in Oct 1867 at MO.[2247]

Known children of Frank M Lyon and Samantha M Collins were as follows:

1262. i. May L Lyon was born in Apr 1866 at KS.[2248]

1263. ii. Cora Lyon was born in May 1888 at NE.[2249]

1264. iii. Pearl Lyon was born in Dec 1891.[2250]

1265. iv. Troy Nelson Lyon was born in Apr 1900 at KS; California Death Index gives birth as 21 Mar 1901 in KS.[2251] He married Mabel (--?--). He married Ruth M (--?--). He died on 30 Dec 1956 at Alameda County, CA, at age 56.[2252]

He was railroad worker. He was also known as Nelson Lyon.

Mabel (--?--)[2253] was born circa 1901 at MS.[2254]

Ruth M (--?--)[2255] was born in 1910 at NE.[2256] She was telephone operator.

+ 1266. v. Howard Lyon was born circa 1905 at NE. He married Elsie Bishop.

1200. Alfred Sheriden Lyon (*Jason, Daniel, Cyrus, John*) was born circa 1866 at IL.[2257] He married Mabel D Wright.

He was house carpenter.

Mabel D Wright was born on 20 Nov 1875 at NE. She died on 27 Nov 1961 at San Jaquin County, CA, at age 86.[2258]

Known children of Alfred Sheriden Lyon and Mabel D Wright were as follows:

1267. i. Deroy J Lyon was born in Dec 1892 at SD.[2259]

1268. ii. Floyd Arthur Lyon was born on 12 Feb 1895 at NE. He died on 16 Aug 1976 at San Jaquin County, CA, at age 81.[2260]

He was photographer.

+ 1269. iii. Claud Maurice Lyon was born on 25 Jul 1897 at Trumbull, Clay County, NE. He married Margaret Elizabeth Ramsey. He died on 27 Dec 1965 at Contra Costa County, CA, at age 68. He was buried at Golden Gate National Cemetery, San Bruno, San Mateo County, CA.

+ 1270. iv. Arlon E Lyon was born in Oct 1899 at NE. He married Pearl (--?--).

1271. v. Vernon Lyon was born after 1900. He died before 1910.

[2246]United States 1900 Census, Glenwood, Phillips County, KS.

[2247]Ibid.

[2248]Ibid.

[2249]Ibid.

[2250]Ibid.

[2251]Ibid.

[2252]California Death Index, Alameda County, CA.

[2253]United States 1920 Census, Chester, Thayer County, NE.

[2254]Ibid.

[2255]United States 1940 Census, Berkeley, Alameda County, CA.

[2256]Ibid.

[2257]United States 1880 Census, Scovllle, Hamilton County, NE.

[2258]California Death Index.

[2259]United States 1900 Census, Thedford, Thomas County, NE.

[2260]California Death Index.

In the 1910 census Vernon's mother said she had had 5 children and 4 were then living. That census listed the four living children who born between 1892 and 1899 all about two years apart. Vernon is assumed to have been born and lived after the 1900 census but died before the 1910 census in either Nebraska or Utah.[2261]

+ 1272. vi. Thelma E Lyon was born on 9 Mar 1915 at Grand River, Emery County, UT. She married Martin Thornesberry. She died circa 26 Feb 2012 at Lodi, San Jaquin County, CA. She was buried at Lodi Memorial Cemetery, Lodi, San Jaquin County, CA.

1273. vii. Richard V Lyon was born on 19 Mar 1917 at Lodi, San Jaquin County, CA. He died on 25 Oct 2004 at Gold Beach, Curry County, OR, at age 87.[2262]

1201. William D Lyon (*Jason, Daniel, Cyrus, John*) was born circa 1868 at IL. He married Afka M Johnson.[2263] He died in 1954.[2264]

There is a William D Lyon in the 1900 census living in Wanda, Adams County, NE with wife Afka. Adams County however is 360 miles from where the William D of interest was born and this connection is suspect.

Afka M Johnson was born in 1875. She died in 1966.[2265]

Known children of William D Lyon and Afka M Johnson were:

+ 1274. i. George Jason Lyon was born on 17 Jun 1894. He married Clara Mary Elizaeth Cullip. He died in Oct 1985 at NE at age 91. He was buried at Riverside Cemetery, Gibbon, Buffalo County, NE.

1202. Lovina Harriett Lyon (*Jason, Daniel, Cyrus, John*) was born in Apr 1869 at IL. She married John E Schertz. She died on 31 Jan 1933 at Nampa, Canyon County, ID, at age 63.[2266] She was buried at Kohlerlawn Cemetery, Nampa, Canyon County, ID.[2267]

She was nurse.

John E Schertz was born in Feb 1853 at IL.[2268]

Known children of Lovina Harriett Lyon and John E Schertz were as follows:

1275. i. Mabel Schertz was born in Jan 1890 at NE.[2269]

1276. ii. Alma Schertz was born in Sep 1893 at NE.[2270]

1277. iii. Melvin Schertz was born in Jan 1896 at NE.[2271] He died before 1910.[2272]

1278. iv. Kate Schertz was born in May 1898 at NE.[2273]

1279. v. Clayton Schertz was born in Mar 1900.[2274] He died before 1910.[2275]

1280. vi. Vera L Schertz was born circa 1902 at NE.[2276]

1281. vii. Josephine E Schertz was born circa 1903 at NE.[2277]

1282. viii. Elva L Schertz was born circa 1905 at NE.[2278]

[2261]United States 1910 Census, Green River, Emery County, UT.
[2262]Social Security Death Index.
[2263]"The Lyon's Tale", May 1979, page 9.
[2264]Ibid.
[2265]Ibid.
[2266]Idaho Death Records.
[2267]Find A Grave.
[2268]United States 1900 Census, Scoville, Hamilton County, NE.
[2269]Ibid.
[2270]Ibid., Scovllle, Hamilton County, NE.
[2271]Ibid.
[2272]United States 1910 Census, Scovllle, Hamilton County, NE.
[2273]United States 1900 Census, Scovllle, Hamilton County, NE.
[2274]Ibid.
[2275]United States 1910 Census, Scovllle, Hamilton County, NE.
[2276]Ibid.
[2277]Ibid.
[2278]Ibid.

1203. Charles Jason Lyon (*Jason, Daniel, Cyrus, John*) was born on 7 Feb 1871 at Loami, Sangamon County, IL.[2279,2280] He married Emeline Deborah Maxson, daughter of Orson Maxson and Adelia (--?--), on 3 Jul 1896.[2281] He died on 5 Sep 1937 at Hastings, Adams County, NE, at age 66.[2282] He was buried at Greenwood Cemetery, Hastings, Adams County, NE.[2283]

Emeline Deborah Maxson was born on 25 Feb 1878 at Farina, Fayette County, NE. She died on 14 Jul 1936 at Hastings, Adams County, NE, at age 58.[2284] She was buried at Greenwood Cemetery, Hastings, Adams County, NE.[2285]

Known children of Charles Jason Lyon and Emeline Deborah Maxson were as follows:

1283.   i.   Ida M Lyon was born in Sep 1896 at NE.[2286]

1284.   ii.   Lola Lyon was born circa 1899 at NE.[2287]

+ 1285.   iii.   William Harold Lyon was born on 23 Nov 1901 at Trumbull, Clay County, NE. He married Iris Irma Wilson on 12 Mar 1922 at Hastings, Adams County, NE. He died on 6 Jul 1995 at Hastings, Adams County, NE, at age 93. He was buried at Greenwood Cemetery, Hastings, Adams County, NE.

1286.   iv.   Raymond L Lyon was born circa 1909 at NE.[2288]

1287.   v.   Doyle C Lyon was born circa 1910 at NE.[2289]

1206. Florence Lucretia Lyon (*Jason, Daniel, Cyrus, John*) was born in 1881 at NE. She married George J Maraott. She died in 1961.[2290] She was buried at Greenwood Cemetery, Hastings, Adams County, NE.[2291]

George J Maraott was born in 1874. He died in 1955.[2292] He was buried at Greenwood Cemetery, Hastings, Adams County, NE.[2293]

Known children of Florence Lucretia Lyon and George J Maraott were:

1288.   i.   Neva Nerine Maraott was born in 1920. She married Lloyd Heye Hinricks. She died in 2012.[2294] She was buried at Greenwood Cemetery, Hastings, Adams County, NE.[2295]

Lloyd Heye Hinricks was born in 1918. He died in 1998.[2296] He was buried at Greenwood Cemetery, Hastings, Adams County, NE.[2297]

1208. Charles L Lyon (*Charles, Alfred, Cyrus, John*) was born on 18 Nov 1856 at New London, Waupaca County, WI. He married Lillian Payton circa 1884.[2298]

He was proprietor of a lumber yard.

[2279]United States 1880 Census, Scovllle, Hamilton County, NE.

[2280]Tombstone.

[2281]"The Lyon's Tale", Jan 2004, page 53.

[2282]Ibid.

[2283]Find A Grave.

[2284]"The Lyon's Tale", Jan 2004, page 53.

[2285]Find A Grave.

[2286]United States 1900 Census, Leicester, Clay County, NE.

[2287]United States 1910 Census, Leicester, Clay County, NE.

[2288]Ibid.

[2289]Ibid.

[2290]Tombstone.

[2291]Find A Grave.

[2292]Ibid.

[2293]Ibid.

[2294]Tombstone.

[2295]Find A Grave.

[2296]Ibid.

[2297]Ibid.

[2298]United States 1910 Census, New London, Outagamie County, WI.

Lillian Payton was born in Apr 1862 at WI.[2299]

Known children of Charles L Lyon and Lillian Payton all born at WI were as follows:

1289.   i.   Sidney Alanzo Lyon was born on 24 Jul 1886.[2300] He died on 1 Feb 1972 at New London, Waupaca County, WI, at age 85.[2301]

He was proprietor of a confectionary.

1290.   ii.   Eddie Lyon was born in Nov 1889.[2302]

1291.   iii.   Robin Lyon was born in Jul 1892. He died in 1906 at WI.[2303] He was buried at Maple Creek Cemetery #1, New London, Outagamie County, WI.[2304]

1210.   Alfred Austin Lyon (*Charles, Alfred, Cyrus, John*) was born on 17 Mar 1864 at New London, Waupaca County, WI. He married Mary Rief circa 1892.[2305]

Mary Rief was born in Jan 1864 at Germany.[2306]

Known children of Alfred Austin Lyon and Mary Rief were as follows:

+ 1292.   i.   Warren Walter Lyon was born on 26 Jan 1893 at New London, Waupaca County, WI. He married Mayme M (--?--). He died on 3 Nov 1973 at Sheboygan, Sheboygan County, WI, at age 80.

+ 1293.   ii.   Earl C Lyon was born in May 1894 at WI. He married Ruth Stichman, daughter of Fred Stichman and Martha (--?--).

1294.   iii.   Arthur E Lyon was born in Jun 1896 at WI.[2307]

1295.   iv.   Viola M Lyon was born in Nov 1898 at WI.[2308]

1212.   Ida Lyon (*Milo, Alfred, Cyrus, John*) was born on 27 Jan 1869 at WI. She married Bert A Lipke on 9 Jul 1889.[2309]

Known children of Ida Lyon and Bert A Lipke both born at WI were as follows:

1296.   i.   Susan Lipke[2310] was born in Aug 1890.[2311]

She was also known as Consualo Lipke.

1297.   ii.   Lucile Lipke was born on 2 Apr 1898.[2312]

1213.   John C Lyon (*Milo, Alfred, Cyrus, John*) was born on 1 Apr 1873 at New London, Waupaca County, WI. He married Mable R Trayser on 18 Oct 1899 at New London, Waupaca County, WI.[2313] He died in 1967 at New London, Waupaca County, WI.

Known children of John C Lyon and Mable R Trayser were as follows:

+ 1298.   i.   Howard M Lyon was born on 5 Aug 1901 at New London, Waupaca County, WI. He married Frances K (--?--). He died on 18 Jul 1965 at WI at age 63.

[2299]United States 1900 Census, Pella, Shawano County, WI.
[2300]World War II Draft Records.
[2301]Social Security Death Index.
[2302]United States 1900 Census, Pella, Shawano County, WI.
[2303]Tombstone.
[2304]Find A Grave.
[2305]United States 1900 Census, New London, Outagamie County, WI.
[2306]Ibid.
[2307]Ibid.
[2308]Ibid.
[2309]Lyon, *Lyon Memorial Massachusetts Families*, page 308.
[2310]United States 1900 Census, New London, Waupaca County, WI.
[2311]Ibid.
[2312]Ibid.
[2313]Lyon, *Lyon Memorial Massachusetts Families*, page 308.

1299. ii. Mildred Lyon was born circa 1912 at WI.[2314]

1226. Mary Etta Lyon (*Emory, John, Reuben, John*) was born circa 1854 at RI. She married Henry Lester Place. She died in 1919 at RI.[2315] She was buried at Pocasset Cemetery, Cranston, Providence County, RI.[2316]

Henry Lester Place was born in 1839 at RI. He died in 1902 at RI.[2317] He was buried at Pocasset Cemetery, Cranston, Providence County, RI.[2318]

Known children of Mary Etta Lyon and Henry Lester Place were as follows:

1300. i. Emery Lester Place was born in 1874. He married Gertrude (--?--).[2319] He died in 1904.[2320] He was buried at Pocasset Cemetery, Cranston, Providence County, RI.[2321]

Gertrude (--?--) was born in 1877.[2322]

1301. ii. Henry L Place was born in 1874.[2323]

1302. iii. Charles Lester Place was born in 1876. He died in 1938.[2324] He was buried at Pocasset Cemetery, Cranston, Providence County, RI.[2325]

[2314]United States 1920 Census, Mukwa, Waupaca County, WI.
[2315]Tombstone.
[2316]Find A Grave.
[2317]Ibid.
[2318]Ibid.
[2319]United States 1910 Census, Providence, Providence County, RI.
[2320]Tombstone.
[2321]Find A Grave.
[2322]United States 1910 Census, Providence, Providence County, RI.
[2323]United States 1900 Census, Providence, Providence County, RI.
[2324]Tombstone.
[2325]Find A Grave.

Generation Six

1231. Daniel H Lyon (*Frank, Willard, Alden, Benjamin, John*) was born in May 1882 at NY. He married Jennie M (--?--).[2326]

Jennie M (--?--) was born circa 1886 at NY.[2327]
Known children of Daniel H Lyon and Jennie M (--?--) were as follows:
+ 1303.   i.   Elrose J Lyon was born circa 1911 at NY.[2328]
+ 1304. ii. Howard D Lyon was born circa 1914 at NY.[2329]
+ 1305. iii. William F Lyon was born circa 1916 at NY.[2330]
+ 1306. iv. Jane A Lyon was born circa 1916.[2331]
+ 1307. v. Marie G Lyon was born circa 1920.[2332]

1237. Margaret L Lyon (*Edward, William, Benjamin, Benjamin, John*) was born circa 1907 at Chenango County, NY. She married Chester McPherson.[2333]

Chester McPherson was born circa 1903 at NY.[2334] He was broker at a stock exchange.
Known children of Margaret L Lyon and Chester McPherson were:
+ 1308. i. Peter R McPherson was born on 7 Mar 1933 at NY. He died on 17 Jul 2006 at Sturgis, Saint Joseph County, MI, at age 73.[2335]

1243. Cora Bell Lyon (*William, Samuel, Reuben, Benjamin, John*) was born circa 1875 at NY. She married Frederick Philley.[2336]

Frederick Philley was born circa 1873 at NY.[2337] He was creamery supervisor.
Known children of Cora Bell Lyon and Frederick Philley all born at NY were as follows:
+ 1309. i. Charles Philley was born circa 1896.[2338]
+ 1310. ii. Burton Philley was born circa 1900.[2339]
+ 1311. iii. Dorothea Philley was born circa 1907.[2340]
+ 1312. iv. Theron L Philley was born circa 1914.[2341]
+ 1313. v. S Janet Philley was born circa 1920.[2342]

1246. Fannie H Lyon (*William, Samuel, Reuben, Benjamin, John*) was born in Jan 1891. She married Raymond Mooney in 1909.[2343]

[2326]United States 1920 Census, Angelica, Allegheny, NY.
[2327]Ibid.
[2328]Ibid.
[2329]Ibid.
[2330]Ibid.
[2331]Ibid.
[2332]Ibid.
[2333]United States 1940 Census, Yonkers, Westchester, NY.
[2334]Ibid.
[2335]Social Security Death Index.
[2336]United States 1910 Census, Windsor, Broome County, NY.
[2337]Ibid.
[2338]Ibid.
[2339]Ibid.
[2340]Ibid.
[2341]United States 1920 Census, Windsor, Broome County, NY.
[2342]United States 1930 Census, Windsor, Broome County, NY.
[2343]United States 1910 Census, Norwich, Chenango County, NY.

Raymond Mooney was born circa 1889 at PA.[2344] He was toolmaker.

Known children of Fannie H Lyon and Raymond Mooney were:

1314.   i.   Dorthy Mooney was born circa 1911 at NY.[2345]

1247. Lisle F Lyon (*William, Samuel, Reuben, Benjamin, John*) was born circa 1902 at NY.[2346] He married Florence A Taylor.[2347]

He was bicycle repairman in 1920.

Florence A Taylor was born circa 1901 at NY.[2348]

Known children of Lisle F Lyon and Florence A Taylor are:

1315.   i.   William F Lyon is still living.

1249. Jessie P Lyon (*"General", Cyrus, Alexander, Cyrus, John*) was born in Mar 1894 at OR. She married John Barton circa 1913.[2349]

John Barton was born on 8 Oct 1884 at Humboldt County, CA. He died on 20 Oct 1951 at WA at age 67.[2350]

Known children of Jessie P Lyon and John Barton were as follows:

1316.   i.   Bessie Barton was born circa 1914 at OR.[2351]

1317.   ii.   Edna Barton was born circa 1918 at OR.[2352]

1318.   iii. Robert Barton was born circa 1921 at OR.[2353]

1319.   iv.   Richard Barton was born circa 1921.[2354]

1261. Fred Rosco Lyon (*Frank, Lucius, Alexander, Cyrus, John*) was born in Feb 1895 at WA. He married Vera D (--?--) say 1935. He died on 22 Jul 1944 at Seattle, King County, WA, at age 49.[2355] He was buried at Evergreen Washelli Memorial Park, Seattle, King County, WA.[2356]

He was architect.

Vera D (--?--) was born circa 1900 at NE. She married Loyd D Crane say 1950. She died in 1992.[2357] She was buried at Evergreen Washelli Memorial Park, Seattle, King County, WA.[2358]

Known children of Fred Rosco Lyon and Vera D (--?--) are:

1320.   i.   William Robert Lyon is still living.

1266. Howard Lyon (*Frank, Jason, Daniel, Cyrus, John*) was born circa 1905 at NE. He married Elsie Bishop.[2359]

Elsie Bishop was born circa 1908 at NE.[2360]

[2344]Ibid.

[2345]United States 1920 Census, Syracuse, Onondago County, NY.

[2346]United States 1910 Census, Norwich, Chenango County, NY.

[2347]United States 1940 Census, Syracuse, Onondago County, NY.

[2348]Ibid.

[2349]United States 1930 Census, South Beach, Lincoln County, OR.

[2350]Washington State Death Records.

[2351]United States 1930 Census, South Beach, Lincoln County, OR.

[2352]Ibid.

[2353]Ibid.

[2354]Ibid.

[2355]Washington State Death Records.

[2356]Find A Grave.

[2357]Ibid.

[2358]Ibid.

[2359]United States 1920 Census, Taylor, Loup County, NE.

Known children of Howard Lyon and Elsie Bishop all born at NE are as follows:

1321.   i.   Clifford Lyon is still living.
1322.   ii.   Clinton Lyon is still living.
1323.   iii.   Rose Lee Lyon is still living.
1324.   iv.   Erma Mary Lyon is still living.
1325.   v.   Bernies Jane Lyon is still living.

1269. Claud Maurice Lyon (*Alfred, Jason, Daniel, Cyrus, John*) was born on 25 Jul 1897 at Trumbull, Clay County, NE. He married Margaret Elizabeth Ramsey. He died on 27 Dec 1965 at Contra Costa County, CA, at age 68.[2361] He was buried at Golden Gate National Cemetery, San Bruno, San Mateo County, CA.[2362]
He was foreman with a railroad.

Margaret Elizabeth Ramsey was born on 5 Nov 1896 at CA. She died on 1 Feb 1988 at San Jaquin County, CA, at age 91.[2363] She was buried at Golden Gate National Cemetery, San Bruno, San Jaquin County, CA.[2364]

Known children of Claud Maurice Lyon and Margaret Elizabeth Ramsey all born at OR are as follows:

1326.   i.   Dorothy M Lyon is still living.
1327.   ii.   Deane A Lyon is still living.
1328.   iii.   (--?--) Lyon is still living.

1270. Arlon E Lyon (*Alfred, Jason, Daniel, Cyrus, John*) was born in Oct 1899 at NE. He married Pearl (--?--).[2365]
He was president of railroad union.

Pearl (--?--) was born circa 1903 at OK.[2366]

Known children of Arlon E Lyon and Pearl (--?--) are as follows:

1329.   i.   Robert Lyon is still living.
1330.   ii.   Anita Lyon is still living.

1272. Thelma E Lyon (*Alfred, Jason, Daniel, Cyrus, John*) was born on 9 Mar 1915 at Grand River, Emery County, UT. She married Martin Thornesberry. She died circa 26 Feb 2012 at Lodi, San Jaquin County, CA.[2367] She was buried at Lodi Memorial Cemetery, Lodi, San Jaquin County, CA.[2368]

Martin Thornesberry[2369] was born circa 1909 at AZ.[2370]

Known children of Thelma E Lyon and Martin Thornesberry both born at CA are as follows:

1331.   i.   Arlon Thornesberry is still living.
1332.   ii.   Elvea Thornesberry is still living.

1274. George Jason Lyon (*William, Jason, Daniel, Cyrus, John*) was born on 17 Jun 1894.[2371,2372] He married Clara Mary Elizaeth Cullip. He died in Oct 1985 at NE at age 91.[2373] He was buried at Riverside Cemetery, Gibbon, Buffalo County, NE.[2374]

[2360]Ibid.
[2361]California Death Index.
[2362]Find A Grave.
[2363]California Death Index.
[2364]Find A Grave.
[2365]United States 1930 Census, Chicago, Cook County, IL.
[2366]Ibid.
[2367]US Cemetery and Funeral Home Collection, Ancestry.com.
[2368]Ibid.
[2369]United States 1940 Census, Lodi, San Joaquin County, CA.
[2370]Ibid.

Clara Mary Elizaeth Cullip was born on 19 Aug 1893 at Kenesaw, Adams County, NE. She died on 31 Jan 1978 at Kearney County, NE, at age 84. She was buried at Kenesaw, Gibbon, Buffalo County, NE.[2375]

Known children of George Jason Lyon and Clara Mary Elizabeth Cullip were as follows:

1333.   i.   Esther G Lyon was born on 7 Dec 1918 at Juniata, Adams County, NE. She married Earl Dancer on 15 Nov 1941. She died on 30 Mar 2005 at Kearney, Buffalo County, NE, at age 86. She was buried at Riverside Cemetery, Gibbon, Buffalo County, NE.[2376]

1334.   ii.   Bernard Dale Lyon was born on 25 Jun 1921 at Kenesaw, Adams County, NE. He married Thelma Wiseman. He died on 8 Sep 2006 at Kearney, Buffalo County, NE, at age 85. He was buried at Riverside Cemetery, Gibbon, Buffalo County, NE.[2377]

1335.   iii.   Dorothy J Lyon was born on 4 May 1927 at Lowell, Kearney County, NE. She married Leo Ash on 6 May 1946. She died on 15 Jun 2007 at Gibbon, Buffalo County, NE, at age 80. She was buried at Riverside Cemetery, Gibbon, Buffalo County, NE.[2378]

1285. William Harold Lyon (*Charles, Jason, Daniel, Cyrus, John*) was born on 23 Nov 1901 at Trumbull, Clay County, NE. He married Iris Irma Wilson on 12 Mar 1922 at Hastings, Adams County, NE. He died on 6 Jul 1995 at Hastings, Adams County, NE, at age 93.[2379] He was buried at Greenwood Cemetery, Hastings, Adams County, NE.[2380]

Iris Irma Wilson was born on 2 Nov 1900 at Osco, Keamey County, NE. She died on 30 Jun 1978 at Aurora, Hamilton County, NE, at age 77. She was buried at Greenwood Cemetery, Hastings, Clay County, NE.[2381]

Known children of William Harold Lyon and Iris Irma Wilson were:

1336.   i.   Robert Harold Lyon was born on 23 May 1922 at Giltner, Hamilton County, NE.[2382] He married Alice Ellen Perrin on 20 Jun 1954 at St Paul, Ramsey County, MN.[2383]

Alice Ellen Perrin was born on 3 May 1930 at St Paul, Ramsey County, MN.[2384]

1292. Warren Walter Lyon (*Alfred, Charles, Alfred, Cyrus, John*) was born on 26 Jan 1893 at New London, Waupaca County, WI. He married Mayme M (--?--). He died on 3 Nov 1973 at Sheboygan, Sheboygan County, WI, at age 80.[2385]

Mayme M (--?--)[2386] was born on 27 Jun 1897 at WI.[2387] She died on 7 Jul 1999 at Outagamie County, WI, at age 102.[2388]

Known children of Warren Walter Lyon and Mayme M (--?--) both born at WI were as follows:

1337.   i.   Arlien Lyon was born circa 1917.[2389]

[2371]"The Lyon's Tale", May 1979, page 9.
[2372]Find A Grave.
[2373]Ibid.
[2374]Ibid.
[2375]Ibid.
[2376]Ibid.
[2377]Ibid.
[2378]Ibid.
[2379]Ibid.
[2380]Ibid.
[2381]"The Lyon's Tale", Jan 2004, page 53.
[2382]Ibid.
[2383]Ibid.
[2384]Ibid.
[2385]Death Records, Sheboygan County WI Death Records.
[2386]United States 1940 Census, Sheboygan, Sheboygan County, WI.
[2387]Birth Records, Outagamie County, WI.
[2388]Ibid.

1338.   ii.   Lyman Lyon was born on 13 Apr 1928. He died on 6 Apr 2000 at Oakland County, MI, at age 71.[2390]

1293.   Earl C Lyon (*Alfred, Charles, Alfred, Cyrus, John*) was born in May 1894 at WI. He married Ruth Stichman, daughter of Fred Stichman and Martha (--?--).

Ruth Stichman was born circa 1894 at WI.[2391]
Known children of Earl C Lyon and Ruth Stichman both born at WI were as follows:
1339.   i.   Wayne E Lyon was born circa 1927.[2392]
1340.   ii.   Joyce Lyon was born circa 1930.[2393]

1298.   Howard M Lyon (*John, Milo, Alfred, Cyrus, John*) was born on 5 Aug 1901 at New London, Waupaca County, WI. He married Frances K (--?--). He died on 18 Jul 1965 at WI at age 63.[2394]

Frances K (--?-) was born circa 1901 at WI.[2395]
Known children of Howard M Lyon and Frances K (--?--) all born at WI were as follows:
1341.   i.   Philip J Lyon was born circa 1928.[2396]
1342.   ii.   Betty M Lyon was born circa 1929.[2397]
1343.   iii.   John H Lyon was born circa 1930.[2398]
1344.   iv.   Robert F Lyon was born circa 1933.[2399]

[2389]United States 1940 Census, Sheboygan, Sheboygan County, WI.
[2390]Social Security Death Index.
[2391]United States 1940 Census, Maple Creek, Outagamie County, WI.
[2392]Ibid.
[2393]Ibid.
[2394]Death Records, Wisconsin.
[2395]United States 1940 Census, Chippewa Falls, Chippewa County, WI.
[2396]Ibid.
[2397]Ibid.
[2398]Ibid.
[2399]Ibid.

Index

Martha (1808-1811)	105
Martha (1869-1936)	49
Martha L (1874-1954)	46, 70
Martha P (1805-1841)	11, 34
Martha Pearl (1903-)	93
Martha Pearl (1904-)	97
Martin Grover (1862-1934)	116, 131
Marvin D (1859-1908)	42
Mary	9
Mary (1701-1753)	1
Mary (1794-)	6, 16, 17
Mary (1807-1865)	107
Mary (1809-1840)	114
Mary (1812-1848)	25
Mary (1830-1919)	59
Mary (1838-)	42
Mary (1838-1915)	42
Mary (1848-)	48
Mary (1859-)	44
Mary (1860-1951)	74
Mary (1864-)	138
Mary (1872-)	59
Mary (Polly) (1768-)	100, 103
Mary A (1858-1941)	27, 49
Mary Alice (1839-1841)	19
Mary Angeline (1830-1919)	35, 59
Mary Ann (1817-1905)	54
Mary Ann (1830-1880)	36
Mary Ann (1831-1870)	42
Mary Ann (1833-)	29
Mary Catherine (1860-1915)	79
Mary Comstock (1828-1897)	108, 117, 118
Mary E (-1929)	120
Mary E (1825-1889)	115
Mary E (1849-)	37, 65
Mary E (1850-1924)	25, 47
Mary E (1859-1922)	65
Mary E (1929-1930)	81
Mary Eliza (1825-)	28, 50
Mary Etta (1854-1919)	128, 139
Mary F (1860-)	135
Mary Frances (1923-1956)	80
Mary Helen (1847-)	31
Mary Isadora (1909-)	91
Mary J (1846-)	61
Mary Jane (1846-1928)	62
Mary L (1882-)	89
Mary L (1903-1987)	78
Mary Lovinia (1880-)	121
Mary M	89
Mary Madeline (1891-1966)	80
Mary Umphrey (1808-1866)	108
Matilda (1876-)	57
Matilda H (1835-1877)	25, 45
Matilda J (1874-1940)	52
Matthew Larwence	98
Maud V (1896-)	78
Maude L (1889-)	76
Maudel (1894-)	81
May Eugenia (Dr) (1861-1936)	51, 71, 72
May Eva (1889-)	49
May L (1866-)	135
Mayme M (1897-1999)	143
Melessia M (1850-1920)	75
Mercy (1774-1862)	9
Merle (1928-2007)	90
Merritt L (1834-)	125
Michael Patrick	97
Mildred (1912-)	139
Mildred I (1903-1974)	84
Mildred L (1909-)	82, 94
Milo (1837-1837)	112
Milo Alfred (1841-1941)	112, 127
Minerva (1837-)	35, 60
Minnie (1864-1936)	42
Minnie Luetta (1874-1954)	85
Minnie M (1902-1966)	90
Miranda (1806-1869)	14, 40
Morgan (1810-1893)	9, 24, 25
Morris Nelson (1898-1963)	70, 88
Morton J (1871-1931)	63
Muriel E	88
Myrna I (1929-)	93
Myron D (1836-)	112, 126
Myron J (1903-)	80, 93
Nabby (1825-)	105
Nancy (1780-)	9
Nancy (1812-1856)	26
Nancy A (1791-)	111
Nancy Jane (1840-)	58
Nellie Burbank	123
Nelson (1900-1956)	135
Nelson Thomas (1843-1872)	26, 48
Nora E (1883-)	66, 83
Nora M (1901-1984)	84
Oliva A (1906-)	77
Olive	36
Olive (1763-1824)	6
Olive (1778-1853)	11
Olive (1798-1893)	29

Bibliography

1812 War Index, New York State, New York State Archives, Albany, NY.

Ancestry Family Trees.

Andrews, Israel Ward LL D. *Centennial Historical Address before the Citizens of Washington County, 4 Jul 1876* Cincinnati: Peter G Thompson, 1877).

Arnold, James N. *Vital Records of Rhode Island 1636-1850.* (Providence RI: Narragansett Press, 1892).

Austin, Emily M., *Mormonism or life among the Mormons* (Madison, WI: 1882).

Barris, Lois M. *Genealogical Information Reported in Dunkirk NY Newspapers.*

Book of Biographies, Biographical Sketches of Leading Citizens of Chenango County NY. (Buffalo, NY: Biographical Publishing Co, 1898).

Broderbund. *World Family Tree.*

California Death Index.

Carpenter, Amos B. *History of the Rehoboth Carpenter Family.* (Amherst, MA: Carpenter & Morehouse, 1898).

Cattaraugus County, NY Cemeteries, 1930.

Chapin, Howard M.. *Rhode Island in the Colonial Wars, A List of Rhode Island Soldiers & Sailors in the Old French & Indian War.* (Providence, RI: Rhode Island Historical Society, 1918).

Charboneau, Milton. *Early Land Owners & Settlers of Livingston County Michigan 1826 to 1870's.*

Chautauqua County NY, Will book 1 1830-1843.

Chenango American Newspaper.

Chenango County, NY, Land Records.

Clarke, Louise Brownell. *The Greenes of Rhode Island* (New York, 1903).

Cooley, J. C., *Rathbone Family* (1898).

Court Deposition ~1860 relative to Mercy Lyon's Pension.

Cranston Town Meeting Minutes.

Cranston, Providence County, RI, Land Records.

Cruikshank, Ernest, *The First American Frontier* (Reprinted Arno Press, 1971).

DAR NY Cemetery, Church, & Town Records.

Death Certificate, Betsey Knapp, 31 Jan 1884.

Downs, John P. *History of Chautauqua County, NY and its People* (Boston: American Historical Society, 1921).

East Greenwich, RI, Land Records.

East Greenwich, RI, Vital Records.

Edson, Obed. *Biography and Portrait Cyclopedia of Chautauqua County, New York. Also known as Biography and History of Chautauqua County* (Philadelphia PA: John Graham, 1891).

Everts & Abbott. *History of Livingston County Michigan* (1880).

Find A Grave www.findagrave.com.

Florida Death Index.

Florida State 1945 Census.

Foster Rhode Island Cemetery records.

Fray, Robert G. *Bradford County, PA Area Deaths* (Allentown, PA: Robert G Fray, 2000).

Gone but Not Forgotten, Oxford Burial Grounds, Chenango Co. Historian, 45 Rexford St., Norwich, Chenango County, NY.

Gorton, Thomas A, PhD. *Samuel Gorton of Rhode Island and his Descendants* (Baltimore, MD: Gateway Press, 1985).

Gregory, Grant. *Ancestors and Descendants of Henry Gregory* (Rutland, VT: Tuttle Publishing Co, 1938).

Hanson, Robert Brand. *Vital Records of Dedham MA* (1989).

Heitman F. B., *Historical Register of the US Army* (Washington, DC: pub., 1890).

Heverly, C F. *History of Monroe Township and Borough 1779-1885* (Towanda, PA: Journal Printing Company, 1885).

Heverly, Clement F.. *Pioneer and Patriot Families of Bradford County, PA 1770-1800* (Towanda, PA: Bradford Star Print, 1913).

Hill, Don Gleason. *The Record of Births, Marriages and Deaths and Intentions of Marriage In the Town of Dedham*.

History of Crawford County Pennsylvania (Chicago, IL: Warner, Beers & Co, 1885).

Howard, Robert J. *Extracts of Chenango County Guardianship Records*.

Idaho Death Records.

Illinois Marriages Record Index.

Iowa 1925 State Census.

Joseph Smith Papers.

Kansas, Cowley County 1885 Census.

King, Col Wm., *Hezekiah King & his Descendants* (1895).

Knapp, Alfred Averill, Dr. *Knapp Family, Aaron Knapp of Taunton, MA in 1638 and Some of his Descendants*. Winter Park, FL: unpublished, 1961).

Ladwig, John W. *Rickertson Burlingame* 1997.

Letter Olive Buckley to Mrs Wells, 27 Apr 1931, Chenango Co. Historian.

Lewis, Helen F. *New York Finger Lake Pioneer Families*.

Lowry, James. *Morgan Lyon, Forgotten Pioneer a Historical and Genealogical Biography* (self published, 2006).

Lynda McGinnis. *Christoffersen Family Chart*.

Lyon Reunion of 1883.

Lyon, A B & G W A. *Lyon Memorial Massachusetts Families* (Detroit. MI: William Graham Printing, 1905).

Lyon, Dr G. W. A.. *Lyon Memorial, NY Families* (Detroit MI: William Graham, 1907).

Lyon, Smith, Klump Family Bible.

Lyons, Ted Thomas. *William Lyon of Roxbury, MA and Some of his Descendants* (Belton, MO: Lyon's Families Association of America, 1997).

Marshall County, IL Marriage Records.

McGinnis Lynda Kay. *Lynda Kay McGinnis Ancestry*.

McRae, Joan M. *Marriage and Deaths Notices Extracted from Warren County, PA Newspapers* (1982).

Michigan Death Records.

Military Minutes of the Council of Appointments of the State of New York, Council of Appointment, Military 1783-1821, 1901, New York State Library.

Missouri Marriage Records.

National Cemetery at Sackets Harbor, NY, (Watertown, NY: Watertown Daily Times, 27 Apr 1946).

New York 1892 State Census.

New York Civil War Records.

New York State 1855 Census.

New York State 1915 Census.

Notes from the files of the Chenango County NY Historian.

O'Callaghan, E B. *The Documentary History of the State of New York* (Albany, NY: Charles Van Benthuysen, 1851).

Peabody, Selim Howard. *Peabody Genealogy* (Boston, MA: Charles H. Pope, 1909).

Pennsylvania Veterans Records.

Perry, Kenneth A. *The Fitch Gazetteer an Annotated Index to the Manuscript History of Washington County NY* (MD: Heritage Books, 1999).

Pollard, Maurice J. *History of the Pollard Family in America, The* (Dover, NH: self published, 1964).

Probate Records, Chenango County, NY.

Reierson, Art. *Burlingame Family.*

Rhode Island Land Records.

Rhode Island Wills.

Rhode Island Colonial Records.

Root'sWeb WorldConnect Project.

Royce, C F. *Biographical and Historical Memoirs of Adams, Clay, Hall and Hamilton Counties, Nebraska.* (Chicago, IL: Goodspeed Publishing Company, 1890).

Smith, James H., *History of Chenango and Madison Counties 1784-1880* (1880).

Social Security Death Index.

Solinda Christoffersen phone and written material.

Suffolk County MA, Vital Records.

Suit Benjamin Gorton vs John Lyon, 1756.

Tiffany, Nelson B.. *Revolutionary War Veterans, Chenango County, New York* (Norwich, NY: Chenango County Historical Society, c 1998).

Tiffany, Nelson, *DAR Revolutionary War Veterans Records, Chenango County, NY* (Chenango County, NY).

Tim Merrill. *Descendants of Alexander Lyon* (2 Dec 1999).

U S Census Mortality Schedule.

U. S. Archives Military Records Group 94, Lt Thomas Lyon III, 1814.

United States Census.

US Army Death Records.

US Army Register of Enlistments 1798-1914.

US Cemetery and Funeral Home Collection, Ancestry.com.

Vermont Secretary of State Records.

Vital Records, Coventry, Kent County, RI.

Vital Records, Foster, Providence County, RI.

Washington State Death Records.

William's Papers, New York State Archives.

Worcester County, MA Land Records.

World War I Draft Records.

World War II Draft Records.